MANAGING FOR SUSTAINABLE

DEVELOPMENT IMPACT

ABOUT THE AUTHORS

Cecile Kusters (MSc) is a Senior Planning, Monitoring and Evaluation (PME) Advisor at CDI, Wageningen University & Research. Her expertise spans the application of the Managing for Sustainable Development Impact (M4SDI) approach in organizations and initiatives, strategic design/Theories of Change, M&E systems design, evaluations, and PME capacity development. She is also the principal author of the CDI publication *Making Evaluations Matter: A Practical Guide for Evaluators.* Cecile has over 25 years of professional experience in the international development sector, including public-private partnerships (PPPs), rural development, agriculture and food security, with a focus primarily on Africa.

Karen Batjes (MPA, Carleton, Canada) is a freelance consultant in the Netherlands. Prior to this, she worked as a senior economist at the Planning Institute of Jamaica. Karen has over 20 years of experience in agricultural development, and more than 10 years in monitoring and evaluation (M&E), impact assessment, and capacity development. She has organized various international conferences on information and M&E. Karen is also a technical writer and has co-authored publications on impact assessment and M&E.

Seerp Wigboldus (MSc) is senior consultant at CDI, Wageningen University & Research. His work experience of 20+ years is mainly related to Asia and Africa and includes the field of strategic planning, monitoring and evaluation. He is currently finishing his PhD on responsible scaling of agricultural innovations.

Jan Brouwers (PhD) works as a senior consultant at CDI, Wageningen University & Research. He is a senior member of the Innovation & Change thematic group, and has a portfolio on multi-stakeholder partnership, social innovation, participatory planning and M&E, policy advice and gender. Jan also coordinates the social innovation research programme for Wageningen University & Research and is actively involved in the conceptual development of Theory of Change thinking and approach.

Sylvester Dickson Baguma (PhD) works for the National Agricultural Research Organisation (NARO) in Uganda. He is a co-facilitator for the CDI course on Managing for Sustainable Development Impact. In NARO, Sylvester facilitates research and development review and planning workshops and heads the information and knowledge management group. Currently, he supports the establishment of NARO's multi-stakeholder innovation partnerships along commodity value chains and develops staff competencies in managing agricultural research for impact. Sylvester uses the Theory of Change approach in NARO and other countries in Africa to develop organizational or corporate strategic plans, research and development proposals and results-oriented M&E systems.

MANAGING FOR SUSTAINABLE DEVELOPMENT IMPACT

Cecile Kusters and
Karen Batjes
with Seerp Wigboldus,
Jan Brouwers and
Sylvester Dickson Baguma

AN INTEGRATED
APPROACH
TO PLANNING,
MONITORING AND
EVALUATION

Practical Action Publishing Ltd
The Schumacher Centre, Bourton on Dunsmore, Rugby,
Warwickshire, CV23 9QZ, UK
www.practicalactionpublishing.org

Wageningen Centre for Development Innovation,
Wageningen University & Research
PO Box 88, 6700 AB Wageningen, The Netherlands
www.wur.eu/cdi

A catalogue record for this book is available from the
British Library. A catalogue record for this book has
been requested from the Library of Congress.

ISBN 978-1-85339-981-7 Paperback
ISBN 978-1-78044-980-7 Library Ebook
ISBN 978-1-78044-981-4 Ebook

Citation: Kusters, C.S.L. and Batjes, K. with Wigboldus,
S., Brouwers, J. and Baguma, S.D. (2017) Managing
for Sustainable Development Impact: An Integrated
Approach to Planning, Monitoring and Evaluation,
Wageningen: Wageningen Centre for Development
Innovation, Wageningen University & Research, and
Rugby, UK: Practical Action Publishing, http://dx.doi.
org/10.3362/9781780449807

Since 1974, Practical Action Publishing has published
and disseminated books and information in support
of international development work throughout the
world. Practical Action Publishing is a trading name
of Practical Action Publishing Ltd (Company Reg. No.
1159018), the wholly owned publishing company of
Practical Action. Practical Action Publishing trades
only in support of its parent charity objectives and any
profits are covenanted back to Practical Action
(Charity Reg. No. 247257, Group VAT Registration No.
880 9924 76).

Wageningen Centre for Development Innovation,
Wageningen University & Research focuses on
supporting the development of sustainable and
inclusive food systems. We link cutting edge processes
of innovation and learning with Wageningen University
& Research's world-leading scientific and technical
expertise. We work with farmers and NGOs, businesses
and entrepreneurs, and governments and international
organizations in many different countries to support
and facilitate processes of innovation and change.

Editor: Jenessi Matturi
Design: reuverandco.com
Printed in the UK by Cambrian Printers, Aberystwyth

FSC
www.fsc.org
MIX
Paper from
responsible sources
FSC® C005094

PART 1: LAYING THE FOUNDATION

ORIENTATIONS:
PEOPLE
LEARNING
CONTEXT

COMMUNICATION

STRATEGIC GUIDANCE

EFFECTIVE OPERATIONS

MONITORING & EVALUATION

IMPACT
FOCUS

CAPACITIES
AND
CONDITIONS

The Managing for Sustainable
Development Impact (M4SDI) Framework

PART 2: CORE M4SDI PROCESSES

ABOUT THIS GUIDE

This guide is about managing development initiatives and organizations towards sustainable development impact. It builds on the work of Guijt and Woodhill in the 2002 IFAD publication *Managing for Impact in Rural Development: A Guide for Project M&E*. Since then, the managing for sustainable development impact (M4SDI) approach has evolved with insights and feedback from CDI colleagues, clients, partners, and over 800 people who have been trained in its use. In addition, the authors have drawn on the work of many others.

M4SDI is an integrated, results-oriented management approach, which can be used across a range of sectors and domains in a variety of contexts, and aims to contribute towards the Sustainable Development Goals (SDGs). It seeks to integrate ideas and practices from a range of approaches and methodologies for planning, monitoring and evaluation, using appropriate methods or tools that engage people in a process of learning and adaptation. It is specifically aimed at strengthening the readiness of leaders, decision-makers and development practitioners to effectively manage their initiatives/organizations in complex settings. M4SDI belongs to a special niche of management approaches, providing relevant perspectives on what makes for effective management for those directly involved in managing initiatives/organizations and wider groups of stakeholders. Many of the people trained in M4SDI have become believers and practitioners of the approach because it addresses several of the most serious concerns in development, such as the difficulty in reaching primary stakeholders, designing effective strategies and related monitoring and evaluation (M&E), focusing on capacity development and change management, and achieving sustainable development impact. The strength of M4SDI lies in its people-centred approach and how it seeks to integrate management processes within a complex environment.

The evolvement of the approach needs to be documented to share lessons learned and support capacity development. And so the principles and practices covered in this guide relate to a variety of development initiatives/organizations in the fields of agriculture, food security, local economic development, value chains, enterprise development, and ecosystem governance. Much of the discussion takes place within the often complex context of development. As such, the guide aims to find a good balance between comprehensiveness and the principle of 'less is more'.

WHO THIS GUIDE IS FOR

This guide is meant to help leaders, managers, decision-makers, M&E staff and other development practitioners navigate their organizations and development initiatives more effectively towards sustainable development impact. It provides ideas, theories and tools which will help practitioners to better:

- understand the context in which the development initiative/organization operates, and tailor M4SDI to this specific context;
- connect sustainable development-related goals to stakeholder perspectives and motivations;
- engage people meaningfully in the initiative/organization and create or maintain a learning environment;
- turn M&E into an effective instrument for strategic guidance towards sustainable development impact.

HOW THE GUIDE IS ORGANIZED

The guide allows readers to orient themselves more easily within the subject of managing for sustainable development impact. It is divided into two parts.

Part 1 (Chapters 1 to 5) provides the core ideas underpinning M4SDI and what it can contribute. We discuss how the world has become increasingly complex and connected through globalization, with more interrelated challenges. We examine the limitations of common development models in addressing such challenges appropriately. We argue for approaches which harness the role that systems thinking can play in helping leaders and development practitioners identify ways of managing towards sustainable development impact.

Chapter 1 outlines the M4SDI approach, the changing context of international development and how M4SDI can help your initiative/organization succeed in this setting.

Chapter 2 is the most conceptual, introducing selected models and theories that have inspired the M4SDI approach. This includes systems perspectives on change in complex systems and frameworks which can help guide initiatives/organizations in situations that are dynamic and unpredictable.

Chapter 3 sets out key orientations that underpin the M4SDI approach. These include people, learning, and context orientations.

Chapter 4 highlights the pivotal role of appropriate capacities and conditions in supporting core M4SDI processes and enabling initiatives/organizations to be people-, learning- and context-oriented. This includes the essential competencies required to successfully manage an initiative/organization towards sustainable development impact.

Chapter 5 explores the role of communication in facilitating M4SDI processes.

Part 2 (Chapters 6, 7, 8 and 9) outlines in detail 'the when and how' of M4SDI. This involves being able to recognize issues and problems that are often multifaceted and knowing when and how to use the core processes strategically to tailor-make your own M4SDI approach. It is crucial to undertake these core processes with a perspective on people, learning and context, whilst ensuring a good communication flow and putting the necessary capacities and conditions in place.

The core processes associated with managing a development initiative/organization for sustainable development impact are covered in depth in Chapters 6, 7 and 8. These interrelated processes include: strategic guidance (**Chapter 6**), effective operations (**Chapter 7**) and monitoring and evaluation (M&E) (**Chapter 8**).

Chapter 9 showcases stories from the field, including narratives from a non-governmental organization (NGO) in Pakistan, a research organization in Uganda and a partnership programme in Ethiopia. The stories reflect the diverse settings in which M4SDI can be implemented.

In the **Annexes** we include: a list of widely-used tools and methodologies; evaluation stories; tips on evaluation design; recommended data analysis procedures; references; and a glossary of terms.

PART 1

LAYING

THE

FOUNDATION

CHAPTER 1

INTRODUCING M4SDI

CHANGING CONTEXT OF INTERNATIONAL DEVELOPMENT

SUMMARY

WHAT M4SDI IS ABOUT

This chapter sets out what M4SDI is about and how it connects to challenges in the management of development initiatives/ organizations, which aim to contribute to the Sustainable Development Goals (SDGs or Global Goals). SDGs represent a universal call to action to end poverty, protect the planet and ensure that all people enjoy peace and prosperity. The 17 interconnected SDGs build on the successes and setbacks of the Millennium Development Goals (MDGs), and their scope has been broadened to include new areas such as climate change, economic inequality, innovation, sustainable consumption, peace and justice. The SDGs call for an integrated approach to address these global challenges. M4SDI, an integrated approach to managing organizations and development initiatives, can help governments, the private sector, NGOs, civil society and individuals respond effectively to these challenges and contribute to the achievement of set goals.

This approach provides ideas on strengthening the capacity of initiatives/ organizations, including the competencies of individuals, to get their act together in responding effectively to complex (global) challenges.

The M4SDI approach has evolved within the context of international development to contribute to the (collective) capacity and competencies of leaders, development practitioners and other change agents to guide development initiatives/ organizations towards fulfilling their mission. M4SDI can be applied in various development settings including projects, programmes, organizations, networks, alliances, as well as in business enterprises. Each form of organization will have its own structure, context, management style and mission, so M4SDI in a development project setting will look quite different from M4SDI in the context of a business enterprise.

The approach was developed particularly for leaders and development practitioners engaged in more complex change processes, where the context is dynamic and unpredictable, requiring a need to respond quickly. It is part of a family of approaches used for well-informed planning and decision-making processes in initiatives/organizations. Others include results-based management (RBM) and managing for development results (MfDR). M4SDI differs from these approaches by actively engaging people in processes of understanding and adapting to the context, partnering in making explicit and adapting the Theories of Change (ToC) and turning M&E into an active instrument for learning and decision-making. M4SDI incorporates ideas and practices from other approaches, and draws on a range of readily available methods/tools. 'Managing' in M4SDI is about navigating complexity towards sustainable development impact.

The M4SDI approach consists of core processes, underpinned by key orientations that determine the nature and scope of these processes, and supported by communication and capacities and conditions to implement these core processes (see Figure 1.1). The core processes include strategic guidance, effective operations and monitoring and evaluation (M&E).

Management processes take place in a specific context and involve people from very diverse backgrounds in terms of their interests, values and perspectives. In M4SDI, it is important to deal with this diversity, and to engage people in a process of shared learning, to gain their commitment, support and perspectives for informed decision-making. This requires people and learning orientation. Further, it is necessary to keep a close eye on the context in order to learn from what emerges, and respond or adapt to any changes in the environment (context orientation). For these processes to function smoothly, key orientations, capacities and conditions and communication are crucial.

Strategic guidance is about managing strategic processes towards sustainable development impact. It includes understanding the situation and its context, making explicit assumptions about how change happens (ToC) and developing strategies towards agreed (visions of) changes. It also includes navigating within a complex and changing context, using information generated through M&E, as well as providing leadership with strategic thinking, strategic foresight and systems thinking.

Effective operations are about turning your strategic plans and ideas into action, and include project management, finance management, human resource management, operational planning, procurement and contract management, maintenance management, information management, and coordination and communication.

Monitoring and evaluation (M&E) are about informing strategic and operational decision-making. This includes monitoring what works and doesn't and what emerges in a complex context.

People orientation is about acknowledging the central role that human interactions play in complex development processes. This involves engaging people meaningfully to understand and work with others in contexts involving different interests, perspectives, relationships, and power dynamics. Strong leadership competencies and facilitation skills are crucial.

Learning orientation is about enhancing learning and creating an environment where learning takes place at the individual, group, organizational and societal levels. This includes not only understanding, but also sense-making to inform strategic and operational decision-making. Engaging people in planning processes and M&E makes these processes more meaningful and enhances the utility of M&E findings and related processes.

Context orientation is about understanding and responding to the internal and external environments in which an initiative/organization operates. This includes understanding: the wider setting (e.g. political dynamics, policies, future trends, key actors, etc.); the specific context (e.g. community setting); organizational structures and processes underpinning the initiative/organization; and the dynamics of staff and stakeholders. Responses to these dynamics need to be situational specific, and require strategic and systems thinking.

Capacities and conditions are about shaping to the readiness of leaders and practitioners to engage in and manage a development initiative/organization towards sustainable development impact. This includes having the capacity and competencies to implement initiatives effectively and responsibly and creating conditions conducive to facilitating change.

Communication is integral to all the M4SDI processes and is the basis for good relationships and collaboration, which are especially important when working in complex contexts.

The various elements of the M4SDI approach operate against the backdrop of maintaining the sustainable development impact focus and much effort is required to ensure that they work in unison to provide successful results (see Figure 1.1). This requires strategic choices on appropriate processes within a particular context.

Figure 1.1 The Managing for Sustainable Development Impact (M4SDI) Framework

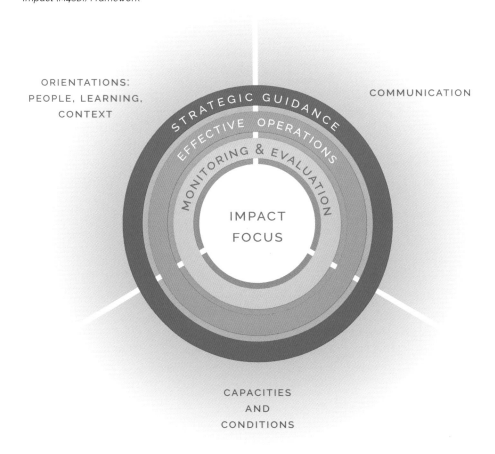

CHANGING CONTEXT OF INTERNATIONAL DEVELOPMENT

A range of factors have had a marked influence on the international development landscape. They include increased global connectivity as seen in globalization, availability and use of mobile technologies, shifting power dynamics in the world, the increasing role of the private sector in development, and a rising demand for evidence of impact. In addition to these, there is increasing focus on scaling, (public–private) partnerships, and interdisciplinary approaches and teams. Together, these factors have resulted in a more complex and multifaceted environment, with important implications for management practices, strategic planning and M&E in development initiatives/organizations. Below are some conditions which shape the context of international development and how M4SDI seeks to connect to them.

Complex challenges

The development landscape has become increasingly complex. Many of the issues that we face, such as poverty (SDG 1), food insecurity and malnutrition (SDG 2), and climate change (SDG 13) call for partnerships to address these sustainable development challenges (SDG 17). According to the United Nations (2017), 'a successful sustainable development agenda requires partnerships between governments, the private sector and civil society. These inclusive partnerships built upon principles and values, a shared vision, and shared goals that place people and the planet at the center, are needed at the global, regional, national and local levels'. And in fact, the private sector is now playing a more active role in partnerships with the government and civil society. These partnerships, however, need good leadership (see Chapter 3) with strategic competencies like strategic thinking (Chapter 4) and systems thinking (Chapters 2 and 4), and call for an in-depth understanding of the situation and continuous adaptation to a changing environment (see Chapter 2, Chapter 3 section 'Context orientation', Chapter 6 section 'Theory of Change' and Chapter 8 section 'Trends in M&E').

To address the problems mentioned above, Buanes and Jentoft (2009: 446) state that 'contributions from many disciplines are needed with inputs that should preferably

A multi-stakeholder partnership (MSP) is defined as 'a process of interactive learning, empowerment and participatory governance that enables stakeholders with interconnected problems and ambitions, but often differing interests, to be collectively innovative and resilient when faced with the emerging risks, crises, and opportunities of a complex and changing environment'.

Source: Brouwer et al., 2015: 18

> Impact is defined as the positive and negative changes produced by a development initiative/organization, directly or indirectly, intended or unintended. This involves the main impacts and effects resulting from the initiative/organization on sustainable development.
>
> *Source:* OECD, 2016

be balanced and integrated. Therefore, interdisciplinarity gains increasing support from scientists, policy-makers and funding agencies', but that structural and cultural barriers need to be addressed to support interdisciplinarity. Scaling is another issue that is getting increasing attention. Wigboldus and Brouwers (2016: 16), refer to scaling as 'strategies and approaches... [aimed at realizing] the potential of relatively isolated inventions, innovations, and developments benefitting people and situations more widely'. Complexities need to be taken seriously in scaling. In the analysis, design, and strategic guidance of envisaged scaling initiatives, a transdisciplinary and multi-stakeholder approach needs to be considered.

Increasing pressure to show results and define Theories of Change

There is growing pressure from both funding agencies and the general public to show concrete results of how development interventions have affected the lives of the people targeted, or the environment they live in. This has resulted in a shift in emphasis from outputs to the demand for reporting on outcomes (i.e. the changes that come about as a result of an initiative, especially behavioural change, but also changes in awareness, motivation, skills, and knowledge) and impact. In relation to this, there has been an increasing request by funders to demonstrate a Theory of Change (see Chapter 6) for a development initiative.

The changing role of M&E

There is increasing demand for M&E though much of this still relates to external reporting requirements (proving) rather than to enhancing the ability to guide processes strategically towards impact (improving). This is perhaps linked to prevailing ideas reflected in some definitions of evaluation (see Chapter 8, section 'Trends in M&E'), which emphasize accountability rather than seeing it more in terms of a dynamic process of evaluative thinking. As a result, the role of M&E in M4SDI is often ignored, along with the information and insights generated. Gradually, however, this is changing and there is recognition that these processes can be used not only for accountability purposes, but also for self-assessment and learning (in terms of what worked and what didn't) and that stakeholders need to be involved in this. More and more initiatives/organizations are engaging multiple stakeholders and forming partnerships and strategic alliances in learning-oriented monitoring and evaluation processes to provide evidence and inform strategic and operational decision making.

M4SDI offers ideas on connecting accountability with self-assessment, learning (from failure, success or emerging issues) and how to engage stakeholders in the various processes. However, whilst knowledge and experience on meaningful M&E have grown, the capacities and conditions to support this still need strengthening. This includes not only M&E competence development, but also streamlining M&E between partners and providing the necessary resources to undertake useful, and evidence-based evaluation.

Scaling

The topic of scaling is high on the agenda of development initiatives. In this context, it is essentially about seeing the benefits of initiatives and innovations go beyond the initial focus groups/areas in which they emerged. However, in many cases development initiatives have not thought this through very well. Theories of Change rarely articulate how scaling is expected to happen, or rather linear perspectives are dominant in which complexities involved in scaling processes have not been addressed. The effects can be twofold: 1) scaling does not happen or only in a very limited way, 2) scaling does happen, but has adverse economic, social, and/or environmental effects. What is good at a small scale or in one place (e.g. a particular country) may not necessarily work out positively at a larger scale or region. This means that we need to take scaling processes more seriously, e.g. by articulating a Theory of Scaling to enhance readiness to engage effectively and responsibly with scaling processes. This includes asking questions such as: Why would this go to scale? What if this goes to scale? Who drives the scaling agenda and who would ultimately benefit? Scaling is rarely a process which can be directed by one group or organization. It usually involves and affects a range of stakeholders as well as processes which cannot be controlled. This means we need to often start thinking in new ways about scaling processes.

Public-private partnerships (PPPs)

Public-private partnerships (PPPs), sometimes referred to as P3s or public finance initiatives (PIFs), are mechanisms or long-term arrangements that governments enter into with the private sector to provide works and services to the public. These may include public infrastructure such as bridges, roads and schools, as well as social services such as the provision of on-the-job training, subsidized housing and health services. PPPs are a good way for governments to procure efficient services. There has been growing interest in PPPs since the financial crisis in 2008, as many cash-strapped governments see the private sector as an additional source of funding to improve infrastructure, provide essential services and share risks and responsibilities. PPPs are also a way to: improve the capabilities of local firms by entering into joint ventures with international firms; introduce new technology to enhance government services; assist in the provision of social services and works where government resources are stretched. Managing PPPs requires strong leadership with strategic competencies to bring about sustainable development impact. Strong management is also needed to ensure that PPPs operate efficiently and transparently.

Integrated approaches/transdisciplinarity
Transdisciplinarity refers to the integration of academic knowledge from various disciplines and non-academic knowledge. Throughout the research process academic and non-academic stakeholders are in dialogue. Societal renewal more and more takes place at the interface of disciplines with synergy between multiple actors. There is growing recognition in the value of sharing insights between disciplines and with people with different experiences in order to bridge the gap between theory and practice, stimulate creativity and out-of-the-box thinking and develop more comprehensive approaches to tackle the problems we face today. However, there are not many examples of transdisciplinary cooperation, which can be attributed in part to structural and cultural barriers. As a result, Buanes and Jentoft (2009: 453) call for a change in the way people review proposals and point to the fact that this is difficult because 'norms, values and worldviews are deeply embedded in this professionalization, and would tend to work against it'. Given that change does not come about overnight, what is important now is for us to start laying the foundation for a culture of transdisciplinarity to emerge. A study by Shahin et al. (2014: 7) for the European Commission proposes a 'smart approach' that includes 'structuring projects [initiatives] in order to enhance the role of the different disciplines' and 'structuring call texts and using additional tools and mechanisms to ensure that useful interaction across disciplines is guaranteed'.

Methodological debate on what is considered evidence
There has been a push towards generating and using credible evidence of meaningful outcomes and impact in order to support policy- and decision-making processes. The methods used to assess such evidence have consequently become very important, sparking the debate on the reliability of the methods used to obtain this evidence. For example, some people believe that only scientific knowledge should be considered as evidence, while others think that socially-constructed knowledge can be used as evidence. In any event, what is clear is that there are different paradigms and theories and this has implications for the methods and approaches used in M&E (see Chapter 8 section 'Trends in M&E').

Proliferation of information
The information and guidance documents on planning, monitoring, and evaluation are countless. This may be overwhelming for many. So, how do you choose what to work with? M4SDI helps navigate the multifaceted options, shows ideas on

connecting or integrating methods and methodologies, and offers ideas on how to make choices in designing a tailor-made approach to manage for sustainable development impact.

SUMMARY

Conditions which shape the context of international development require a reconsideration of how we manage development initiatives/organizations. The M4SDI approach responds to this. This includes responding to complex challenges (SDGs) as well as the demands on development initiatives/organizations to prove impact. Making a meaningful contribution to sustainable development involves a willingness to learn, to network and connect across sectors, scales and domains and be prepared to adapt to change. This often requires working on new capacities and competencies which are discussed in this guide.

The chapters that follow further explain the M4SDI approach and how it can support initiatives/organizations dealing with challenges in a complex environment.

CHAPTER 2

UNDERSTANDING COMPLEXITY

A SYSTEMS APPROACH TO DEALING WITH COMPLEXITY
   A systems perspective
   Complex systems
   Systems thinking
   Power in systems

MAKING THEORIES OF CHANGE EXPLICIT
   Options for change strategies

SUMMARY

DEALING WITH CHANGE IN COMPLEX SYSTEMS

- Understand what complexity is
- Understand how to use the systems approach to deal with complexity
- Understand the role Theories of Change can play in enhancing readiness to think and act strategically in the face of complexity

Managing for sustainable development impact is about change in complex systems, and involves understanding the adaptive management processes that are needed when you try to intervene in complex systems.

Jim Woodhill, personal communication, 15 January 2017

Sustainable development involves change processes which are dynamic and often difficult to predict i.e. complex. Developing a good understanding of what is going on and what can be anticipated involves a multifaceted and complex reality. Managing for sustainable development impact (M4SDI) is an integrated approach to managing development initiatives/organizations, aimed at supporting leaders and practitioners to navigate such complexity appropriately and effectively. And using M4SDI enhances the contributions initiatives/organizations make towards achieving the Sustainable Development Goals (SDGs). Systems thinking alerts decision-makers to the connectedness of these dimensions and related phenomena, events, factors and actors, and thus underpins the M4SDI approach.

In this chapter, we first discuss ways of understanding complexity in nature and society and options for engaging strategically with complexity. We then explain how a systems approach helps make sense of complexity to inform management decision-making. This includes recognizing how power plays out in complex systems. We conclude this chapter with a brief introduction to the role Theories of Change (ToC) can play in enhancing readiness to think and act strategically in the face of complexity. This chapter is a stepping stone towards more elaborate discussions on key orientations of the M4SDI approach in Chapter 3 and the articulation of ToC in Chapter 6.

The work of Kurtz and Snowden (2003) is helpful in showing how to deal with management challenges in complex systems. They developed a decision-making tool, the Cynefin framework (Figure 2.1), which distinguishes between four key types of situation: simple; complicated; complex; and chaotic. In this framework, the level of complexity is related to the nature of the relationship between cause and effect, and this requires different forms of analysis, planning, monitoring and management. An explanation of these four types of situation is presented within the context of the framework developed by Snowden and Boone (2007) to guide leaders and practitioners in their decision-making and management styles.

Simple context – the domain of practice
In simple contexts or 'known knowns', there are limited, stable interactions, and cause-and-effect relationships are predictable and clear to everyone. In this context leaders/development practitioners must first assess (sense) the facts of a situation, then categorize and respond to it. Simple contexts are often heavily process-oriented, such as the processing of loan payments. Following strict procedures and using 'best practices' will generally lead to the same result. In this situation, decisions can be delegated and the appropriate actions taken and so close monitoring is not needed. To avoid complacency and to keep on top of new changes, leaders/development practitioners need to communicate regularly with

Figure 2.1 The Cynefin sense-making framework
Source: Kurtz and Snowden, 2003

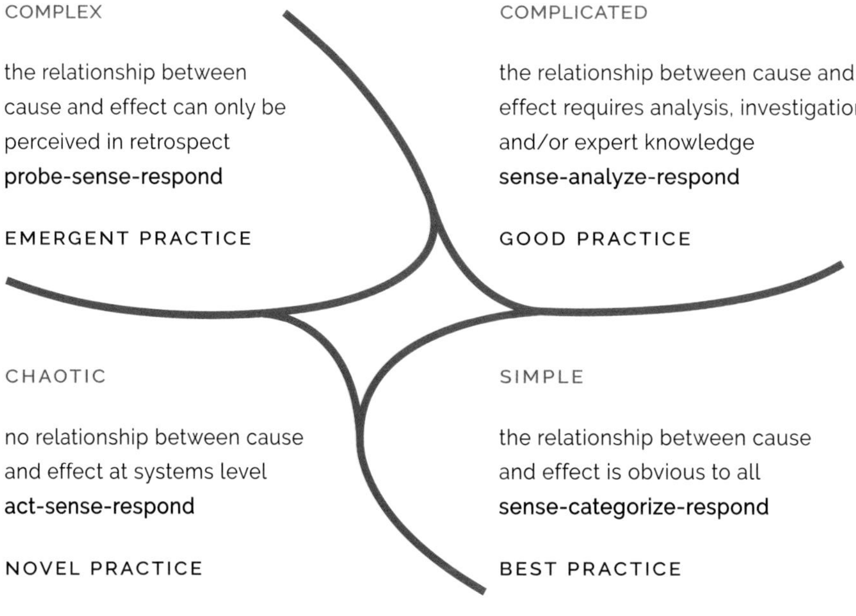

COMPLEX	COMPLICATED
the relationship between cause and effect can only be perceived in retrospect **probe-sense-respond**	the relationship between cause and effect requires analysis, investigation and/or expert knowledge **sense-analyze-respond**
EMERGENT PRACTICE	GOOD PRACTICE
CHAOTIC	SIMPLE
no relationship between cause and effect at systems level **act-sense-respond**	the relationship between cause and effect is obvious to all **sense-categorize-respond**
NOVEL PRACTICE	BEST PRACTICE

staff and stakeholders and have an open-door policy towards those with innovative ideas on improving processes (see Table 2.1).

Complicated context – the domain of experts

In complicated contexts or 'known unknowns', there is a clear relationship between cause-and-effect, but not everyone can see it, and there may be multiple right answers to problems that may arise. In this situation, leaders/development practitioners need to sense, analyse and respond to the situation. Experts can help to analyse the situation, and investigate options. For example, a sick child can be diagnosed and treated by a medical doctor, or an irrigation engineer can be called upon to help find solutions to irrigation problems. Within this context, monitoring needs to be supported by those with the specific expertise in question.

Complex context – the domain of emergence

In complex contexts or 'unknown unknowns' cause-and-effect relationships may be identifiable in retrospect, but cannot be predicted with any certainty. Here, dealing with multiple challenges requires to first probe, then sense and respond to a situation. Examples include dealing with climate change, food security or HIV/AIDS where solutions are not known beforehand but need to be discovered through the collaboration of different experts and practitioners (e.g. interdisciplinary or transdisciplinary research). In this situation, outcomes may be unforeseen and this requires initiatives to be flexible and closely monitored to adapt quickly when results prove negative. This also requires room to conduct safe-fail experiments, so that instructive patterns can emerge. It also involves working closely with key stakeholders to understand what is happening, how planned interventions are progressing, and practising adaptive management.

Chaotic context – the domain of rapid response

In chaotic contexts or 'unknowables', cause-and-effect relationships are impossible to determine because they shift constantly and no manageable patterns exist, only turbulence. Leaders are expected to first act to establish order, then to sense where there is stability and instability and respond in a manner that transforms the chaotic situation into a complex one, or even into a simple situation. Examples include crises like the September 11, 2001 attack, drought, or war. In crisis management, communication is crucial and has to be direct and top-down as there is no time to consult people. It is important to transform this situation from chaos to a complex one where identification of emerging patterns can help discover new opportunities and prevent similar situations happening in the future.

Each of these types of context requires a different decision-making and management style with implications for the way M&E is carried out (see Table 2.1).

Context characteristics	Role of leader/ development practitioner	Danger signals	Response to danger signals	Implications for M&E
SIMPLE				
Stable environment Cause-and-effect relationships Clear Standard procedures	Sense, categorize, respond Delegate Draw on best practices Communicate in a clear, direct manner Fact-based management	Complacency Seeking to make complex problems simple Overreliance on best practices if context shifts	Create communication channels to challenge the status quo Stay connected without micro-management Do not take for granted that things are simple Recognize the value and limitations of best practice	M&E is fairly straightforward and simple since cause-and-effect relationships are generally known
COMPLICATED				
Relatively stable environment Expert diagnosis with related options required Clear cause-and-effect relationships but not evident to everyone initially	Sense, analyse, respond Get expert advice; seek additional views from other stakeholders Listen to conflicting advice (from both experts and non-experts/ stakeholders) Fact-based management	Experts overconfident about their own solutions Views of a wide cross-section of stakeholders excluded	Encourage stakeholders to challenge expert opinions to open up to new ways of thinking Use different tools to get people to think out of the box	Experts need to be involved in M&E to assess the implementation of selected options, preferably in collaboration with stakeholders

Table 2.1 Decision-making and management styles

Source: Adapted from Snowden and Boone, 2007

Context characteristics	Role of leader/ development practitioner	Danger signals	Response to danger signals	Implications for M&E
COMPLEX				
Environment dynamic, unpredictable No right answers: trial and error, emergent instructive patterns Need for creativity and innovation Many, often competing, ideas	Probe, sense, respond Allow for safe fail experiments, so that patterns can emerge Increase level of interaction and communication between experts and stakeholders Get the views of a wide cross-section of stakeholders. Use methods that help stimulate/ create ideas Allow for failure Pattern-based management	Temptation to fall back on conventional management styles, based on command and control Temptation to look for facts rather than allow for experimentation and patterns to emerge Seeking to resolve problems quickly	Be patient and allow time to critically reflect Ensure stakeholders are involved in experimentation and sharing of lessons learned so that patterns can emerge	Monitor different strategic options and (safe fail) experiments closely and stimulate sharing lessons learned and sharing different views to discover patterns that emerge Developmental evaluation (Patton, 2011) addresses complexity
CHAOTIC				
Turbulent and chaotic environment, difficult to predict No clear cause and effect relationships Crisis, no time to think or consult people	Act, sense, respond Look for what works, since there is no time to seek right answers or to think and analyse properly Take immediate action to re-establish order, since there is no time for much consultation. Provide clear, direct communication across the board Pattern-based management	Command and control approach longer than needed Missed opportunity for innovation Not transforming the chaotic situation to a more stable situation	Put in place mechanisms to take advantage of emerging opportunities Encourage staff and stakeholders to challenge your point of view once the crisis is over Work to shift the situation from chaotic to complex Keep an eye open for unexpected needs in chaotic situations	No time for extensive M&E; instead focus on quickly understanding what works

As discussed earlier, managing for sustainable development impact involves dealing with complexity and complex systems in which cause-and-effect relationships can often only be known retrospectively. In order to make good management decisions, you need to make sense of such complexity to avoid becoming overwhelmed by it, or neglect its implications. You also need to make decisions which make sense in view of such complex dynamics. A systems approach helps equip decision-makers to do so.

A systems perspective

According to Williams and Hummelbrunner (2010: 16), 'there is no single, concise, and generally agreed definition' for a system. For them, a system consists of interrelated elements with a boundary that determines what is inside of a system and what is outside (context or environment). So systems can be defined at various levels of complexity e.g. from a plant cell to an organization, and from a society to an ecosystem. It all depends on where you define your boundaries. Essentially, a systems perspective is about considering things in their connectedness and coherence and not as isolated elements or phenomena.

As stakeholders, it is important to agree on what is considered to be within the system focus, and what is outside of it. In other words, consider what to take into account and what connections and dynamics are part of the focus of your initiative/ organization. Consciously defining the boundaries of the system you want to focus on creates awareness of what your initiative/organization contributes to, and how it is affected by the conditions and changes occurring outside the scope of your system focus.

Complex systems

Brouwer et al. (2015: 49) state that 'systems can be relatively simple, with changes in inputs, resulting in easily predictable changes and outputs, but they can also be highly complex, with a vast network of interrelationships'. They further indicate that (*ibid*: 173) 'a complex system has the following features:
· It involves large numbers of interacting elements.
· The interactions are nonlinear, and minor changes can have disproportionately major consequences.
· The system is dynamic, which means solutions cannot be imposed on it, but instead arise from the circumstances. This can be referred to as emergence'.

According to Hummelbrunner (2011: 395) development initiatives have become multilayered and multifaceted i.e. more complex, due to a range of challenges and situations:

- Achievement depends on the interaction of different resources and the type of collaboration that exists between the main actors who control these resources.
- These actors are diverse as they have different values, needs and interests.
- The context in which these initiatives operate is often dynamic and unpredictable, making it difficult to make strategic choices.
- For development to take place, resources, technology, knowledge and an open change process are necessary, but it is difficult to know in advance what is needed, so it is crucial to have regular adaptation and shaping of the initiative in response to changing contexts and lessons learned.

Hummelbrunner (2011: 395) attributes this complexity to various elements – such as 'actors, actions, factors' – 'and their linkages'. If changes occur in one element, this can influence other elements often with unexpected consequences. In complex contexts or complex systems, change therefore happens in unexpected and surprising ways and cannot be fully controlled or managed. This requires establishing close relationships with and between stakeholders, allowing experimentation and the sharing of lessons so that patterns can emerge, and responses tailored to the situation.

Systems thinking

Williams and Hummelbrunner (2010) state that dealing with complex systems requires thinking and acting from a systems perspective, which involves not only describing, but also making sense of complex and complicated situations (see Figure 2.1). Key concepts in systems thinking that distinguish a systems approach from other approaches dealing with complexity, include interrelationships, perspectives (of a situation), and boundaries (i.e. who defines what is in or out of a system). 'So thinking systemically [or systems thinking] is about making sense of the world rather than merely describing it. It is fundamentally a sense-making process that organizes the messiness of the real world into concepts and components that allow us to understand things a bit better' (ibid: 18).

Brouwer et al. (2015) further describe systems thinking as the ability to view problems and events in relation to whole systems, while Stroh (2015: 16) defines systems thinking 'as the ability to understand interconnections in such a way as to achieve a desired purpose'. His book Systems Thinking for Social Change is based on the idea that 'applying systems thinking principles and tools enables you to achieve better results with fewer resources in more lasting ways' (ibid: 1). Stroh (2015) identifies ways in which systems thinking can help foster change and

support managing for sustainable development impact, some include the need to:
- Become aware of your role in contributing to the problem you want to address, and reflect on and shift your own intentions, thinking and actions.
- Support stakeholders in recognizing that they collectively contribute to the problem despite their best efforts.
- Focus on a few coordinated changes over time to obtain significant and sustainable system-wide impact, instead of trying to do too much with too little resources.
- Embrace continuous learning, which is a key characteristic of any meaningful change in a complex system.

Systems thinking, therefore, helps you to probe more deeply into problems and not accept things at face value. It involves asking questions and collaborating with others to understand situations as part of wider conditions in which actors and factors are interconnected. It also considers the role you can play within the wider context of issues being addressed.

Applying systems thinking in M4SDI therefore leads to three key orientations: people, learning and context. This involves understanding and engaging (with) stakeholders, learning from emerging patterns and processes, and responding in a dynamic and unpredictable context. Engaging stakeholders is about understanding their perspectives, relationships, and power relations, and how these factors influence change in complex systems.

Power in systems
As explained earlier, the Cynefin framework helps you to understand and work with different situations, including complex contexts. Systems thinking is useful in understanding and making sense of complexity, how different elements of a system (i.e. problems or issues) are interrelated, and what emerges in a dynamic and often unpredictable context. This sense-making can help to strategically guide the initiative/organization towards sustainable development impact. Green (2016: 15–16) brings an additional dimension to the discussion by arguing that 'in complex systems, institutions are needed to keep the playing field level enough to encourage the dynamism at its heart – for example, through competition policy, access to information, enhancing general technological skills, or credit and other support for small firms...' and that 'the state and other institutions must find ways to push markets to pursue socially desirable goals, such as greater equality, human rights, or long-term sustainability, without undermining the dynamism of the market system'. See Chapter 6 section 'Situation analysis' for more on institutional analysis.

Green (2016: 20-22) also formulated the following principles for working in complex systems, some of which have already been mentioned:

- Be flexible: This will allow you to respond to emerging events and signals of change.
- Seek fast and ongoing feedback: This will help you to pick up and deal with signals of change.
- Success is often accidental: Provide feedback quickly in order to detect and respond to unexpected success.
- Undertake multiple parallel experiments: For example, set up lean businesses based on best guesses on what will work, and then have a fairly rapid low-cost cycle of experimentation and adaptation until something is successful.
- Learn by doing (and failing): This includes fast feedback on what works and how, as well as on unintended consequences.
- Identify and discuss your rules of thumb: Make these rules explicit as well as regularly review them.
- Convene and broker relationships: This includes thinking about who to invite to the table and creating space for dialogue.

Many of the issues mentioned above are also in line with organizational learning principles e.g. Senge's (2006) five disciplines (see Chapter 3 section 'Learning orientation').

Green also calls us to pay attention to power in order to identify opportunities and possibilities for change. He points to the work of Rowlands (1997) who developed an all-embracing approach to promote change rather than limit focus to visible power and bemoan the fact that some power is hidden and invisible. For instance different gender roles may express differences in power. If women are not able to have access to credit or own land they are excluded in their society from becoming an agricultural entrepreneur. This model has four aspects (Green, 2016: 33): the power within (i.e. sense of self-confidence and awareness of one's rights); power with (based on the power of collective action and solidarity); power to (the ability to decide and act on decisions); and power over (refers to hierarchical power and domination). He goes on to state that 'unless people first develop a sense of self-confidence and a belief in their own rights (power within), efforts to help them organize (power with) and demand a say (power to) may not bear fruit' (*ibid*: 33).

It is therefore important to address underlying power dynamics between conflicting interests, which, according to Green, can determine people's capacity even to participate, never mind influence outcomes (see Chapter 3 section 'People orientation').

Everyone has ideas about how change takes place, whether or not these ideas have been made explicit (see Chapter 6). This is referred to as 'Theories of Change' (ToC). It is useful to make explicit any underlying assumptions about how change happens, so that decision-making processes can be better informed and strategic choices made more transparent. In an effort to improve development practice at Oxfam GB, some staff members from the Programme Policy Team examined their Theories of Change. Eyben et al. (2008) present the four ways of conceptualizing change that they identified as part of the process: **the innovation-diffusion model**; the **'archetypes'** framework; **complexity theories of societal change**; and **Western sociological theories** of change.

Eyben et al. suggest the first of these, the innovation-diffusion model, which was developed by Everett Rogers. According to Rogers (2003: 5), diffusion is a 'process in which an innovation is communicated through certain channels over time among members of a social system'.

Next, Eyben et al. (2008: 202-203) identify how meaningful intervention leads to social reform. In this context they describe eight 'archetypes' that can bring about change:
- The Ladder: Fulfil the immediate needs of people and allow them to collect resources and have a voice.
- Intellectual Elites: Persuade those holding power to create openings for change to happen. Persuasion techniques can include perceived self-interest or even threats to make institutions and policies more responsive.
- People in the Streets: Build political pressure from the bottom to ensure institution accountability and equity across the various levels.
- A Good Example: Aim for localized success as this creates belief and provides safety for individuals, institutes, and countries to follow suit. In other words, lead by example.
- Shock to the System: Stay grounded when unpredictable events (e.g. economic or natural disasters) lead to failure of the power structures. New institutions and leaders will emerge.
- Follow the Leader: Inspire others. This will lead to exponential results.
- The Power of Belief: Increase awareness of rights and call on basic dignity and values.
- Good Old Fashioned Democracy: Promote democratic processes (political parties, elections) at various levels (e.g. communities, town councils, neighbourhood committees).

In relation to complexity theories of societal change, Eyben et al. (2008: 203-204) indicate that change is emergent and unpredictable, which requires flexibility to change in response to new opportunities and challenges.

Western sociological theories of how history is shaped include: change in society results from the unintended consequences of individual actions; the interaction between environmental opportunities (i.e. education) and technology affects how history happens; different beliefs and values interact to shape and change social behaviour; people are individually and collectively able to change their lives if they focus their actions; change results from contradictions in the way society is structured (Eyben et al., 2008: 204-206).

In a development initiative/organization, different stakeholders will have different ideas about how change could or should happen (their personal theories of change). To face this together and make it a shared effort, stakeholders need to operate on the basis of a shared ToC, even though they may hold different ideas in relation to particular parts of the envisaged change processes. This is why it is important to make your ToC or underlying assumptions explicit (see Chapter 6).

Options for change strategies

As suggested by Waddell (2014), in making explicit your ToC, it is important to keep in mind the unpredictable and emergent nature of complex systems, as this requires experimenting and using multiple strategies. He further goes on to say that in complex contexts, 'action choices are opportunity, power and value driven' and 'based upon addressing issues such as fairness, achievability, ownership, human rights, and the importance of the natural environment' (*ibid*: 9). Waddell offers four principles that can help guide the way initiatives are managed (*ibid*: 14): think long term (at least 25 years) when framing short-term policy; think beyond more than one domain (e.g. agriculture, water, health, conflict) and various actors (organizations) at different levels (local-to-global); focus on learning-by-doing and putting learning into practice; have a wide range of options (wide playing field) (Rotmans et al., 2001).

In addition to these principles, Waddell (2014: 14) suggests four change strategies that interact with each other (see Figure 2.2): forcing change through radical action by those who have been dispossessed; driving change through legitimate means such as imposing legal sanctions, joining labour unions and having strikes; allowing change through e.g. capital investments, rules and regulations; promoting change, e.g. through education and outreach activities, so as to raise awareness and support for action. These strategies and actions differ in terms of the extent to which there is collaboration or confrontation, and the insider-outsider power structure, where the insider traditionally holds power.

Figure 2.2 Change strategies
Source: Waddell, 2014, adapted
from Waddell, 2001

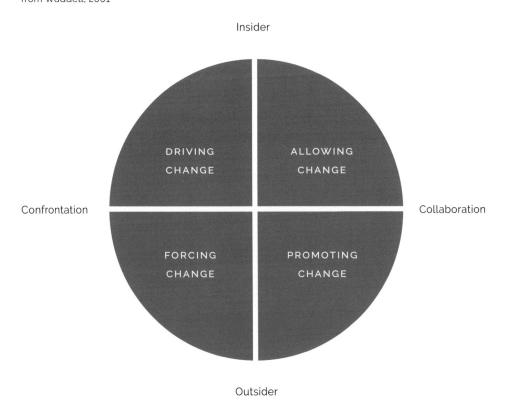

SUMMARY

Sustainable development involves change processes which are complex. Developing a good understanding about what is going on and what you can anticipate involves understanding a multifaceted and complex reality, as reflected by the 17 SDGs, which are interlinked and integrated. The Cynefin framework helps leaders/development practitioners to understand different levels of complexity and how to respond in complex contexts. A systems approach is useful when dealing with complexity and involves collaborating with others to make sense of situations where a diverse range of actors and factors are interconnected. Systems thinking also requires understanding power relationships and recognizing the role leaders/ development practitioners can play within the wider context of issues they are trying to address.

In thinking through theories on how change happens, you need to make explicit your underlying assumptions about how change happens, and plan how best to deal with complex contexts. Often this will involve the need to facilitate experimentation, use multiple strategies at different levels and with different stakeholders, deal with power differences and stimulate learning. It also involves providing fast and continuous feedback through close monitoring of what emerges, and what changes, and responding to this.

CHAPTER 3

PEOPLE ORIENTATION
> Understanding and working with individuals
> Understanding and working with groups
> Understanding and stimulating stakeholder engagement, commitment and ownership
> Managing diversity, conflict and power
> Leadership
> Summary: People orientation

LEARNING ORIENTATION
> What is learning?
> Kolb's experiential learning cycle and learning styles
> Organizational learning: triple-loop learning
> Organizational learning – Senge's five disciplines
> Summary: Learning orientation

CONTEXT ORIENTATION
> Situational responsiveness
> Developing and maintaining a context perspective
> Situation (context) analysis
> Summary: Context orientation

KEY ORIENTATIONS

Managing for sustainable development impact (M4SDI) requires thinking through what needs to be done to facilitate the core processes.

Given that traditional approaches to managing development initiatives/organizations are no longer adequate, and that new ways are required to meet today's challenges, we therefore need to pay attention to the following key areas:

· **People** play a pivotal role in shaping processes within systems – relationships and people's background, interests and actions matter. Engaging people is an important part of enhancing core M4SDI processes and helps us understand their attitudes, behaviour, values, and interrelationships to gain insight into problems and influence change.
· Since we cannot control systems, we should try to influence them by embracing **learning**. Creating a learning environment where people can share their experiences will help build capacities, equip us to better adapt to change and enhance performance.
· Taking a systems perspective helps us understand **context** – the environment in which the initiative/organization operates, the root causes of problems, and what can be done to address them.
· Developing **capacities and conditions** (see Chapter 4) to support the work of the initiative/organization is key. To manage for impact, organizational capabilities and requisite competencies are needed to create the conditions for an initiative/organization to perform and contribute towards sustainable development.
· Effective **communication** is crucial in any development initiative/organization (see Chapter 5). It helps us understand and connect with stakeholders and is the foundation for people-, learning- and context-orientations and core M4SDI processes. Communication also enhances commitment and cooperation and helps prevent or address conflict.

In this chapter, we explore what it means to be people-, learning- and context-oriented – perspectives that underpin core M4SDI processes and influence their implementation (see Chapters 6–8).

PEOPLE ORIENTATION

For change to happen in the lives of people living in poverty, they need to be given the opportunity to participate in decision-making processes that matter most to them (Burns et al., 2013). To transform their lives, they also need strong support to build their knowledge and organizational capacity, and create spaces for dialogue where inequalities can be redressed (*ibid*; Narayan et al., 2000). People orientation means that people processes must be part and parcel of the culture of any initiative/organization.

Dealing with people (staff and stakeholders in M4SDI) means dealing with diversity – different beliefs, backgrounds, knowledge, experiences, personalities, interests and views which influence our motivations to engage meaningfully in development initiatives/organizations. So how can leaders and practitioners engage people in development processes in spite of these differences? In this section we address this very question by examining how individuals and groups function, the theory behind stakeholder engagement and how to stimulate it, how to manage diversity, conflict and power, and the critical role leadership can play in supporting people processes, especially multi-stakeholder processes, and enabling initiatives/organizations to become people-oriented.

Understanding and working with individuals

Every individual is different, with a distinct personality and identity, partly formed genetically. Outside influences such as upbringing or education, and professional and personal experiences, have an impact on people as well. All these factors influence our thinking and behaviour, but we often fail to take them into account when designing development initiatives. To get a basic understanding of your own personality in relation to other personality types, try taking a personality test (NERIS Analytics Ltd, 2017) to help understand yourself and the people you work with. Crucially, take time to also get to know your stakeholders and appreciate the diverse range of perspectives they bring to the table.

Understanding and working with groups

People are individuals in their own right, but also operate in groups in various settings. How well these groups function will largely determine the initiative/organization's success. The work of Tuckman (1965) provides some insight into how groups function and develop over time. His 1965 model identified four stages of team development: 1) forming; 2) storming; 3) norming; 4) performing. In the 1970s he added a fifth phase − adjourning (see Figure 3.1). All these phases are necessary for the team to grow, face challenges, find solutions and deliver results.

Figure 3.1 Stages of group development
Source: Adapted from CULCokpalad, 2015
and based on Tuckman and Jensen, 1977

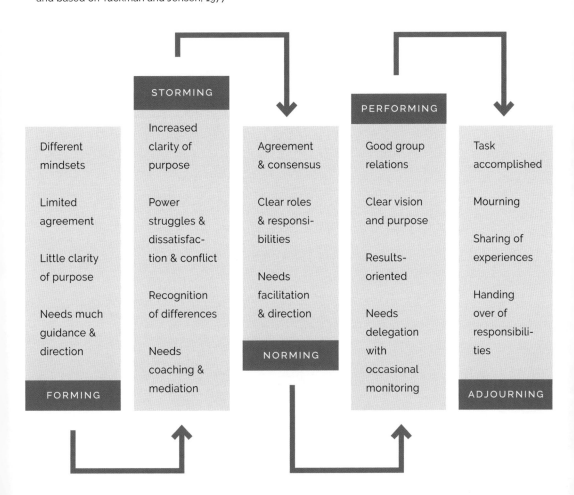

Table 3.1 presents an overview of the various phases of group formation. During each phase, leaders guide groups towards achieving results. While it is important to understand how teams develop over time, it is also crucial to know what roles a leader can play. To be able to fulfil this role, specific leadership competencies are required such as strategic thinking, strategic foresight, facilitating learning and engagement, and effective communication (see Chapter 4).

Groups work well if there is a good mix of team roles. Belbin (2015) defined a team role as 'a tendency to behave, contribute and interrelate with others in a particular way' (*ibid*: 1), identifying nine such team roles that underlie team success. By understanding your role within a particular team, Belbin suggests that you can develop your strengths and manage your weaknesses to improve your contribution to the team (see Table 3.2). Team leaders and development practitioners can use the Belbin model as a guide to create more balanced teams. It is crucial to bear in mind, however, that behaviour and interpersonal style within a group depends on the situation, type of work and interrelationships within the group.

Furthermore, consider the learning styles of the individuals in the group and how they relate to one another. The Kolb learning cycle highlights the different ways in which people learn (see section 'Kolb's experiential learning cycle and learning styles').

Table 3.1 Group formation, characteristics, expectations and leadership roles
Source: Adapted from Kusters et al., 2011

CHARACTERISTICS & EXPECTATIONS	ROLE OF LEADER/PRACTITIONER
Stage: forming This is when group members come together for the first time, with different expectations and mindsets about the task(s) at hand and the people they have to work with. There is yet no clear guidance on the task and how this can be achieved.	Be sensitive to what motivates stakeholders to get them involved and accepted by the group. Be actively involved in leading the group in discussions, clearly setting goals and shaping expectations.
Stage: storming This phase is difficult for all. Although there is increasing clarity on what needs to be done, roles and responsibilities are not yet defined. This may lead to a struggle for power (to influence how things are done) or some people withdrawing from the task altogether. Dissatisfaction, frustration and conflict are very common in this phase.	Coaching or mediation is needed to help the group work past their differences and resolve conflicts quickly. Help the group by focusing on the task, while balancing group dynamics. Consider personalities, competencies and possible group roles. Assist in developing the required competencies (e.g. PME and leadership competencies). Be aware that in diverse groups some members will not be very open. Also stress the importance of tolerance and respect of each other's strengths and weaknesses.
Stage: norming There is agreement and consensus among members of the group with respect to roles and responsibilities. Members can now focus on the task(s). Leadership comes mainly from within the group.	Be clear about the roles and responsibilities of each member. Play more of a facilitating or enabling role, and less of a directing role.
Stage: performing During this phase, the group functions as a well-oiled machine. Members have a clear vision and purpose with agreed roles and responsibilities, which helps them to perform the task(s). They can easily engage with each other without any serious conflict. This is when results are being achieved.	The emphasis should be on delegating tasks, monitoring progress and providing leadership when necessary.
Stage: adjourning At this stage, the task has been fulfilled and the group can be dissolved. This can take time and bring grief to members.	Make room for group members to share experiences (positive and negative). Allow members to take distance and hand over responsibilities.

Table 3.2 Summary of Belbin's team roles

Source: Adapted from Belbin, 2015

TEAM ROLES		STRENGTHS	ALLOWABLE WEAKNESSES
ROLE: ACTION ORIENTED	Shaper	Challenges team to strive for success despite constraints. Dynamic, thrives on pressure. Has the drive and courage to overcome obstacles and keep the team moving and not losing focus or momentum.	Can be abrasive or impatient with people. Can also be provocative and offend people's feelings.
	Implementer	Doer. Can put ideas into action and a workable strategy. Reliable and efficient.	May not be flexible and open to new ideas or respond quickly.
	Completer Finisher	Ensures that the work is completed properly. Can be conscientious and anxious. Polishes and perfects to the highest standards of quality control.	Finds it difficult to delegate, and can worry unduly.
ROLE: PEOPLE ORIENTED	Coordinator	Mature, confident, identifies talent. Clarifies goals. Good delegator.	Can be seen as manipulative and might offload his/her share of the work.
	Teamworker	Co-operative, perceptive and diplomatic. Listens and averts friction, flexible and supportive. Helps the team to gel and complete the work required.	Hesitant in taking decisions in difficult situations. Avoids conflict.
	Resource Investigator	Outgoing, enthusiastic, networker. Explores opportunities and ideas and develops contacts.	Might be over-optimistic, and can lose interest once the initial enthusiasm has passed.
ROLE: THOUGHT ORIENTED	Plant	Creative, imaginative, free-thinking, rich in ideas, good problem-solver, uses unconventional ways.	Often too caught up in thought to communicate properly with others.
	Monitor Evaluator	Sober, strategic and discerning. Sees all options and judges logically, accurately and impartially. Crucial for making informed decisions.	Finds it difficult to inspire people, often serious, critical.
	Specialist	Provides specialist knowledge and skills needed to support efforts. Can be single-minded, but also self-starting and dedicated.	Contribution can be limited to the technical arena and can dwell on technical details.

Understanding and stimulating stakeholder engagement, commitment and ownership

M4SDI is about working with staff and stakeholders to achieve results which motivate those involved to stay committed and engaged. But what motivates them to actively engage in initiatives/organizations?

Cultivating commitment is about ensuring that staff and stakeholders are positive and motivated, establishing a clear sense of teamwork and collectively working towards achieving results. To cultivate commitment and create ownership, it's important to think through who to engage in the core M4SDI processes, for what purpose and how to go about it.

In diverse settings, however, collaboration may be even more challenging because of the increased likelihood of conflicting interests and different perspectives. To get around these issues, development efforts need to focus on where there is demonstrable commitment to change (James and Wrigley, 2007) and engaging stakeholders actively and creatively at all levels to boost ownership and commitment.

'Participation is a right held by all people to engage in society and in the decisions that impact their lives. Participation is thus a political endeavor that challenges oppression and discrimination, in particular of the poorest and most marginalized people. Participatory processes enable people to see more clearly, and learn from the complexity that they are living and working amid. Through participation people can identify opportunities and strategies for action, and build solidarity to effect change.'

Institute of Development Studies, 2016

Participation

Much work has been done trying to understand how and why people participate. As a result, a number of typologies of participation have been developed, derived mainly from Arnstein's 1969 ladder of citizen participation (Arnstein, 2004; see Figure 3.2). Some of these typologies include Hart's (1992) young people's ladder of participation and Pretty's typology of participation (1995) shown in Figure 3.3.

Arnstein's model describes the different levels of participation as ranging from manipulation to informing and consultation, to power and control. The eight rungs of the ladder are set out hierarchically, and grouped into three categories – non-participation, tokenism and citizen control. Here Arnstein argues that the only measure of participation is the power to make decisions (i.e. citizen control). While these typologies are useful, it is also important to capture the dynamic and emergent nature of participation in development initiatives (Tritter and McCallum, 2006), the reasons for it and the role of power (see section 'Managing diversity, conflict and power'). Cornwall (2008: 269) suggests that we also need to pay attention to who is participating, in what, and for whose benefit. According to Oxford Policy Management (2013), we also need to '... create an understanding of the conditions under which participatory approaches may further development objectives, and to aid the design of specific interventions'.

There are a number of participatory methods available for inclusive social development that we can draw on in order to understand participation. See annex 1 for methods and approaches. Wageningen University & Research's M4SDI portal and MSP portal and the IDS website on participatory methods also provide examples. While these methods are useful and can be adapted to suit the situation, it is important to think about why and how we engage people.

Stakeholders

A stakeholder is an agency, organization, group or individual who has a (direct or indirect) interest in a development initiative/organization, or who affects or is affected positively or negatively by the implementation and outcome of it. Different stakeholders can have different stakes and even people in the same stakeholder group may not necessarily share the same interests. Personal situations may affect people's motivations and decisions and how they react in particular situations. For example, the Ebola outbreak in Guinea, Liberia, and Sierra Leone led people to change their attitude and behaviour in many ways, ranging from the manner in which they greeted each other to the way they buried their dead. Some NGOs also had to divert their focus from environmental to health issues in order to address and prevent further spread of the disease.

To better manage for sustainable development impact, it is important to understand local realities, perspectives and stakes for a deeper insight into what influences people's personal change process. Also, think strategically about who to engage in the process of planning and design, implementation, and M&E, and when and how to engage them. Stakeholders need not be engaged in the same way throughout all these processes. For example, a funder can be involved in the initial stages of project design to ensure it is in line with the funder's criteria, and during key M&E events such as yearly stakeholder workshops to reflect on the past year and plan for the next.

Figure 3.2
Arnstein's ladder of citizen
participation
Source: Arnstein, 2004

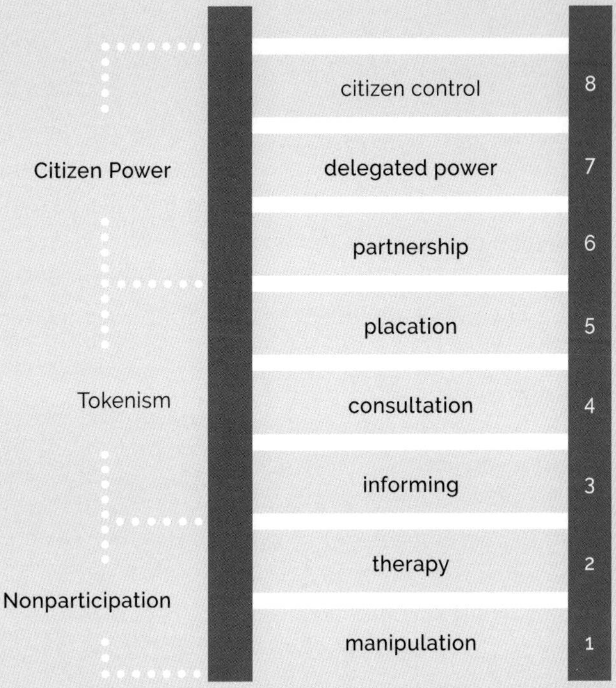

Citizen Power

citizen control	8
delegated power	7
partnership	6
placation	5

Tokenism

consultation	4
informing	3

Nonparticipation

therapy	2
manipulation	1

Figure 3.3 Participation
typologies by Hart (1992)
and Pretty (1995)
Source: Oxford Policy
Management, 2013

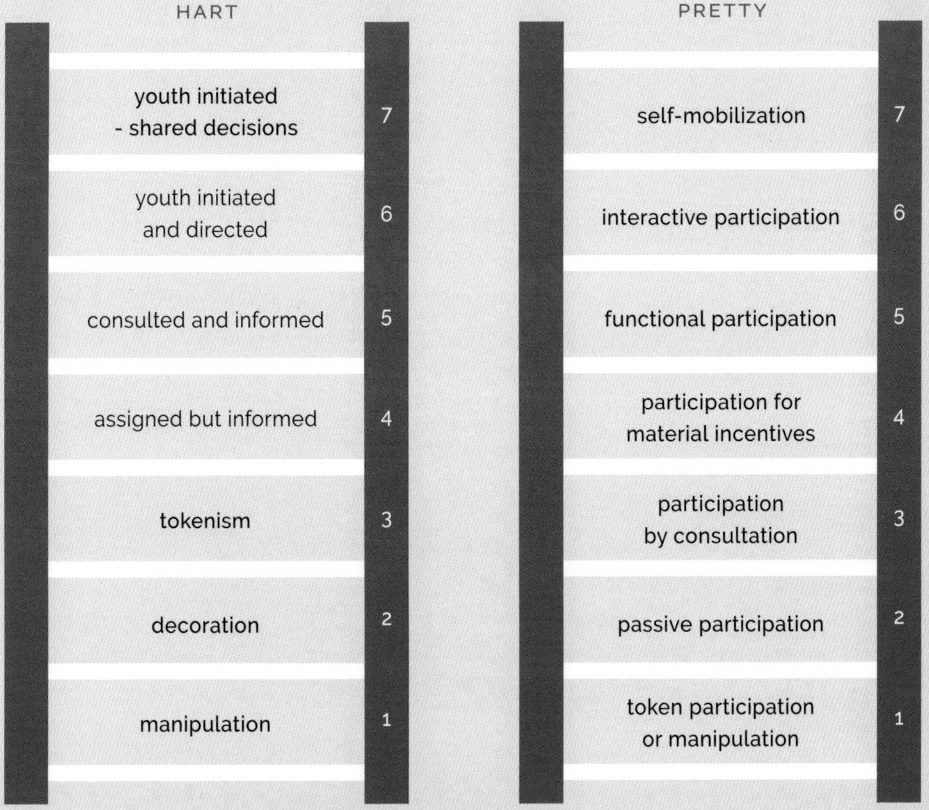

HART

youth initiated - shared decisions	7
youth initiated and directed	6
consulted and informed	5
assigned but informed	4
tokenism	3
decoration	2
manipulation	1

PRETTY

self-mobilization	7
interactive participation	6
functional participation	5
participation for material incentives	4
participation by consultation	3
passive participation	2
token participation or manipulation	1

Managing diversity, conflict and power

Engaging people is particularly challenging and involves managing diversity in terms of personalities, backgrounds, experiences, education, interests, values and mindsets. Managing diversity also includes dealing with conflict and power although it may not always mean that we need to search for common ground. Rather, we need to accept and work with our differences. Below we explore the subject of conflict and the importance of power and rank.

Conflict

There are different definitions of conflict. For many people, conflict is considered something negative to be avoided. Coser (1967 cited in Moore, 2014: 23) defines conflict as the 'mental and emotional states and interaction of two or more people who disagree, compete, or struggle over perceived or actual differences in beliefs or values or to attain status, power or scarce resources'. Wertheim, Love, Peck and Littlefield (cited in Manning, 2015) think of conflict as 'occurring when there are real or perceived differences in interests (i.e. wants, needs, fears, concerns) that cannot be simultaneously satisfied'. Tillett (2000) indicates that there are different types of conflict: intrapersonal conflict (e.g. individuals have competing loyalties and needs); interpersonal conflict (i.e. between two people); intragroup conflict (e.g. between political factions); intergroup conflict (e.g. conflict between different community groups) and that conflicts arise for such things as beliefs, ethics, ideologies, morals and values.

So, conflict comes about mainly when there is disagreement between two parties. It can emerge gradually, or develop rapidly in response to significant events. Work carried out by the FAO (2005) on negotiation and mediation techniques for natural resource management shows that as differences increase and intensify, conflict can arise (manifest) to become a full-blown public issue that is difficult to avoid. In the manifest stage, the differences between the individuals/parties become more

Figure 3.4 Conflict stages Source: FAO, 2005

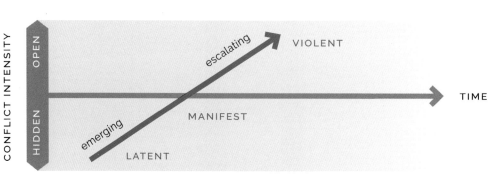

obvious, dominating group dynamics. As disagreements become more visible, they can permeate issues and discussions. You may see opposing parties beginning to define themselves according to their differences, resulting in 'us' versus 'them' situations. These differences can be used to mobilize support for a particular 'cause'. At this stage, manifest conflict can spiral into violence, which could lead to counter-violence and further escalation of conflict. Attempts should be made to tackle conflict at the latent stage (see Figure 3.4). It is important to note that at the manifest stage, conflicts can also result in a stalemate or impasse. Table 3.3 sets out the different types of conflict that Moore (2014) has identified and the possible ways of addressing them.

Table 3.3 Types of conflict and ways of addressing them

Source: Adapted from Moore, 2014

Conflict type		
DATA	• Lack of information • Misinformation • Differences in interpretation • Difference of opinion in relation to the relevance of the data	• Agree on what data are important. • Agree on a process of gathering information. • Develop common criteria to analyse data. • Get outside opinion from independent experts.
INTERESTS	• Real or imagined competitive interests • Procedural interests • Psychological interests	• Try to concentrate on interests, not positions. According to Fisher and Ury (1991: 24) 'your position is something you have decided upon. Your interests are what caused you to so decide'. • Look for ways to address and increase the options available. • Develop a set of trade-offs to satisfy people, taking into consideration the way in which people have been treated.
RELATIONSHIP	• Strong emotions • Poor communication • Repetitive negative behaviour • Stereotyping	• Use procedures and ground rules to control the way emotions are expressed. • Improve communication. • Find ways to encourage and reinforce positive behaviour. • Provide a way for people to express their feelings and allow for dialogue.
STRUCTURAL	• Unequal control and distribution of resources • Unequal power • Time constraints	• Redress control and distribution of resources. • Devise fairer and mutually agreed decision-making processes. • Try to get the time needed.
VALUE	• Different standards used to evaluate ideas and behaviour • Different ways of life, attitudes (mindsets), ideology	• Allow people to agree to disagree. • Search for common ground to build on.

Not all conflicts are negative. Indeed, conflicts can lead to better group performance if the members are able to explore the issues fully and openly and use the opportunity to bring about change. When dealing with conflict we can learn from each other, sometimes even more than from harmonious dialogue. Conflict is therefore part of life and can bring about growth and transformation.

Ways of dealing with conflict
There are many ways of dealing with conflict, but we have found the Thomas Kilmann conflict mode instrument (TKI) useful. The TKI tool explores an individual's behaviour along two dimensions: (1) assertiveness, the degree to which an individual is driven to achieve his goals or objectives; and (2) cooperativeness, the degree to which an individual is willing to let the other person achieve his goals or objectives. Within these two dimensions are five different modes or styles for responding to conflict situations (Kilmann Diagnostics, 2016):

Avoiding: Low assertiveness and low cooperativeness characterize this mode. The person does nothing to address the conflict. Avoidance may mean ignoring the issue, or delay dealing with the problem. This mode is useful if the problem is minor, but if the issue is significant, conflict will develop and resentment might build up.

Competing: Assertiveness and uncooperativeness characterize this mode. The person seeks to address his/her own concerns at the expense of others and uses whatever means or power available to get ahead, by arguing, using sanctions or rank. This mode is particularly useful in times of chaos when decisions need to be taken quickly and decisively. It is not suited to long-term situations as it can lead to a build-up of resentment.

Accommodating: This means being unassertive and cooperative and is the direct opposite of competing. In this mode, the person will put aside his/her own concerns for the benefit of the other person. This can easily develop into a situation where the accommodating person can be taken advantage of. Resentment may also build up as a result of having to deny one's own needs.

Compromising: In this mode both the level of assertiveness and cooperativeness is moderate. This mode is often used to find a mutual solution that often doesn't fully satisfy both sides, since each has to make concessions. Compromising is useful in situations where both sides have similar goals, but should not be used as a long-term strategy as it may hide more important underlying issues.

Collaborating: This is when a person has a high level of assertiveness and cooperativeness. This mode can be likened to a win-win situation and is the complete opposite of the avoiding mode. Collaborating is a time-consuming process to explore and learn from each other to find solutions that meet the concerns of all involved.

We can all use these five conflict modes. However, some modes are more commonly used than others perhaps because we rely on them either out of temperament or practice. Our conflict behaviour at the workplace, for example, is largely the result of our personal predispositions as well as the demands of the situation.

Another useful model is the continuum of conflict (Figure 3.5) developed by Moore (2014). This model shows that with increasing intensity and complexity, different strategies are needed to deal with conflict. This may range from private decision-making at one end of the continuum where conflicts are still easy to solve, to legal, third-party decision-making at the other. Of course the sooner you address the conflict, the less chance it has of developing into a large-scale problem. People may experience the same conflict differently and so may have other views on how the conflict should be resolved. In M4SDI, it is critical to understand the perceptions and interests of the parties involved in conflict. The nonviolent communication (NVC) model is a tool that can be used in such situations (see Chapter 5).

Power and rank

Managing diversity is also about dealing with power and rank (see Box 3.1). Everyone has power and rank. In fact, we are probably more aware of other people's power than of our own. Arnold Mindell (1995: 42) describes rank as 'a conscious or unconscious, social or personal ability arising from culture,

Figure 3.5 Continuum of conflict management and resolution approaches and procedures
Source: Moore, 2014

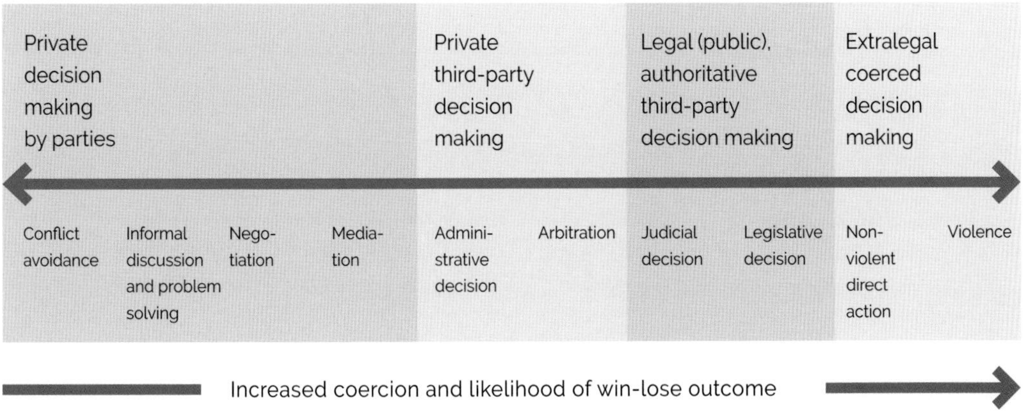

Private decision making by parties				Private third-party decision making		Legal (public), authoritative third-party decision making		Extralegal coerced decision making	
Conflict avoidance	Informal discussion and problem solving	Nego- tiation	Media- tion	Admini- strative decision	Arbitration	Judicial decision	Legislative decision	Non- violent direct action	Violence

Increased coercion and likelihood of win-lose outcome

community support, psychology, and/or spiritual power'. He also says that rank is 'the sum of a person's power and privileges' (*ibid*: 28). Our sense of power depends on who we are interacting with in any given situation at any particular moment. Rank differences therefore play a role in social situations and conflicts. Being aware of our rank helps us to understand why we may feel less powerful around people of higher rank. Awareness can also help those of a higher rank reduce the likelihood of using their position in a way that is considered hurtful or abusive to someone of a lower rank.

BOX 3.1 MORE ABOUT RANK

Individuals earn some of their power and privilege by facing life's challenges and overcoming them. Sometimes, rank is unearned, i.e. acquired by birth or social position. Rank is not constant and can change from moment to moment in a particular situation. It may be difficult, however, to change our social and situational rank, but we have the ability to change our psychological and spiritual rank. To function properly and effect change, leaders, staff and stakeholders need to feel empowered to contribute meaningfully to M4SDI processes. For this to happen, we need to empower those with less rank and power.

Descriptions of the different types of rank are:

Situational rank is specific to an individual's position in a particular situation, e.g. one's position in an organization. However, someone's high social rank in one situation may not apply in another, e.g. being a leader in your local community, but holding a low-level position within your organization.

Social rank is generally unearned and its relative powers and privileges are supported by social norms covering areas such as gender, class, ethnicity, colour, wealth, nationality and education.

Psychological rank has to do with our level of self-awareness and the way we feel about ourselves. This is linked to how we feel about past experiences, such as surviving difficult and challenging situations, e.g. traumatic experiences in childhood. A high psychological rank means understanding oneself and having a strong sense of self or self-esteem.

Spiritual rank is power that is independent of culture, family and the world. It is described as the feeling of connection (i.e. to a higher power, to nature or to the environment) and conviction of inner self resulting from positive past experiences. For some people it comes from religious belief or divine experience.

When you are aware of your rank, you can use it to your own benefit and to the benefit of others.

Source: Based on Mindell, 1995

Leadership

We have looked at how individuals and groups function, how to engage and motivate people, and how to deal with diversity, conflict and power. These have implications for the type of leadership and competencies needed to manage for sustainable development impact.

Leadership, according to Kotter (2013) is 'associated with taking an organization into the future, finding opportunities that are coming at it faster and faster and successfully exploiting those opportunities'. People with leadership qualities are needed throughout the initiative/organization to inspire and engage people at all levels. Managers, on the other hand, play a key role by ensuring that the necessary competencies, capacities and conditions are in place so that PME and decision-making processes are effectively implemented (see Chapter 4). Both leadership and management qualities are essential in managing for sustainable development impact.

Leadership styles

Leaders can adopt different styles based on the people they are dealing with and the task at hand. The Hersey-Blanchard Situational Leadership Model (Hersey and Blanchard, 1993) states that to be successful in navigating the demands of increasingly diverse groups, leaders and development practitioners need to be flexible in their leadership styles with respect to the maturity of the people they're leading and the details of the task. They can draw on the situational leadership model1 to help them decide where to place more or less emphasis on the task, and on the relationships with people. The model also provides a framework for leaders to help staff and stakeholders grow and develop. Hersey and Blanchard list four main leadership styles (labelled S1 to S4 in Figure 3.6):

- Telling/directing (S1): Leaders provide direction on what, how, when, and where to do tasks. Communication is generally one-way. This style is applicable when followers' performance readiness (i.e. people's ability and willingness to perform a task) is very low.
- Selling/coaching (S2): Leaders define roles and tasks. However, there is more communication as leaders ask followers for ideas and suggestions. Leaders "sell" their message to followers to get their support and coach them on the task (less directing), and help them learn how to deal with problems. This style is used in situations where the performance readiness is moderately low.

1] Situational Leadership® is a registered trademark of the Center for Leadership Studies. See more at: http://tinyurl.com/zo5bbvj [accessed 27 February 2017].

- Participating/supporting (S3): Leaders and followers have a closer relationship in this situation. There is less emphasis on direction since followers already have a good understanding of the task. Leaders and followers work and take decisions together. A supporting leadership style is needed in situations where performance readiness is moderately high.
- Delegating (S4): Leaders entrust followers with most of the responsibility for the task, since they are both competent and willing to do the job. Leaders monitor progress, are involved in goal setting, but there is limited interference. This is most suited to situations where the readiness of followers is high.

Figure 3.6 Situational leadership styles

Source: Based on Hersey and Blanchard, 1993

Figure 3.6 illustrates how leadership styles closely follow the competence of team members for a particular task. High levels of competence are associated with delegating and supportive leadership styles, whilst low levels of competence require more directing and coaching. Brouwer et al. (2015) present six aspects of leadership that are useful when managing for sustainable development impact. They are:

Convening leadership: We have mentioned throughout the guide that leaders and development practitioners need to communicate effectively, framing issues in a way that inspires and motivates stakeholders. Successful leadership requires a respected and trusted person who is able to network and build relationships among stakeholder groups.

Constituency leadership: Constituents refer to staff and stakeholders who look to leaders and development practitioners for leadership. It is important in M4SDI that leaders actively engage stakeholders and genuinely represent their interests. This means listening to them, understanding their needs and responding to them within the context of the initiative/organization.

Supporting leadership: Strong support from influential people not necessarily directly involved in the initiative/organization is crucial, e.g. a well-known benefactor with a special interest in seeing the initiative/organization succeed. Keeping them abreast of developments can sustain their interest and continued support.

Organizing leadership: Organizing has to take place on all fronts to support the proper functioning of the initiative/organization. This includes arranging stakeholder meetings, conducting field visits, identifying staff with key competencies, and ensuring that there is adequate funding available.

Informing leadership: Leaders will need to ensure that staff and stakeholders have access to good information to support decision-making, e.g. during the strategic guidance process. Access to information and taking part in multi-stakeholder processes can also empower and enhance the motivation of staff and stakeholders. Communicating effectively (a strategic competence) with different audiences is also crucial.

Facilitating leadership: We mentioned earlier how useful participatory methods can be in helping leaders and practitioners engage stakeholders and promote learning. Facilitation, a key strategic competence in M4SDI, must play a key role in this process.

SUMMARY: PEOPLE ORIENTATION

In managing for sustainable development impact, being people-oriented helps to better understand and work with the people (staff and stakeholders) involved in an initiative/organization so as to be more effective in bringing about change. People orientation is about interacting with staff and stakeholders, individually and collectively, bearing in mind the diversity of personalities, attitudes, beliefs, backgrounds, experiences, knowledge, interests and perspectives. It also involves leading individuals, groups and multi-stakeholder processes effectively and engaging people to share their views and experiences, and actively contribute to change processes. Being people-oriented also means dealing with conflict and power.

Leadership is also key in managing people processes and inspiring people for change. Strong leadership goes hand in hand with strong management. Leaders need to be visionary and inspire staff and stakeholders to realize a shared vision. They also need to be sensitive to the needs of those they serve and understand when and how to adjust their leadership style to any given situation. There are six key aspects of leadership to bear in mind; they include convening, constituency, supporting, organizing, informing and facilitating leadership. Strategic thinking, effective communication, strategic foresight, and facilitating learning and engagement are crucial competencies for engaging people effectively.

> As the world becomes more inter-connected and business becomes more complex and dynamic, work must become more "learningful". It is no longer sufficient to have one person learning for the organiza-tion, a Ford or a Sloan or a Watson or a Gates. It's just not possible any longer to figure it out from the top and have everyone else following the orders of the "grand strate-gist". The organizations that will truly excel in the future will be the organizations that discover how to tap people's commitment and capacity to learn at all levels in an organization.'
>
> *Senge, 2006: 4*

LEARNING ORIENTATION

Learning is increasingly being recognized as an important vehicle for development initiatives and organizations to improve their effectiveness and adapt to change. Senge (2010) reinforces this by suggesting that learning needs to take place at different levels within an organization on a continuous basis so that people can expand their capacity to get the desired results. Much of the rationale for this is linked to systems thinking discussed in Chapter 2, where Senge points out that many managers have, to a large extent, lost touch with what it is they are meant to be contributing to, because they are not able to see the context of their efforts. Systems thinking offers them a way to understand the importance of learning collectively and discovering that people, events and other parts are related and influence each other in unpredictable ways. This deeper understanding makes them realize that they too can contribute to solving problems and changing behaviour.

The initiative/organization needs to integrate learning into all aspects of its work, such as engaging key stakeholders in strategic guidance, effective operations and M&E processes. However, before this can happen, conditions have to be laid for learning. Once a learning environment is created, it will be possible for people to learn individually or collectively inside or outside the initiative/organization. Important competencies supporting learning orientation therefore include systems thinking, facilitating learning and engagement, and communication.

In this section, we focus on what learning means, how people learn, how learning can be stimulated at the individual, organizational and societal (collective) levels, and what it means to be a learning initiative/organization. First, we clarify what we understand by the terms information, knowledge and wisdom, as they are intricately linked to learning.

Information is defined as 'data given context, and endowed with meaning and significance' (CTA 2012: 2). Britton (2002: 8) describes knowledge as 'systematically organized information which, by the processes of analysis, comparison, testing and generalizing can be used to answer complex questions'. He goes on to define wisdom as 'the combination of the facts and insights of knowledge with practical experience in a way that can usefully guide action' (*ibid*: 8). Figure 3.7 highlights the relationship between information, knowledge and wisdom. And while some knowledge is accessible, much of the wisdom of individuals remains tacit (unvoiced). The challenge for us is how to access the tacit knowledge and wisdom of staff and stakeholders. Learning-oriented organizations are particularly keen to engage staff and stakeholders in ways that allow them to access information and translate this into knowledge and wisdom. They are also committed to converting their tacit knowledge into explicit knowledge through a process of articulation (e.g. facilitation and documentation) and reflection (e.g. critical reflection).

What is learning?

The Oxford dictionary (2016) defines learning as 'the (acquisition of) knowledge, [wisdom] or skills through study, experience, or being taught'. Ambrose et al. (2010) suggest that this definition has three components to it:
· Learning is a process, not a product.
· Learning refers to a change in attitudes, behaviours, beliefs, knowledge.
· Learning is not something done to people, but something that people themselves do.

Figure 3.7 Difference between data, information, knowledge and wisdom

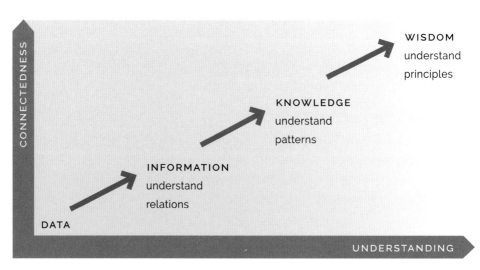

> **BOX 3.2 EXAMPLES OF QUESTIONS FOR CRITICAL REFLECTION ON M&E FINDINGS**
>
> **What**: What succeeded/failed?
> **Why**: Why have we succeeded or failed?
> **So what**: So what are the implications for the initiative/organization?
> **Now what**: What action(s) can we take now to make improvements for the future?

In other words, learning is a mental process through which people acquire and improve the ability to change their ways of thinking and/or behaviour. Learning involves reflection on experiences and applying lessons learned to future strategies and actions, thereby providing the basis for another cycle of learning.

Within the context of a development initiative/organization, this means that staff and stakeholders should be involved in learning-oriented M4SDI processes. Some of the reasons for learning that we have already mentioned include gaining knowledge and bringing about change, but Tilbury (2011: 104) indicates that learning also means:

- asking powerful questions, e.g. for critical reflection (see Box 3.2, Chapter 5, and Chapter 8 section on 'Agree on critical reflection and sense-making');
- understanding one's own values;
- envisaging positive and sustainable futures (futures thinking);
- thinking systemically;
- applying lessons learned.

Learning opportunities inside and outside an initiative/organization can take place in various ways (see Box 3.3). According to Tilbury (2011: 104) these opportunities include: processes that engage the 'whole system' (e.g. to increase synergy among stakeholders); processes of active and participatory learning (e.g. role play, debates, group discussions, field studies); processes of collaboration and dialogue (this includes multi-stakeholder and intercultural dialogue, and collaboration to maximize capacity and increase engagement); and processes that innovate curriculum, teaching and learning experiences. Learning can support getting people on board in change management processes, by drawing valuable lessons learned from work/experience, M&E and any other learning or knowledge management processes. It means making M4SDI processes more reflective and learning-oriented to make sense of findings, determine future strategies and actions, and generate and document lessons learned.

Learning takes place at different levels – at the individual (intra-personal) and inter-personal level, i.e. project, programme, organizational and even societal (multi-stakeholder) levels. There are many learning theories that we can draw on

BOX 3.3 LEARNING OPPORTUNITIES

- Encourage reporting that includes staff giving their opinions.
- Go into the field and ask stakeholders for their views.
- Provide constructive feedback.
- Seek feedback from the people you work with, and try to set an example.
- Reward critical feedback if possible.
- Value field and exchange visits.
- Include the expectation of critical reflection in job descriptions, terms of reference and memoranda of understanding so that when people come into the organization or partner with it, they do not see it as an obligation, but as part of the organizational culture.
- Engage in safe fail trials and experiments.

to understand how better to interact with people at the different levels and get more meaning from the learning processes described earlier. It is impossible to cover many of these theories here, so our discussion is limited to Kolb's learning model which deals with learning at the individual and initiative levels. We also cover organizational learning, with special reference to triple-loop learning and Senge's five disciplines, simply because we have found them to be useful.

Kolb's experiential learning cycle and learning styles[2]

David Kolb developed the experiential learning theory and learning styles model, which give valuable insight into how people learn.

Experiential learning cycle

The experiential learning cycle suggests that learning is a four-stage cyclical process, where knowledge and wisdom are 'created through the transformation of experience' (Kolb, 1984: 38). The stages are:
- Stage 1: learning from concrete experiences (feeling)
- Stage 2: learning from reflective observation (watching)
- Stage 3: learning from abstract conceptualization (thinking)
- Stage 4: learning from active experimentation (doing).

Although the model is presented as a series of stages, in reality it is possible to enter the cycle at any stage and follow it through sequentially. It is important to complete the cycle because as you move from one stage to the next, you build on your learning and improve. Stage 1 is about having a concrete experience – 'feeling'. For example, certain activities of an initiative/organization did not work out in a particular year. In Stage 2, this experience is reflected on ('reflective

2/ *Source:* Making Evaluations Matter: A practical Guide for Evaluators. Kusters et al., 2011

observation' – 'watching') in order to gain information about what happened. In an initiative, we can relate this to the monitoring process –collecting information on similar activities and finding out whether what is happening in one area is also happening in other areas. Stage 3 involves thinking, analysing or planning ('abstract conceptualization' – 'thinking'). Here, we try to make sense of the information available and draw conclusions or develop theories. In an initiative/organization this often relates to or informs decision-making based on critical reflection on M&E findings. The information (and ideas) generated during the sense-making processes (such as yearly stakeholder meetings) informs the adaptation of existing plans or the development of the next annual work plan. The fourth stage ('active experimentation' – 'doing') involves planning and working with these new ideas, e.g. a work plan (see Figure 3.8). Experimentation in this instance means the implementation of the annual plan. And so the cycle continues. The learning cycle has proved to be a very helpful tool in problem-solving and project management and can be used in all the core M4SDI processes.

Learning styles

We have seen that learning takes place in different ways. Peter Honey and Alan Mumford (1986) identify four distinct learning styles or preferences – and many

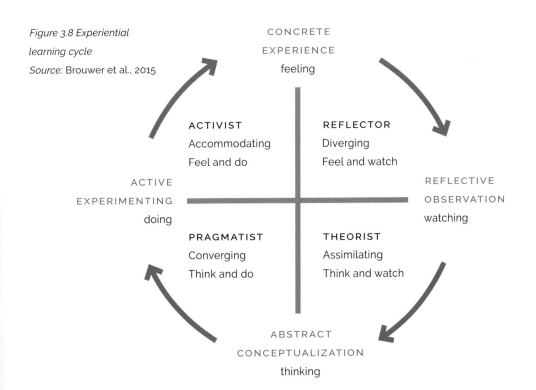

Figure 3.8 Experiential learning cycle
Source: Brouwer et al., 2015

CONCRETE EXPERIENCE
feeling

ACTIVIST
Accommodating
Feel and do

REFLECTOR
Diverging
Feel and watch

ACTIVE EXPERIMENTING
doing

REFLECTIVE OBSERVATION
watching

PRAGMATIST
Converging
Think and do

THEORIST
Assimilating
Think and watch

ABSTRACT CONCEPTUALIZATION
thinking

Table 3.4 Honey and Mumford's learning styles
Source: Adapted from University of Leicester,
2016 and Sarabdeen, 2013

CHARACTERISTICS	LEARNING METHODS
Activists learn by doing and participating. They like challenges and tend to jump in with both feet first. They are usually open-minded in their approach to learning, and impartial with respect to new experiences. Often you find 'explorers' and 'innovators' in this category.	• Brainstorming • Problem solving • Group discussion • Puzzles • Competitions • Role-play
Reflectors learn by observing and thinking about what happened. They prefer to observe from a distance and ponder on experiences from various perspectives. They like to collect data to analyse and reflect upon, as well as consult stakeholders. However, reflectors often delay reaching conclusions. You will often find researchers and M&E staff in this category.	• Models • Statistics • Stories • Quotes • Background information
Learners in this category like to understand the theory behind actions and think things through. You can engage these people in learning processes by using models, concepts and facts. They are naturally objective, preferring to analyse and synthesize, and put this new information into coherent theory. Managers and other decision-makers are often found in this category. Much of their decision-making style can be described as rational.	• Thinking about how to apply theories to reality • Problem solving • Discussion
Pragmatists like to seek and try out new things they have learned and put them into practice. Abstract concepts and plans are not considered important unless they can be put into action. Pragmatists like to try out ideas, theories and techniques to see if they work. Often you find implementers in this category.	• Paired discussions • Self-assessments • Personality tests • Coaching • Interviews

of us tend to follow one or two of these. The learning styles are activist, theorist, pragmatist and reflector, and the main characteristics of each are presented in Table 3.4. These learning styles (see Figure 3.8) are closely associated with the Kolb learning cycle. So an activist might be primarily interested in experiencing new challenges and not in taking the time to critically reflect and draw lessons from experiences. To become a better learner, s/he should engage with other stages of the learning cycle.

It is crucial when engaging people in M4SDI to think about their preferred learning styles and how to make the best use of them. This involves using different methods (see Table 3.4) such as reading and observation (reflectors), or testing and experimenting (pragmatists). When forming groups internally and externally, it is useful to have a mix of people with different learning styles.

Organizational learning: triple-loop learning[3]

Triple loop learning, inspired by Argyris and Schön (1974), is considered an important aspect of organizational learning. We can identify three levels of learning which may be present in an organization (see Figure 3.9):

- **Single-loop learning** consists of one feedback loop, which involves observing that a problem or error needs to be fixed and adapting our behaviour or actions to correct or improve the situation. This type of learning does not delve deeply into the root causes of a problem and is mainly concerned with looking at the symptoms.
- **Double-loop learning** reflects on why things work or fail. People are observers of their own actions. Learning involves asking questions about how things are done and what needs to change for better results.
- **Triple-loop learning** takes place at a much deeper level than single- or double-loop learning. Organizations that engage in triple-loop learning experience changes in the relationship between their organizational structure and behaviour over time, as they learn more about themselves and the wider environment and how to respond to change. For example, an organization may question its purpose and even its very existence, resulting in far-reaching changes to its internal structure, culture and practices in response to changes in the external environment. In M4SDI, a key consideration is deciding what is right. This entails reviewing the rationale behind the organization or development initiative. Understanding and questioning these deeper values, paradigms, and visions that influence our thinking and choices can help us review our options for adapting in a dynamic environment.

3| Adapted from: http://www.knowledge-management-tools.net/organizational-learning-theory.html

BOX 3.4 ORGANIZATIONAL BARRIERS TO LEARNING

Internal barriers
- Failure to recognize that learning is important to an initiative's/organization's development and its ability to respond to the needs of its stakeholders
- Lack of incentives and rewards for learning
- Existence of a blame culture where accountability is associated with blame
- Rigid structures with very little room for flexibility and change
- Weak structure to support access, storage, transfer and dissemination of lessons learned
- Poor institutional memory due to high staff turnover, or heavy reliance on short-term consultants

External barriers
- Donor priorities
- Unequal nature of the donor-beneficiary relationship which puts the donor in the driving seat, inhibiting the free flow of information and the formation of a true partnership
- Pressure to demonstrate low overheads
- Competition for funding

Source: Kusters et al., 2011

Figure 3.9 Levels of learning in an organization – triple-loop learning
Source: Brouwer et al. 2015, based on Argyris and Schön, 1974

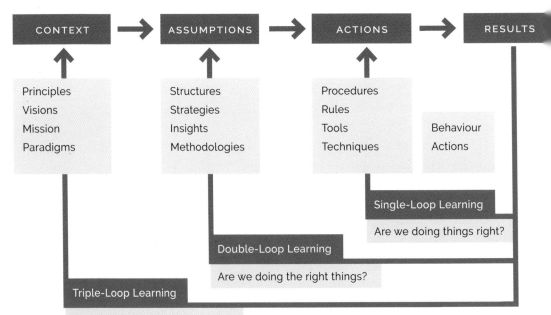

Effective learning alternates between these three types of learning. Single-loop learning will take place more often as practitioners critically reflect on events that take place within their initiative/organization. Strategic choices relate more to double-loop and triple-loop learning. At the same time, to be truly effective, the environment in which an initiative/organization operates needs to be conducive to learning. Some barriers to learning that we need to be aware of are listed in Box 3.4.

Organizational learning – Senge's five disciplines

Senge's (2006) concept of the learning organization helps us understand what is involved in building effective organizations in which both people and achievements can flourish. There are a number of views about what a learning organization truly is. Senge's five disciplines provide key ideas to developing organizations that can truly 'learn' in order to continuously enhance their capacity to realize their highest aspirations – sustainable development impact. These five disciplines are outlined below.

Personal mastery: Personal mastery is the discipline of continually clarifying and deepening our personal vision, of focusing our energies, developing patience and of seeing reality objectively. Applying this to M4SDI involves inspiring people to become personally engaged in and committed to a change process, and actively contribute to understanding reality, working towards a shared vision, and reflecting on the change process and adapting to a changing environment.
Mental models: Mental models are deeply ingrained assumptions, generalizations or even pictures or images that influence how we understand the world. Very often, we are not consciously aware of our mental models or the effects they have on our behavior. Being aware of them helps us probe more deeply and gain insight into people's actions and the consequences of their behaviour. It is therefore important to create an environment where people can question and share their ideas and views freely.

A shared vision: If any one idea about leadership has inspired organizations for thousands of years, it is the capacity to hold a shared vision or concern of the future we seek to create. In M4SDI, this means engaging staff and stakeholders in developing a common vision for their initiative/organization.

Team learning: When teams are truly learning, not only do they produce extraordinary results, individual members also develop their competencies more rapidly. In M4SDI, learning together in a group results in better performance and improved individual competencies.

Systems thinking: Systems thinking helps us to look at an initiative/organization holistically in order to understand how people and issues are related. It is for this reason that systems thinking is known as the all-important "fifth discipline". In complex situations, it helps us to see interrelationships in new ways and to identify the underlying structures and processes. Initiatives/organizations that are continuously in touch with their environment are better able to develop, adapt and transform themselves in response to changes around them.

Conversely, Senge (2006) also lists some pitfalls to learning for people and organizations:

- 'I am my position'. With this attitude, individuals in the initiative/organization focus too closely on their own positions and responsibilities, thus missing out on the bigger picture and inter-unity.
- 'The enemy is out there'. This attitude is about blame-shifting and leads people to find an external agent to blame for shortcomings.
- 'The fixation on events'. With this attitude, we get bogged down focusing on short-term events instead of long-terms visions and aspirations.
- 'The parable of the boiled frog'. When change gradually happens, we tend not to notice the larger shift which happens over time, much like a frog in a pot will relax into drowsiness as the water is slowly heated.
- 'The delusion of learning from experience'. Given that some effects are beyond the current limits of our awareness (e.g. effects in time, non-linear effects), we do not experience many of the effects of our actions.
- 'The myth of the management team'. This is about the danger of pretending and keeping up appearances. With this disability, management protects itself from the threat of appearing uncertain or ignorant in the face of collective inquiry, resulting in "skilled incompetence" (people who are incredibly proficient at keeping themselves from learning).

SUMMARY: LEARNING ORIENTATION

Learning orientation is a key part of any initiative/organization managing for sustainable development impact. To become learning oriented, a concerted effort to integrate learning into the core M4SDI processes is required. For example, learning must play a key role in guiding strategies, strengthening M&E processes (e.g. during data collection and sense-making processes) and enhancing the use of M&E findings. Learning should also inform the leadership role, the decisions leaders take and how they connect the wider environment with what is happening in the context of their initiative/organization.

A culture of learning entails having a set of conditions (i.e. leadership, organizational values, processes and practices) that encourage people to share experiences, gain knowledge and wisdom, enhance competencies and improve overall performance. Much of this is captured in Senge's five disciplines for the learning organization. Some ideas to consider when managing for sustainable development impact include: engaging key stakeholders in learning at all levels; making full use of Kolb's experiential learning cycle and dealing with different learning styles; building in regular critical reflection moments that question not only our behaviour and actions, but also what assumptions, strategies, values and visions underpin these (triple-loop learning); being aware of the barriers to learning and finding ways to overcome them. For an initiative/organization to be learning-oriented, strategic competencies in systems thinking, facilitating learning and engagement, and effective communication are essential.

CONTEXT ORIENTATION

Every situation and organization is unique. For example, tackling nutrition insecurity in a rural area in Ghana, West Africa, is very different from dealing with the same issue in an urban area in India. The underlying causes are different and some groups may be more affected than others. Also, there will be different actors trying to address the situation, and they may all have a particular perspective on how the situation can be addressed. When managing a programme which addresses nutrition insecurity, broad and specific contextual factors need to be taken into account, as well as the views of individuals, groups and institutions.

Every development initiative/organization therefore requires tailoring, taking into consideration the contextual realities. Context includes understanding the wider setting and the conditions which have a direct bearing on the initiative's/organization's interests. It is also about identifying future trends and developments, and being able to anticipate and be pro-active in response to any changes in the environment. So context orientation is particularly important in guiding strategic processes. Systems thinking is crucial in understanding the context of an initiative/organization, particularly when the context is complex (see Chapter 2).

Assessing contextual issues includes doing a proper situation analysis (see Chapter 6 section 'Situation analysis'), and this will need to be informed by engaging a wide range of stakeholders to get a better understanding of different contextual issues at the local, national, or international level.

While an initial situation analysis may provide a solid basis for designing a development initiative, we know that things can quickly change in dynamic environments. For example, a government-run agricultural project may have been designed to address food insecurity in a particular region, but it can be affected by factors like drought, policy changes, or civil conflicts. Internal influences such as staff changes, office conflicts, internal policies and procedures, may affect how well the development initiative is implemented. It is therefore important to regularly review the environment in which you are operating so that you can respond and adapt to changing circumstances.

In the following sections, we will discuss the importance of an initiative/ organization being situational responsive and developing and maintaining a context perspective. How to go about conducting a situation analysis, including stakeholder analysis and institutional analysis, is discussed in Chapter 6 (section 'Strategic guidance').

Situational responsiveness

Situational responsiveness is the ability of an initiative/organization to respond to internal and external factors and adapt to changes or developments in its environment. This ability is essential if the work of the initiative/organization is to be relevant and effective. Staff and stakeholders play a critical role in influencing how well an initiative/organization is able to respond to situations, by actively engaging them in understanding and responding to these dynamics. Organizational capacity is another factor which influences how a situation is dealt with. For example, there will be differences in staff competencies and conditions in every initiative/organization (see Chapter 4). However, to be situational responsive, key competencies such as strategic thinking and strategic foresight are required. Figure 3.10 shows how to stay connected to your context and adapt plans accordingly.

Developing and maintaining a context perspective

To develop and maintain a context perspective, the following five dimensions of context can be useful:

Dimension 1: The **wider context** in which the development initiative/organization functions. This involves policies, political dynamics, governance structures, drivers of change, trends (social, economic, environmental), (social) conflict, societal concerns, available knowledge, key players and their (planned) interventions. Taking a wider context perspective will help identify opportunities and constraints facing the initiative/organization.

Figure 3.10 Staying connected to the context during implementation

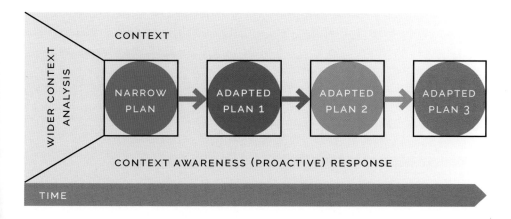

Dimension 2: The **specific context** in which the initiative/organization operates. This may be a particular community, district, country or region. You may see this as a specification of the same issues mentioned under the wider context. Of particular interest are formal and informal institutions with which you engage (see Chapter 6).

Dimension 3: What **individuals** bring to the initiative/organization. Working together within and across organizational boundaries will involve interacting with different individuals. A basic understanding of people's mindsets and ideas about how change happens, their (cultural) identities and personalities, emotions and perceptions, as well as their individual competencies, resources and practices is useful. In Chapter 4 we discuss the strategic competencies that relate to this dimension. See also section 'Understanding and working with individuals').

Dimension 4: What (organized) **groups** bring into the initiative/organization. This relates to the collective capabilities, the mix of individual competencies and conditions (i.e. capacity), the relationships, interactions, including connections to other institutions that can affect the work of the initiative/organization. See also section 'Understanding and working with groups'.

Dimension 5: The **organizational structures and processes** underpinning the initiative. These cover how organizational systems, processes, procedures, and infrastructure work together in terms of flexibility, administrative pressure, hierarchy, role definitions, job descriptions, collective sense-making, etc. Secondary processes and structures such as the existence of financial buffers, diversity of funding, and job security, are also included.

Situation (context) analysis

A situation (or context) analysis is used to obtain a good understanding of the context in which the initiative/organization operates, and serves as a good basis for planning development initiatives. A situation analysis will need to include an institutional and stakeholder analysis, an analysis of issues and problems, and possibly an exploratory look at options for the future. A stakeholder analysis, for example, helps identify the key stakeholders and assess their respective interests. There are a number of tools that can be used to identify and describe stakeholders on the basis of their attributes, interrelationships and interests in any given initiative/organization. Details on how to conduct a situation analysis are provided in Chapter 6 section 'Strategic guidance'.

SUMMARY: CONTEXT ORIENTATION

Every initiative/organization is different. Initiatives/organizations need to be context-oriented to ensure that their design and management are situational responsive and adaptive. Being context-oriented is particularly important in complex, dynamic environments where opportunities may spontaneously arise and quickly disappear, or where changes in the environment may have a detrimental effect on the initiative/organization. Context orientation is therefore particularly important for strategic guidance and decision-making processes, and to adaptively manage in changing environments.

Conducting a thorough situation analysis prior to the design of any initiative, and monitoring the internal and external context at regular intervals during the lifetime of an initiative/organization, is important to keep abreast of any changes that might occur. In developing and maintaining a context perspective, you will need to consider the wider and specific contexts, the stakeholders (individuals and groups), as well as your organizational structure and processes. Important competencies needed to support a context-oriented organization include strategic thinking and strategic foresight.

CHAPTER 4

WHY ARE CAPACITIES AND CONDITIONS IMPORTANT?

DETERMINING CAPACITIES AND CONDITIONS USING THE 5CS FRAMEWORK
  Capability to act and commit
  Capability to adapt and self-renew
  Capability to achieve development objectives
  Capability to relate
  Capability to achieve coherence

COMPETENCIES
  Technical competencies
  Strategic competencies

SUMMARY

CAPACITIES AND CONDITIONS

LEARNING OBJECTIVES

· Understand key terms such
  as capacity, conditions,
  competencies
· Understand the importance
  of having appropriate
  capacities, conditions and
  competencies in place to
  support M4SDI
· Recognize what is needed
  to enhance capacities and
  conditions necessary for
  M4SDI

Over the last two decades there has been increasing focus on supporting capacity development efforts with special reference to development strategies and processes. For example, one of the highlights of the 2005 Paris Declaration on Aid Effectiveness was the commitment of partner countries to integrate their capacity strengthening objectives into national strategies and funders agreeing to play a supportive role. This was followed by the endorsement of the Accra Agenda for Action in 2008 by funders and partner countries, which stated (in part) that 'Without robust capacity – strong institutions, systems, and local expertise – developing countries cannot fully own and manage their development processes' (OECD, 2008:16). Clearly, the capacity to support strategic planning, monitoring and evaluation (PME) processes to manage development initiatives and provide evidence to inform policy, programmes and projects is crucial for realizing development objectives and bringing about social change. However, despite billions of dollars spent annually to strengthen organizational capacity, progress has been slow. Some of the reasons for this are due to management reforms not going far enough (*ibid*), and the inability of some leaders and development practitioners to respond to these new challenges. A key objective of this chapter is to demonstrate to leaders and development practitioners the importance of capacities and conditions and how to enhance them for sustainable development impact in initiatives and organizations. As a first step, we need to ask basic questions. What do we understand by capacity and why is it important? How can we as leaders and development practitioners identify and strengthen the capacities needed to manage initiatives and organizations for sustainable development impact? How can we work in situations or conditions that we cannot control or change and how can we create conditions internally that enhance sustainable development impact?

Capacity is not an easy term to define. A cursory survey of literature shows that capacity means different things to different people. Fowler and Ubels (2010: 22) refer to capacity as 'a multi-faceted phenomenon... based on different competencies or capabilities that combine to shape the overall capacity of a purposeful human system… Ways in which elements are present and combine can vary enormously within and between types of organization [and initiative]'.

There are other definitions of capacity. For example, OECD (2010: 1) refers to capacity as 'the ability of people, organisations and society as a whole to manage their affairs successfully'. Keijzer et al. (2011: 13) define capacity as the 'overall ability of an organisation or system to create value for others', whereas Baser and Morgan (2008: 3) describe it as 'that emergent combination of individual competencies, collective capabilities, assets and relationships that enables a human system to create value'. These definitions underscore the view that initiatives/organizations are living systems operating within an even bigger dynamic system, as mentioned in Chapter 2, and that while capacity is enabling, it is also the outcome of complex interactions of actors in the system, and is unpredictable and emergent in nature. Box 4.1 defines some key terms used in this chapter.

To better understand capacities and conditions and develop appropriate actions in relation to initiatives and organizations, we need to take a systems perspective. From this perspective, we recognize that we should not take things at face value, but instead ask probing questions to get a fuller picture of what an initiative/organization is about, and should be doing, within the context of its environment and available resources. Only then can we ask what the implications are with respect to capacities and conditions. The European Centre for Development Policy Management (2009: 123) suggests looking 'beyond the formal capacities to deliver development results – such as technical and managerial competencies – and to identify other factors that drive organisational and systems behaviour'. The latter include resources, assets, formal policies as well as hidden factors, such as informal policies and power structures, culture, connections, and principles. Pushing ourselves to look at capacities and conditions in this way will help us understand the ins and outs of our initiative/organization, especially as we become more and more aware of our organizational needs, strengths and weaknesses, and as we improve our organizational learning and capacity to bring about change.

For a system or initiative/organization to work, we need competent staff committed to getting results. Further, the required collective capabilities should be in place. Several other factors, including a robust support structure (with adequate resources), also contribute to the proper functioning of a system. So, capacity as we understand it emerges as a result of individual competencies of stakeholders, collective capabilities of an initiative/organization, and associated conditions. Conditions refer to the circumstances internally and externally that come about as a result of a number of factors such as culture, formal and informal policies, power relations, principles or values, and resources. Capacities and conditions

BOX 4.1: DEFINITIONS OF KEY TERMS

Capacity is the emergent outcome of a system. It is the combination of the individual competencies of leaders, staff of an initiative/organization, development practitioners and other key stakeholders involved in an initiative/organization, the collective capabilities, assets and relationships that enable an initiative or organizational system to create social value. (Adapted from Baser and Morgan, 2008)

Capacity development is the process through which the capacity of an initiative, organization and key stakeholders is enhanced. It is also the change that focuses on improvement in the wider society or environment. (Adapted from Baser and Morgan, 2008)

Capabilities are the collective abilities of an initiative/organization to do something either within its system or externally. Capabilities are the result of conditions and collective competencies of an initiative/organization. (Adapted from Keijzer et al., 2011)

Competencies refer to the energies, mindsets, skills and motivations of leaders, development practitioners and other key stakeholders. (Adapted from Keijzer et al., 2011)

Conditions refer to the circumstances internally and externally that come about as a result of, for example, a combination of assets, connections, formal and informal policies, resources, culture, power relations, principles or values.

are therefore not static as there is interaction within the system in the form of feedback loops. Consequently, the system improves as organizational learning takes place. In addition, as a system's capacity increases, an initiative/organization within that system will increasingly be able to handle more complexity effectively over time (Baser and Morgan, 2008).

In the following sections, we discuss the importance of capacities and conditions in relation to the core processes and key orientations. We then present the five core capabilities framework (also referred to as the 5Cs framework) developed by Baser and Morgan (2008), which draws heavily on systems thinking. We have found this framework to be particularly useful in helping leaders and development practitioners assess the capabilities of an initiative/organization, as well as determine the competencies – technical PME-related, as well as more strategic competencies – and conditions needed to contribute to the building of capacities. In addition, we discuss the competencies required to support M4SDI processes and to strengthen the ability of an initiative/organization to adapt to changes within its environment. Attention is paid to the enabling role that leadership and strategic competencies play in enhancing capacities and conditions required within an initiative/organization and among key stakeholders, and in seeking innovative ways to enhance capacity development.

WHY ARE CAPACITIES AND CONDITIONS IMPORTANT?

Managing an initiative/organization for sustainable development impact means being agile and resilient to change, even in complex situations. It means being able to manage your initiative/organization in an integrated and systemic way given the inter-dependencies between the core processes and key orientations.

At the practical level, managing for sustainable development impact entails:
• ensuring that strategies developed are based on in-depth and shared understanding of how change happens in a particular context and the intended cause-effect relationships, and ensuring that the underlying assumptions being made during strategy development are sound and explicit;
• focusing on and promoting results-oriented learning processes of stakeholders, drawing on sound data and information collected through a combination of qualitative and quantitative approaches;
• having in place multi-directional accountability systems that enable a strong sense of responsibility and ownership among implementing partners and stakeholders;
• establishing a monitoring and evaluation (M&E) system that encourages people to be open, honest and to critically question successes and failures and actively share this knowledge and the lessons learned.

To meet these challenges, it is vital to pay attention to the capacities and conditions as they relate to an initiative/organization. It is also crucial to have committed leadership with the relevant competencies and access to reliable information about the initiative/organization, its stakeholders, activities, outputs, outcomes, failures and successes, and the overarching environment in which it operates. Central to this are the PME processes which can be likened to the pulse of an initiative/organization, signalling how well it is doing. PME processes are also referred to as the core processes in this guide. They include strategic guidance, effective operations and M&E (see Chapters 6–8). It would be impossible to carry out these processes effectively if the appropriate capacities and conditions were not in place including the related key orientations that are essential for managing for sustainable development impact. Figure 1.1 in Chapter 1 shows how the core processes, orientations and capacities and conditions are interlinked.

Key orientations have been dealt with at length in Chapter 3, but it is worthwhile mentioning them briefly here in relation to the role they play in the M4SDI process and what this implies for capacities and conditions.

People orientation: Different stakeholders bring to the table different beliefs, experiences, personalities and views. To manage multi-stakeholder processes such as engagement, participation and conflict, you need to understand and deal with people, both individually and in groups, to get the best out of them for the desired impact. Therefore, good leadership (including effective communication and facilitation skills) is essential in managing multi-stakeholder processes successfully. Managing people processes is particularly important during PME processes.

Learning orientation: An environment where people can discuss openly and learn from each other within and outside an initiative/organization is an important element in facilitating learning processes. These processes help to critically reflect on, and make sense of, the situation the initiative is facing, as well as to learn from the organization's failures and successes and so increase the relevance and effectiveness of your work. Learning is essential throughout the PME processes. Without it, responding to changes that affect your initiative/organization would be difficult. It is important that conditions, both internally and externally (with stakeholders), are conducive to learning and that there is expertise in-house to facilitate learning processes.

Context orientation: This involves understanding the (internal and external) environment in which a development initiative/organization is operating. It helps you understand how the initiative/organization fits within the bigger picture so you can strategically target your efforts to take advantage of opportunities, and to predict, adapt and respond to new situations. This is particularly important during the strategic guidance and M&E processes. Being able to think strategically and systemically is essential.

Addressing the capacity and conditions of an initiative/organization, while taking the above-mentioned aspects into consideration, will not be easy. Some of the things that you will need to think about include:
- human resource needs (Do you have the necessary skills in-house to manage the initiative? If not, what competencies do you need? Do you require external expertise (consultants) to carry out specific tasks?);
- developing hierarchies, mandates, procedures and rules and regulations where appropriate;
- establishing a clear PME structure with roles and responsibilities and clear annual work plans and budget (AWPBs);

- developing an equitable incentive system to motivate staff, bearing in mind that intrinsic motivation is often much stronger than extrinsic motivation because it personally connects an individual to behaviour (Are staff members motivated? What incentives (i.e. skills training, recognition) are in place?);
- putting in place a management information system (MIS) to support information needs;
- determining whether there are sufficient finances and resources to run the initiative/organization;
- developing a communication strategy that will serve as a guide to help engage and maintain close ties with staff and other key stakeholders.

There are different ways to go about assessing an initiative to find out which changes are necessary for it to have the desired impact. Some of the models used include the sustainable livelihood model (DFID, 1999) which explores the interplay between assets and other change dimensions, and the organizational/task-oriented 7S model (McKinsey & Co., 2008). However, as mentioned earlier, we have found that the 5Cs framework (Baser and Morgan, 2008) provides a good basis for assessing organizational capacities and conditions and identifying areas for action.

DETERMINING CAPACITIES AND CONDITIONS USING THE 5CS FRAMEWORK

Many people have difficulty seeing their organization in its entirety. The 5Cs framework helps initiatives and organizations to objectively look at how the different parts operate and are interlinked. You can also use the framework to identify the areas within an initiative/organization that need to be addressed to strengthen M4SDI processes and ultimately sustainable development impact. The framework singles out capacity or capacities as 'producing social value', while the five core capabilities act together to result in certain capacities and conditions. So, for an initiative to achieve its goals, it must have five basic capabilities. These are the capability to act and commit, the capability to adapt and self-renew, the capability to achieve development objectives (perform), the capability to relate, and the capability to achieve coherence. Figure 4.1 presents an adapted version of the original 5Cs framework. In our model, we show that the capabilities of an initiative are at the same level, reinforcing each other to perform and focus on sustainable development impact.

PME processes are integrated into the 5Cs model, especially in the capability to act and commit, and the capability to adapt and self-renew (M&E for adaptive management). The competencies needed to manage for sustainable development impact are briefly mentioned under each capability. The technical and strategic competencies needed to manage for sustainable development impact are described more explicitly later on (see section 'Competencies').

The 5Cs framework outlined below presents areas of an initiative/organization you could focus on to determine where attention is needed to strengthen capacities and conditions in your organization and manage for sustainable development impact. At the end of each section are questions you could ask about your initiative/ organization.

Capability to act and commit

This capability is concerned with the extent to which an initiative/organization is able to function properly. How well is it able to self-organize to carry out its mandate and act responsively and responsibly? Is leadership committed to moving the initiative/organization forward despite the challenges faced in the external environment and can leadership help provide the necessary directions? What are

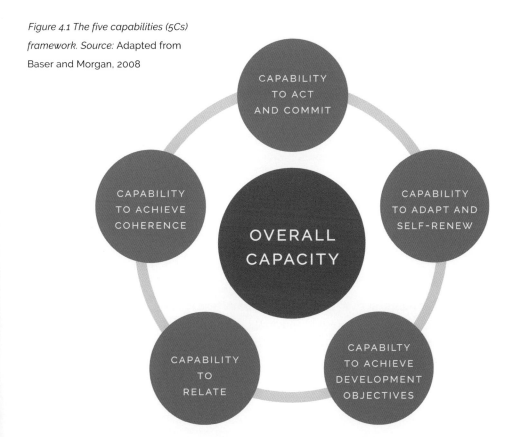

Figure 4.1 The five capabilities (5Cs) framework. Source: Adapted from Baser and Morgan, 2008

the competencies, incentives and resources needed to be able to act responsively and adequately and be ready for implementation?

Important elements that need to be considered include:

Inspiring leadership

Leaders and development practitioners need to have a range of competencies to effectively run an initiative for results. These include being able to scan the environment (systems thinking and situation analysis competency), think strategically, and most importantly inspire and motivate people into action. To do this you should be sensitive and responsive to the needs of staff and other stakeholders, be a good communicator to engage and gain the trust of stakeholders internally and externally, (i.e. strategic thinking, managing change and facilitating learning and engagement competencies are needed). During the strategic guidance process, it is important that leadership is people-, learning-, and context-oriented (see section 'Strategic competencies').

Key questions to help you think more deeply about the leadership in your initiative/organization are: What kind of leadership style does the initiative/ organization have? Is it responsive, inspiring and sensitive to the needs of staff? Is it able to engage staff and create an atmosphere of trust?

Strategic and operational guidance

This relates to the ability to provide strategic direction (see Chapter 6). To do so, strategic competencies are needed, such as strategic thinking, systems thinking and strategic foresight. This will help the initiative/organization to develop adequate strategic and operational plans which need to be supported during implementation.

Key questions to ask are: To what extent do leaders provide strategic guidance? To what extent are operations in line with strategic plans? Is leadership prepared to be open and alert for emerging and unexpected futures? Is the organization able to adapt?

Staff and stakeholders with adequate competencies and motivation

To carry out the plans mentioned above, think about whether there is an adequate incentive system in place to motivate staff and other relevant stakeholders to improve performance. Consider whether staff have the technical (subject matter) competencies to carry out specific tasks, e.g. possessing agricultural extension competencies when training farmers. For PME-related tasks, specific technical competencies required include the ability to analyse the situation in which the initiative is operating, develop a strategy, and collect and analyse data (see section 'Technical competencies'). Staff should be properly trained and if the necessary expertise is not available in-house, consider hiring additional expertise (consultants) if resources permit. There should also be opportunities for staff development to support the work of the initiative/organization.

Other incentives include: clear roles and responsibilities and a good work plan; sufficient resources made available to carry out the work and limit the bureaucracy in getting things done; fair remuneration, perhaps including health benefits, use of a vehicle, clothing allowance, transportation allowance, etc.; room for advancement and professional training; and opportunities for creativity and innovation.

Some important questions to ask include: Do staff have the necessary competencies and skills to carry out their work properly? Are there training opportunities? What is the level of staff turnover?

Mobilization of financial resources
Financial resources are necessary to support human resources, staff activities, as well as key systems (e.g. management information system (MIS)), training, transportation, etc. Efforts should be made to diversify funding as much as possible and funds should cover different time periods to increase the initiative's sustainability. Developing clear procedures for getting funding and ensuring that staff are aware of them will promote inclusiveness and increase the chance of acquiring additional funding.

A budget for PME would include items such as:
• recurrent labour costs (staff, both permanent and temporary);
• contracts for consultants and enumerators (fees, travel expenses, allowances);
• training of team members, i.e. capacity building;
• cost of organizing workshops and field visits, i.e. venue, materials, allowances;
• communication and reporting costs.

Strategic guidance and effective operations processes, as well as key orientations, are important when mobilizing financial resources. Important competencies include situation analysis, strategic planning and operational management. Key questions to ask include: Is adequate funding in place? Are there multiple funding sources covering different time periods? Are proper procedures in place to pursue new funding opportunities?

Capability to adapt and self-renew

Many initiatives are not always able to adjust to changes in the external environment. For instance, there may be poor internal communication, a lack of openness and incentives that promote learning, or the inability to scan the environment to identify changes.

To develop the ability to respond to change successfully and incorporate new ideas, consider whether the initiative/organization:
· has an adaptive management culture;
· understands and responds to results and changes in the external environment;
· has staff adequately trained in PME;
· is open to learning and critical reflection;
· is open to new ideas from staff and other stakeholders;
· has a well implemented internal communication strategy;
· engages target groups and stakeholders in learning;
· has a system in place to signal and understand the trends and shifting context in its environment;
· uses the information obtained to develop future strategies.

Strategic guidance and M&E processes are crucial here. For both processes to work properly, conditions within an initiative have to be conducive to enhancing people- and learning-oriented processes and there has to be a system in place to inform strategic and operational decision-making processes. Competencies in areas such as actor and situation analysis, M&E design, data collection, data analysis and sense-making for use, are especially important in supporting M&E functions. Other competencies such as strategic planning, strategic thinking, systems thinking, strategic foresight, and change management are also key.

Questions to ask include: Is M&E being used effectively to assess activities, outputs, outcomes and impact? Are individual M&E competencies in place to support M&E functions? Does M&E effectively inform strategic and operational decision-making? Does critical reflection take place on a regular basis to learn from successes and failures? Are staff able to freely share their ideas in relation to the achievement of objectives? Is there a system in place to help the initiative/organization keep abreast of changes or developments in the environment?

Capability to achieve development objectives

The main issue here is whether the initiative/organization is able to produce what it was set up to do. For a project, this may mean achieving development objectives.

For an organization, this may involve ensuring that specific products or services are delivered. For example, a university delivers competent students for the labour market or a ministry formulates and implements policies.

Key considerations include:
- the establishment of clear operational plans to guide staff in their day-to-day operations;
- a focus on quality and efficiency;
- the implementation of activities in line with ambitions to deliver the expected results;
- the existence of agreed standards and performance measurements;
- the existence of feedback mechanisms with client satisfaction ratings that are followed up.

Effective operations and M&E processes and the related technical competencies are important here. Operations competency is needed to be able to carry out operational planning and implementation of activities while M&E competencies are required to monitor progress and report critical issues.

Useful questions to ask are: Does your initiative/organization have properly set out operational plans for carrying out projects or providing services/products? Are operations based on the cost-effective use of resources and the extent to which outputs are delivered? Are mechanisms in place to determine whether the products and services meet the needs of the stakeholders? Does the initiative/organization balance efficiency requirements with the quality of its work? Are internal audit procedures in place?

Capability to relate

The capability of an initiative/organization to relate to other stakeholders within the context in which it operates is essential and underscores the importance of internal relationships. It is particularly useful to engage stakeholders in developing policies and strategies that benefit the initiative/organization. Strengthening the relationship with your stakeholders through partnerships or some form of informal alliance can make an initiative/organization more effective in its delivery of products or services, as well as increase the chance of attracting additional funding. Relationships with strong networks and partners therefore matter. Cultivating good relationships with your target groups and developing strong internal connections are key to helping your initiative/organization deliver effectively. The main considerations here are whether the initiative/organization is seen as a credible, reliable partner, and whether it can communicate well with its stakeholders and maintain good relationships with them, as well as with funders. This requires a committed leadership that is open in its relations with stakeholders.

Strategic guidance and M&E processes, and learning and people orientations are paramount here. Competencies such as strategic thinking, systems thinking, strategic foresight and facilitating learning and engagement are also important.

Key questions to consider include: Does the initiative/organization cultivate and maintain relations with its stakeholders? How often do staff go into the field to see how the target group is doing and engage them in dialogue? How well does the initiative/organization communicate with stakeholders as well as include them in key decision-making processes? Is the initiative/organization open to new stakeholders? Does the initiative/organization have a clear mandate?

Capability to achieve coherence

Organizations need a variety of competencies, systems and structures in place when operating within a dynamic context where there are a wide range of stakeholders, as well as a variety of views and ways of thinking. And yet, some measure of cohesiveness is required to ensure initiatives/organizations remain focused on what it is they are supposed to do.

This can be achieved through:
• a clearly developed vision, mandate and strategy, which are regularly revisited (and revised when necessary) by management, staff and key stakeholders;
• a well-defined set of operating principles and procedures put in place, supported and used by management;
• diversity within the organization in terms of its staff, consortia or partnerships;
• consistency between the organization's ambition, vision, strategy and operations;
• activities and projects that are complementary, i.e. in line with the vision and mandate of the organization and mutually supportive.

This capability relates to the core PME processes and people orientation. PME competencies and strategic leadership competencies are needed to ensure coherence. Important questions include: Are the vision, mission and strategies discussed on a regular basis? Are projects, strategies and operations in line with the vision and mission? Are there operational guidelines and procedures in place? Does the organization have complementary strategies?

COMPETENCIES

We have seen that each initiative/organization operates within a different context so it is only natural to expect that the required capacities, conditions and competencies will vary accordingly. Different types of competencies are required when managing for sustainable development impact, depending on the situation and tasks. In unfamiliar situations, and when facing unfamiliar problems, we may sometimes need to set aside what we consider 'best practice' or 'good practice' and instead develop a fresh appreciation of what would help to make good decisions about what to do. In other cases, we may need to bring together new combinations of good practices. Leaders and development practitioners therefore need to have the requisite competencies that will enable them to apply their knowledge and skills to various situations effectively. Interestingly, Mulder (2012) has observed a marked shift from the traditional transmissive approach to education, which is primarily concerned with teachers and experts deciding on the curriculum content for graduates, to emerging transformative forms of education or competence-based education. Here students get the relevant knowledge they need to contribute to socio-economic development, and attention is also given to developing competencies based on authentic tasks and issues that require knowledge in action. We can also learn from this by further enhancing the competencies of staff and stakeholders by encouraging them to become active learners and providing opportunities for activities such as field trips, internships and experience-sharing and collaboration in specific areas.

In this section, we focus on what we consider the most important competencies in managing for sustainable development impact. These competencies can be divided into two main groups: technical and strategic. Technical competencies or skills are the things we learn mostly in vocational training, whereas strategic competencies are about our interpersonal, intrapersonal and social skills, our thinking and sense-making abilities, and our capacity to link them to the roles and responsibilities needed for M4SDI. Both types of competencies are discussed in more detail below.

Technical competencies

Technical competencies support the implementation and day-to-day running of an initiative/organization. Managing for sustainable development impact means that the technical competencies within an initiative/organization also support PME processes. The main competencies therefore include subject-matter related competencies and technical PME-related competencies.

Subject-matter related competencies. If the initiative/organization is concerned with agriculture or health, for example, then the initiative should have competencies in these areas.

Technical PME-related competencies. These include competencies in situation analysis, strategic planning, operational planning, M&E design, data collection and data analysis, sense-making and reporting for use (see Figure 4.2).

Below is an explanation of (technical) PME competencies:

Situation analysis: This entails understanding the initiative and its environment. Good analytical skills are needed for this. Key analysis themes might include stakeholders, issues or problems, biophysical setting, environmental issues, and institutions. For example, you would want to know about your stakeholders, so some of the questions you would ask are: Who are the relevant stakeholders? What are their perceptions of the issue to be addressed? What hinders their work? Who might be affected by the initiative and in what way?

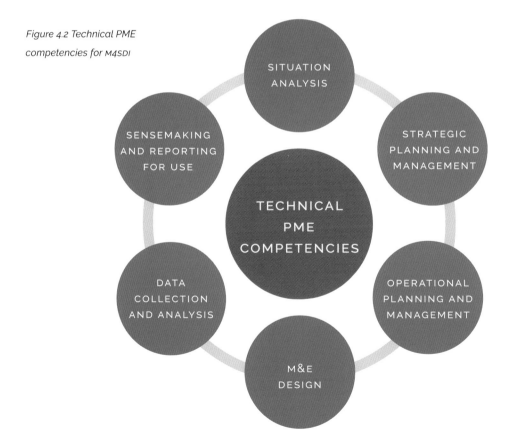

Figure 4.2 Technical PME competencies for M4SDI

Strategic planning & management: Special skills are needed to guide and manage the strategic planning process. Knowledge on how to develop and adapt the Theory of Change of your initiative/organization and how to use logic and foresight models is important.

Operational planning & management: Once the strategy or strategies have been developed, you will need to make them operational and think through the details in terms of time and resources. Operational planning and management competency (see Chapter 7 section 'Key competencies supporting effective operations') touches on project management, financial management, human resource management (HRM), operational planning, procurement and contracting, maintenance management, information management, and coordination and communication. This competency facilitates and strengthens effective operations processes and fosters interactions among staff, partner organizations and primary stakeholders.

This involves ensuring:
- an optimal structure for M4SDI responsibilities:
  - M4SDI roles and responsibilities of staff, implementing partners and primary stakeholders are clearly defined with PME staff allocated clear lines of authority.
  - There is a strong link between the management of a development initiative/ organization and PME staff so that M&E findings are used to inform decisions.
  - PME functions are represented at a high strategic and resource management level and incorporated into the approaches and activities of all project implementers.
  - PME staff act as facilitators of learning.
  - Consideration is given to where the M4SDI functions in a project/organization structure are positioned (with primary and implementing partners): Is the PME unit centralized, or are PME tasks shared?
- adequate finances and other resources in place to support M4SDI processes for:
  - contracts for consultants or external expertise;
  - fees and travel expenses;
  - physical, non-contractual investment costs such as equipment, computers and software, publications, etc.;
  - training and study opportunities for M4SDI-related capacity-building;
  - labour costs for permanent staff, temporary support staff and technical assistance;
  - non-labour operational costs for expenses such as accessing data, allowances for primary stakeholders and project implementers, stationery, meetings, and special evaluation events.
- clear guidelines in place to guarantee that procurement and contracts are in

keeping with agreed rules and regulations;

· development of a maintenance strategy for equipment, furniture and office buildings;

· an organized information system to support communication processes and easy access to data. Provisions have to be made for information to be collected and stored.

M&E design: Expertise in M&E is essential. You must be able to connect situation analysis, strategic and operational planning to M&E, and determine whether the initiative is able to engage in and guide the M&E process (see Chapter 8).

Data collection and analysis: Often data collection and analysis go hand in hand. Strong analytical skills as well specialist as knowledge in quantitative and qualitative methodologies and methods are essential. The ability to design and administer surveys, conduct interviews and facilitate group discussions is also crucial. These skills are particularly important for the design and implementation of mixed methods to support evaluation studies. Not all initiatives/organizations will have access to such expertise. Therefore, you should ensure there is access to this type of expertise when the need arises (see Chapter 8).

Sense-making and reporting for use: It is important to be able to work with stakeholders to make sense of the findings and determine in a participatory way what actions will be needed in the future. This information will then need to be effectively communicated and reported to various stakeholders. The use of the findings will also need to be further stimulated.

Strategic competencies

While it is important that staff and other stakeholders involved in a development initiative or an organization have the necessary technical competencies, it is also crucial that leaders and development practitioners have strong strategic competencies that will allow them to navigate challenges, particularly within settings that are highly dynamic. The strategic competencies are particularly relevant in strategic guidance (Chapter 6) as they help leaders and practitioners to think through how change does/can happen and to keep track of, and respond to, what's happening in the environment.

Leadership and strategic competencies

Numerous studies have sought to identify the competencies leaders need for effective leadership. But before we go any further, we need to explain what we understand by the term leadership because it is often used interchangeably with management. For a start, leadership does not necessarily mean 'being in charge'.

Field staff may not have been involved in developing the strategic framework of their organization, but if they are to make those around them understand the importance of collaboration, they will need to be able to communicate, act, inspire and respond as leaders. Leadership is therefore often described in terms of doing the right things by asking the right questions, whereas management is concerned with doing things right.

In M4SDI, strong leadership, along with strong management and dedicated staff are required, otherwise there is a good chance that your initiative/organization will not perform well. Leadership has an important role to play in managing an initiative/organization for sustainable development impact in a dynamic environment. This means that leadership needs to be adaptive and there are several leadership frameworks that you can draw on to develop your own leadership style. We have found the Situational Leadership®[1] Model (Hersey and Blanchard, 1998) to be useful for understanding which leadership style to adopt depending on the amount of supervision needed and the readiness of the person to carry out a particular function/task. To learn more about leadership styles and their implications see Chapter 3 section 'Leadership'.

While there are quite a range of competencies that are important for leadership, the strategic competencies (Figure 4.3) that leaders and development practitioners are expected to demonstrate in M4SDI have been grouped as follows and discussed below: strategic thinking; systems thinking; strategic foresight; managing change; facilitating learning and engagement; and strategic communication. These strategic competencies are also necessary for the effective functioning of the five different capabilities that make up the capacity of an initiative/organization.

These competencies are particularly important because they support the core PME processes and key orientations of the M4SDI approach. It is therefore desirable that leaders and development practitioners possess many of the competencies mentioned. However, if these competencies are not available within the organization, the right expertise (consultants) should be hired or staff trained.

Strategic thinking competency
Strategic thinking is essential to the strategic guidance process and context orientation. Without this competency, it would be difficult to come up with ideas that help shape the direction of an initiative/organization or to develop innovative strategies and ways to implement them that will cause the least disruption.

1] *Situational Leadership® is a registered trademark of the Center for Leadership Studies. - See more at: http://www.mindtools. com/pages/article/newLDR_44.htm#sthash.WqInxVtH.piutCfmm.dpuf*

Experiences in the field suggest that strategic thinking does not come easily to everyone, but you can always improve yourself.

Conway (2009: 15–18) defines strategic thinking as '... identifying, imagining and understanding possible and plausible future operating environments for your [initiative] and using that knowledge to expand your thinking about your potential future options about how to position your [initiative] effectively in the external environment in order to make better informed decisions about [what] action to take'. She goes on to say that strategic thinking means thinking 'deep' (how you interpret and give meaning to information) and 'long' (continuously scanning the environment for various connections and interacting with a wide range of stakeholders) about future possibilities or future courses of action, strategies or pathways that the initiative might take based on the knowledge at hand.

*Figure 4.3 Strategic
competencies for M4SDI*

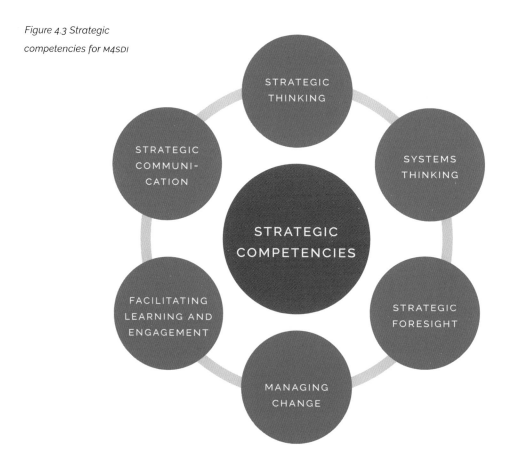

Strategic thinking is therefore useful in facilitating the planning process and provides a reference framework for M&E, which in turn supports management in navigating the future so that the vision can become a reality.

If you find strategic thinking difficult, the following points, adapted from Gorzynski (2009), are particularly helpful:
· See the 'bigger picture'.
· Think 'outside the box'.
· See things in context.
· See shades of grey rather than black and white.
· Reflect on your thinking and the assumptions you make.
· Synthesize a range of information, events, experiences and draw meaning and patterns from this.
· Cope with paradox and ambiguity.

Strategic thinkers are also considered to be systems thinkers and life-long learners. They are interested in making room for experimentation and creativity and innovation. They also know how to focus on key areas, are adaptable and future-oriented. Factors that could undermine the strategic thinking process include: the danger of wanting immediate results without considering the implications; being complacent and accepting whatever is being done; being overly confident to the extent that you overlook critical issues that directly affect your initiative/organization; and oversimplifying the real problem by focussing on what seems most feasible rather than what is most important. As a leader or development practitioner, it is important to recognize these potential pitfalls so you can avoid them. There are a number of methods and techniques which may help strengthen the ability to think strategically, or at least to create an environment for strategic thinking.

These include:
· visual thinking, visualization tools;
· scenario thinking;
· modelling and simulation techniques;
· creating systems perspectives to understand connections, causalities, relationships, boundaries, e.g. rich pictures (soft systems methodology);
· explaining situations using metaphors;
· using storytelling to connect events and changes meaningfully;
· listening and asking questions;
· appreciative inquiry which begins by identifying success factors and encouraging people to look for everything that works in the initiative/organization. This generates positive energy to shape the vision and spark action for change.

We often ask too few questions and quickly assume we know and understand. Strategic thinking means asking questions which in turn expands our thinking (e.g. What might happen if...?). Asking questions also shows that you are interested in people and in their perspectives and experiences. Strategic thinking and critical reflection are closely linked and, taken within the context of systems thinking, they can help you make sense of the situation that your initiative/ organization is addressing.

Creative thinking is closely linked to strategic thinking and enriches the strategic process, making it more effective and fruitful. Creative thinking is the ability to look at a situation with 'fresh eyes' in order to generate new ideas.
Linus Pauling, a double Nobel laureate, once said:

If you want to have good ideas, you must have many ideas.

Within the setting of a development initiative, this means intentionally and actively encouraging stakeholders involved in the process to develop multiple solutions to a particular problem.

One way to stimulate creative thinking is to use the divergent thinking technique. Palmer and Kaplan (2007: 8) point to the enabling role that divergent thinking plays in the strategic planning process and bemoan the fact that 'many organizations find it hard to step back and diverge... [even though] they could have far greater impact' if they take the time to do so. Development practitioners, along with management and other key stakeholders can, for example, engage in divergent thinking – to explore new areas and to think creatively. Generating innovative ideas is particularly important in the Theory of Change process.

Creative thinking is of immense value and is a vital competence in challenging settings, such as conflict situations and where there is scarcity of resources. Leaders and development practitioners need to be able to think creatively and/or be able to harness the creativity of staff and other stakeholders especially during the strategic planning and managing for change process. Some techniques that you can use to spark creative thinking include brainstorming, mind mapping, rich picturing, envisioning the future and engaging in role play.

Critical reflection is another competency that is closely related to strategic thinking. It helps you to see the situation that the initiative/organization faces from different perspectives. It also helps you to make connections at different levels. Critical reflection is a process of reviewing what happened in the past and the actions taken, and also involves thinking deeply in order to draw lessons, learning from what worked and what did not work. Asking questions like what happened, why, what this means, and what can be done about it, are crucial to critical reflection. This competency is particularly important in learning during the Theory of Change process, and thinking strategically about how to adapt towards sustainable development impact.

Systems thinking competency

Although we have already discussed systems thinking in some detail in Chapter 2, it is worth mentioning here again because it supports our ability to think strategically, learn, plan and manage change within complex situations. John Muir (1911: 110) famously wrote:

When we try to pick out anything by itself, we find it hitched to everything else in the universe.

In other words, problems do not exist in isolation. Systems thinking helps you to understand the root causes of problems by exploring their inter-relationships and picking up trends, or patterns of change, so that you can work with stakeholders to find ways of addressing them. Taking a systems perspective will help you think strategically and critically reflect during PME processes and also encourage you to be context- and learning-oriented.

Strategic foresight competency

Many researchers working in the field of strategy believe that foresight is a critical competency for leaders and development practitioners. This is because it strengthens strategic thinking that informs the strategic guidance process, which is responsible for ensuring that any strategy developed is geared towards the future. During this process as well, articulating your Theory of Change can be seen as connecting the past to the future. It is for this reason that it is important to stay on top of trends and ongoing developments.

Traditional approaches to strategy development have tended to focus on formulating strategies for initiatives/organizations operating in environments with a high degree of predictability, but as we have seen, the environment is often dynamic and unpredictable. For example, when the initiative/organization encounters a problem, the tendency is to react to the crisis in the best way possible (reaction-oriented). Using foresight will help you think systemically about the future of your initiative or organization and plan for it by identifying appropriate responses to changes in the environment (future-oriented). Table 4.1 shows the differences between questions asked depending on whether your initiative is reaction-oriented or future-oriented.

Table 4.1 The differences between reaction-oriented and future-oriented questions.
Source: Adapted from Conway, 2016

REACTION-ORIENTED	FUTURE-ORIENTED
What happened?	What is going on? In which direction are things moving?
Why did it happen?	What is fuelling the changes that will have an impact on the future of the initiative?
	What are the possible futures?
How do we react now?	What should we do today?
	What are the possible long-term consequences of actions taken today?
What are we going to do?	What will make us ready to act?
Assess after the event	**Anticipate the event**

There are strategic foresight frameworks/models and methods or tools that can help you strengthen your competency in this area. To be able to use them, it is important to be aware of the various categories of futures/foresight methods open to you, such as strategic, long-range planning (the more common role of foresight in organizations); forecasting and technical analysis (which may relate to, e.g. market research); and strategic foresight (which relates to making strategies and planning more future-proof). Long-term futures studies, for example, give a long-range perspective on events that help you to prepare for changes in the environment. The OECD (2012) warning about the consequences of inaction in view of the environmental outlook to 2050 is a case in point. Other futures studies, such as described in the Scenarios for the Future of Technology and International Development report (Rockefeller Foundation and Global Business Network, 2010), also help to find out what critical uncertainties you need to respond to, and to prepare new development agendas by picking out the most important trends that need to be addressed. Examples of tools for foresight analysis are strategic foresight and predictive surveys such as the Delphi method (Helmer, 1967), scenario planning, trend extrapolation and learning curves.

Futures thinking can therefore help proactive leaders and development practitioners create new outlooks on strategy. By understanding the alternatives, development initiatives and organizations can become far more innovative. The emphasis is not so much on predicting correctly or getting the right strategy, but more about creating a deeper realization of the dynamics in which to position your efforts. By doing so, you are likely to create new windows of opportunity.

Managing change competency

Change can be quite unsettling for those involved in an initiative/organization, especially if it is managed in an environment where conditions are not in place that allow and nurture change processes. Not surprisingly, many initiatives find implementing a new strategy to be challenging, often fraught with obstacles.

To manage a change process successfully, you will need to be strategic in your actions, as well as inspiring, empathetic to people's needs, be able to communicate effectively, build coalitions of support, tackle any resistance to change and facilitate change processes effectively. Instrumental to all of this is the creation of an environment which promotes creativity, knowledge and learning. This implies that bringing about change or transformation is not something that can come about overnight – it takes a lot of time, years even.

Your managing for change competency doesn't just begin to 'kick in' once the strategy for your initiative/organization has been formulated. It starts much earlier, at the start of the strategic planning process. Developing a good understanding of the issues facing your initiative, being constantly on the lookout for opportunities and being aware of situations and relationships that you can take advantage of later during the change process are crucial to this competency.

We can learn much from Kotter's (2007) 8-step process for leading change (see Table 4.2). It highlights a number of stages that build on each other and eventually lead to an initiative successfully implementing change for sustainable development impact. What is outlined in these eight steps has implications for much of what is decided during the strategic planning process and any strategy developed would have to consider seriously how it can incorporate these stages into its plan.

STAGE	ACTION TO TAKE	POSSIBLE PITFALLS
Create a sense of urgency	The environment is constantly changing and there is a continuous need to keep up with this change. Successful change efforts begin when key persons start to look at the initiative critically and recognize that there is need for change. Convince the majority of your top-level managers of the need for change. Acknowledge fear of the unknown.	Underestimating how difficult it is to address resistance and convince people of the need for change and get them on board. Becoming overwhelmed by the risks change brings. Not maintaining a sense of urgency throughout the process especially when you see signs that the initiative is embracing change.
1		
Build a powerful guiding coalition	This entails forming a group committed to the change process and sufficiently powerful enough to lead the change effort. This group should ideally include not only senior officers but also a mix of other staff such as M&E officers and practitioners with different roles and responsibilities. Retreats are usually a good way of getting the group to build trust and enhance communication among its members. The group has to be able to work as one outside of the normal hierarchy. Members of the group need to maintain a close relationship and keep each other informed, so as to be able to respond to emerging issues.	Limited experience in consultation and working in groups. Lack of willingness to assign responsibility to the most capable person regardless of position.
2		
Create a vision	Create a vision that conveys the change you want to bring about. Use strategies developed and agreed during the strategic planning process.	Not presenting your vision in a clear way so that the people concerned understand what it is.
3		

Table 4.2 An 8-step process for leading change in a development initiative. Source: Adapted from Kotter, 2007

STAGE	ACTION TO TAKE	POSSIBLE PITFALLS
4 Communicate the vision	Use every communication channel possible to convey the new vision and strategies being implemented. The guiding coalition should also be involved in helping people change their behaviour through communication and by reminding them about the desired behaviour.	Not communicating your vision to staff and stakeholders properly. Managers and key staff involved in leading the push for change taking actions that contradict the change effort.
5 Empower staff and stakeholders to act on the vision	Assess the capacities and conditions of the initiative. Identify areas of strengths and weaknesses. Remove barriers that prevent people achieving the vision even if you think this may lead to the loss of a valued individual. Provide training and increased exposure in the field where possible. Create an open environment where people feel free to discuss ideas and to be creative/innovative. Get more and more people on board by actively engaging and encouraging them. Give some room for failure and to freely admit mistakes.	Allowing powerful actors to undermine the change effort.
6 Create early wins in the change process	Create short-term goals that you can achieve and celebrate. This will also help to convince those who are not yet on board and encourage those who are already convinced, and to maintain the momentum needed to sustain the change process.	Leaving short-term successes to chance.
7 Consolidate improvements and produce more change	Use the early wins to push the change process even further, e.g. changing systems, structures and policies that continue to undermine the vision.	Declaring too early that change is embedded in the initiative's culture when in fact it is not.
8 Ensure that change is part of the initiative's culture	Show people how the new systems, structures, policies and new behaviours and attitudes have helped the initiative to achieve more sustainable development impact.	Not creating social values that are consistent with the new vision. Not identifying successors of leaders who support the change process.

Facilitating learning and engagement competency

Learning is perhaps the most important competency of all as it unlocks most other competencies. Facilitating learning and engaging people therefore makes it possible for people to learn either by themselves or with other people within or outside the organization, such as collaborating with partners (see Chapter 3 section 'Learning at different levels'). Ensuring shared learning within an initiative/organization can enhance its relevance and effectiveness by engaging people in the design, implementation, and M&E processes.

For an initiative to be effective, good facilitation – we consider this 'the act of making something easier' – is required. A good facilitator plays a neutral role in planning, guiding and managing group events or processes in order to ensure that objectives are effectively met. Whether the facilitator comes from within or outside the organization, it is important for the person to step back from all the details of

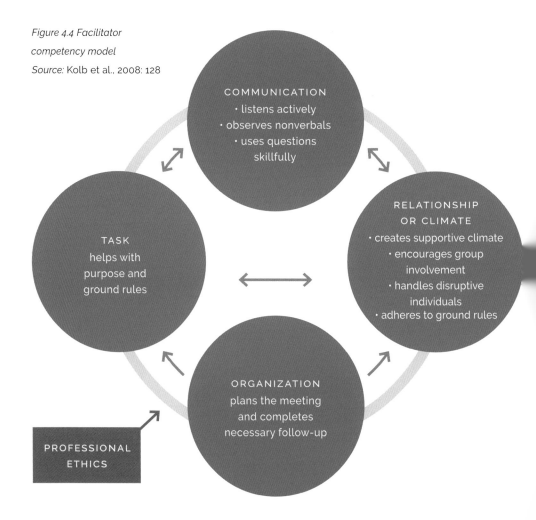

Figure 4.4 Facilitator competency model
Source: Kolb et al., 2008: 128

the initiative/organization and any personal views, and focus entirely on the group processes used to manage participant discussions and bring the event or process to a successful end.

A study conducted by Kolb et al. (2008) highlighted several competencies that facilitators considered important in facilitating processes in small groups. The researchers grouped the top competencies into three cluster categories – task, communication and relationship – and showed how these related to each other. The work of earlier researchers, as reviewed by Kolb et al., has established an interdependent (Fisher, 1980; Kelly and Thibaut, 1954) and reciprocal (Engleberg and Wynn, 1997) link between the task and relationship competency categories. Kolb et al. further determined that there was an interrelated and reciprocal relationship among the three clusters as indicated by the arrows in Figure 4.4. For example, listening actively, which is part of the communication cluster, also influences relationship and task competencies. The three clusters have a collective effect on the facilitation process. The initiative/organization provides the framework through which meetings are organized and implemented, and actions followed up. Professional ethics form an important basis for guiding the way facilitators act and take decisions.

In larger group settings where there are multi-stakeholder processes, Brouwer et al. (2015) identify three main roles that facilitators play to promote collaborative innovation: a convener brings together the relevant actors and stimulates interaction; a moderator gets the stakeholders to collaborate by managing their differences and supporting processes of mutual learning; and a catalyst stimulates stakeholders to think outside the box and to develop and implement new and bold solutions. No one person can fulfil all of these roles, so a team of facilitators is often needed. In forming a balanced team, think about issues like gender, culture and professional background. To be able to perform these roles, Brouwer et al. (*ibid*) indicate that facilitators need competencies in understanding the context, knowing and developing themselves, envisioning the process, choosing methods and tools, and working in teams.

Bearing in mind the above discussion, the facilitating learning and engagement competency can help further M4SDI processes, i.e. strategic planning, managing change, monitoring and evaluation and knowledge management processes, as well as people and learning orientations. M4SDI involves working with different stakeholders often in multi-stakeholder processes, and this calls for the creation of an environment where there is trust so that stakeholders can freely share and learn from each other and work to increase the relevance and effectiveness of their initiative/organization (see Box 4.2).

BOX 4.2 FACILITATING MEETINGS AND ENGAGING STAKEHOLDERS

To facilitate and engage stakeholders to manage for sustainable development impact, you will need to do the following:

Gather background information beforehand to find out what the purpose of the facilitation is, the desired outcome, the context and participants involved.

Design the meeting to ensure success using the most appropriate tools that will best help in facilitating the group towards the desired outcome.

Create the right climate and norms with the participants so that everyone can feel comfortable discussing issues openly.

Guide and manage group processes to enforce norms and influence participants' actions. This includes actively listening to participants, ensuring that there is effective participation and a common or shared understanding on issues. Make sure that participants' contributions are considered and included in the ideas, decisions, or strategies developed. It is also important that participants feel part of the process and share responsibility for the outcome. Ensuring that group processes flow well will most likely result in more ideas, solutions and decisions.

Properly document discussions, outcomes, actions and outstanding questions with clear follow-up actions and roles and responsibilities.

Staiger-Rivas et al. (2015) also argue that this competency can contribute to ensuring tangible outcomes despite the diversity of stakeholders. It is important to note, however, that no matter how good the facilitator, there are limits to what he or she can do. According to Kolb et al. (2008: 131) other factors that contribute to the success of group facilitation include: the provision of organizational and supervisory support, the availability of adequate resources, the knowledge that participants bring to the process, and their personal characteristics.

Strategic communication competency

According to Wageningen University & Research (2016), strategic communication is about 'connecting people in complex environments'. It refers to 'individual or organisational efforts to address or engage audiences for the advancement of organisational, societal or political goals'. Any approach taken in strategic communication should be context-oriented, interdisciplinary and practical. It is a crucial competency for leadership and for those engaged in an initiative/ organization. It helps tie PME processes together and engage people in meaningful ways without losing sight of the context (see Chapter 5).

SUMMARY

Capacity is the combination of individual competencies of stakeholders, collective capabilities, assets and relationships, enabling the initiative/organization to create social value. For an initiative/organization to operate effectively, individual competencies as well as appropriate capacities and conditions need to be in place to support core M4SDI/PME processes and key orientations. There is no blueprint for developing requisite competencies, capacities and conditions to support M4SDI processes as each initiative/organization is different. It is important to note that capacities and conditions are not static; there is interaction within the system in the form of feedback loops. However, as the system develops and improves as a result of organizational learning, the initiative/organization is better able to deal with complex issues.

To better understand capacities (and conditions), we have found the five core capabilities (5Cs) framework useful in analysing an initiative/organization in an integrated and systemic way. To manage for sustainable development impact, initiatives need to have in place certain technical and strategic competencies to support core M4SDI processes, key orientations and to find new ways of enhancing capacity development. Technical (PME) competencies include situation analysis, strategic planning, operational planning, M&E design, data collection and analysis, and sense-making and reporting for use. The strategic competencies that we consider important are strategic thinking, systems thinking, strategic foresight, change management, facilitating learning and engagement, and strategic communication.

CHAPTER 5

ROLE OF COMMUNICATION IN M4SDI

UNDERSTANDING COMMUNICATION

OVERCOMING OBSTACLES TO COMMUNICATION
Asking powerful questions
Generative listening
Giving feedback
Non-violent communication (NVC)

DEVELOPING A COMMUNICATION STRATEGY

SUMMARY

COMMUNICATION

LEARNING OBJECTIVES

· Understand what
communication is
· Explain why communication
is important in M4SDI
· Understand the different
communication models,
the obstacles to effective
communication and ways of
overcoming them
· Understand why a
communication strategy
is important and how to
develop one

Communication is part of everyday life. It is the way in which we convey our ideas, thoughts and actions. Not surprisingly, many leaders and development practitioners often underestimate the valuable role it can play in managing their initiative/organization effectively. Communication is a multifaceted process that helps to engage people and develop understanding, consensus, ownership, meaningful alliances and strong partnerships with a view to increasing sustainable development impact. Communication is the thread that binds everything together, and helps to shape M4SDI processes through everyday conversations and dialogue. And it is important that leaders/development practitioners lead by example – in the way they communicate and engage people in core M4SDI processes, and in how they go about preparing and facilitating meetings and dialogue (see section 'Understanding communication').

Knowing how communication processes operate and how they can be harnessed will help improve engagement and interaction of people and enhance management of the initiative/organization for sustainable development impact. This chapter explains perspectives on the role of communication in M4SDI, what it is and how the thinking on communication has changed over time to reflect the complexities of our everyday world. Perspectives on the challenges to effective communication, and ways of overcoming them are presented, including asking powerful questions, generative listening, providing feedback and using the nonviolent communication (NVC) model. We then look at how to develop an effective communication strategy.

Effective communication is essential to every aspect of M4SDI and can play a cementing role in linking and supporting the core M4SDI processes (see Chapters 6-8). Leadership is key in setting an example for providing guidance and support to communication processes. In fact, communication is considered a strategic competency in M4SDI. For example, the strategic guidance process entails engaging people in dialogue to develop a common understanding of problems, share experiences, create a shared vision of the future, develop strategies, and get people on board to deal with complexity and influence change processes. In effective operations, communication helps to get people's views on how best to implement the initiative and agree on activities, timing, roles and responsibilities and the required budget. This can sustain commitment and motivate people to carry out operations that support the initiative/organization. Communicating with stakeholders during monitoring and evaluation (M&E) is essential, especially when deciding what data to collect and how, and in making sense of findings for informed decision-making.

During the core processes, leaders and practitioners need to monitor the internal and external contexts (context orientation), and keep each other informed about relevant changes and adapt accordingly. Communication is also important in people processes (people orientation) - engaging in dialogue and discussion, building relationships and trust, stimulating creativity and innovation and dealing with diversity, power and conflict. Furthermore, communication is essential in facilitating learning processes (learning orientation) at the interpersonal and organizational levels and among stakeholders (see Chapter 3).

UNDERSTANDING COMMUNICATION

In this guide we refer to communication as the act of communicating. Communication can be intentional and verbal (e.g. speaking), but also unintentional and non-verbal (e.g. facial expressions). It is the exchange of thoughts, information and feelings between individuals or groups. Effective communication includes the ability to express ideas effectively and various methods can help to get your message across. Examples include person-to-person engagement, email, reports, radio, television and web-based campaigns (The Communications Network, 2010). Table 5.4 provides an expanded list of communication methods.

Dialogue and sense-making processes (see Chapter 8) are also useful in making communication effective in enhancing learning and innovation. According to

Brouwer et al. (2015: 96), dialogue is 'A conversation in which people think together in a relationship, suspend their judgment, and together create something new (new social realities). People who are in dialogue set out to understand the other person's perspective, even if they don't agree with it'.

Our understanding of communication has evolved over the years. In the early 1940s, Shannon and Weaver described communication in purely linear terms – messages are encoded by the sender and sent to the receiver through a communication channel. The receiver then decodes or interprets the information received, after which feedback takes place (objective model of communication, see Figure 5.1).

Later, it was recognized that people's interpretation of the message was often different from what the sender originally wanted to convey (subjective model). This was attributed to people having their own frames of reference based on unique experiences and cultural norms. For example, the language we speak/write, the words we choose, the way in which we phrase things, all influence how a message comes across. This message is then interpreted based on the experiences and cultural norms of those receiving it. So, if you want the other person to understand what you wish to communicate, you have to be able to place yourself in their world and be prepared to listen to what they have to say as well (Dervin, 1981). However, over time we have learned that even when we do try to understand others, people can still remain indifferent to messages or unwilling to accept them. This has given rise to the construction model which suggests that those receiving the information interpret things differently because of the knowledge they bring to the situation,

Figure 5.1 Traditional, linear model on communication

Source: Based on Shannon and Weaver, 1964 and Communication Theory, 2010

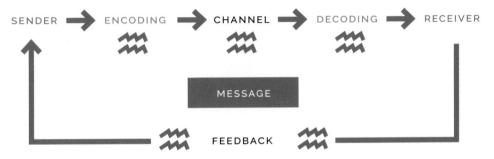

potential 'noise': anything that distorts, distracts or interferes with the communication process

Communication aspect	Objective (linear) model	Subjective model	Construction model
People involved in communication	Individuals	People with different ideas and backgrounds	Diverse people in a relational and historical setting
Meaning of the message	Message is fixed, determined by the person sending it. The leader/practitioner has a clear idea of the message to communicate to stakeholders.	Leaders/practitioners and stakeholders have different ideas and interpretations of messages.	Leaders/development practitioners strategically engage people to share ideas, develop a common understanding, make sense of facts and perspectives, and take decisions within the context of the initiative/organization and the external environment.
Reason for communication	To influence the other person, and to get a message across	Determine the different ideas people have and tailor the communication accordingly	To come to a shared agreement on the purpose of communication, and how it can serve a bigger purpose (e.g. communication for enhanced learning and adaptive management)
Main cause of differences in interpretation	Noise in the communication channels	Different past experiences, paradigms, mindsets and cultures	Different values, interests and struggle for power/influence
What theorists' implicit communication ideal is	Effective transfer of particular meanings	Discussion on the meaning of the communication	Aim for a higher ideal. Open, free exchange of communication; and dialogue and agreement on how to bring about change
Time perspective	Present	Past and present	Past, present and (anticipated) future
Effects of communication	Receiving a message, fully or partly	Adapted meanings and related actions (or inactivity)	Adapted meanings, relations and influence with various impacts
Key conditions for 'effective' communication	Exactness of the message and quality of the channel	Anticipation and empathy	Strategy of combining communication and other resources like making time available for key staff and stakeholders (including experts) to actively engage with each other in deep dialogue and (generative) learning and communication processes
Transmitters of communication	Symbolic signals (i.e. messages that don't necessarily lead people to act) transmitted via various media	Symbolic signals exchanged via various media	All forms of actions that people engage in or that can be accessed via various media

Table 5.1 Three conceptual models of
communication within the M4SDI context
Source: Adapted from Leeuwis and Aarts, 2011

including their beliefs, world view, relationships with those involved in the communication process, special interests, and the power/influence of other people in their environment (see Table 5.1 for a comparison of the three models).

According to Leeuwis and Aarts (2011: 25), 'in the "construction model" communication itself is regarded as an action that has direct consequences to the [real] world'. In other words, the meanings that come about within a complex environment are actively constructed and are not impartial, e.g. relationships may be developed and conflicts may arise, etc. This model tries to explain how people can come together to make sense of complex situations and agree upon actions to be taken. For example, during M&E, shared sense-making of findings can guide future directions, decision-making and shared actions.

Leeuwis and Aarts (2011) also point out that the role of communication can no longer be thought of in terms of 'diffusing' information, but instead as a process occurring within the context of our work. They also indicate that we need to recognize that everyday communication between people is equally, if not more, important than the efforts by leaders/development practitioners. The latter, they argue, need to play more of an enabling role. This includes facilitating exchanges (i.e. conversations and dialogue), learning and sharing experiences, mediating in conflicts, and building networks that can help foster change.

OVERCOMING OBSTACLES TO COMMUNICATION

Given that communication is 'constructed', rather than 'fixed', we also need to view obstacles to communication in the same way, and not just in terms of clarity of message or identifying appropriate methods and channels. In M4SDI, a similar approach is also taken, especially with respect to understanding and working with people, and creating a learning environment. Brouwer et al. (2015) identify a number of these obstacles to communication:

• **Having divergent views:** People often hold a different set of beliefs and have different cultural norms (some of which they themselves are not aware of) and this in itself can lead to misunderstandings.
• **Having preconceived ideas and judging others:** We often have perceptions about people – why they say the things they do and why they act in a particular way.

- **Not listening to each other:** Sometimes we are so busy trying to get our points across that we don't really listen to what others have to say.
- **Allowing our emotions to govern our responses:** We can become emotional when discussing sensitive issues, thereby failing to grasp what is being said.
- **Having an environment (e.g. at the work place) where it is difficult to openly discuss issues and share experiences.** Leadership is required to create conditions conducive to discussing and sharing experiences openly and freely.

Engaging people in the core M4SDI processes and enhancing their learning can help overcome some of these obstacles. However, it is also useful to ask powerful questions, engage in generative listening, provide feedback and use the nonviolent communication (NVC) model (Rosenberg, 2003). Box 5.1 offers practical guidance for effective communication with stakeholders in with a context that upholds cultural issues.

Asking powerful questions

Asking powerful questions in a variety of settings (i.e. within an organization or in larger group settings) is a good way to actively get staff and stakeholders to start conversations and engage in deep dialogue, to learn from each other and develop new insights. Vogt et al. (2003) describe a powerful question as one that: stirs curiosity; provokes conversation; is thought-provoking; brings assumptions to light; invites creativity; generates energy and pushes the group forward; stays with stakeholders; and elicits more questions. They documented a number of questions that they and their colleagues found useful under three broad themes:

Questions aimed at concentrating collective attention: What is important about your situation and why do you care? What key opportunities/dilemmas do you see in your situation? What assumptions come to the fore and how should these be challenged?

Questions for linking ideas and probing more deeply: What picture is emerging as a result of our discussions? What have we learned so far, and are there any new insights? Did you hear anything that surprised or challenged you?

Questions aimed at identifying future action: What is needed to foster change on this issue? What challenges are we likely to face and how can we overcome them? What conversations should we be having that could help change mindsets and create new possibilities?

Generative listening

Many of us find it difficult to really listen to others. Hanlon and Rigney (2011: 2) suggest it is because 'we are mentally too busy' to pause and listen, or 'unwilling or unable to let go', listening only superficially. They also claim that 'most of us are unable to limit the interpretive biases in any of our listening... In other words, we filter constantly through our internal processes which draw heavily on our experiences and biases or preferences' (*ibid*: 3). They refer to Otto Scharmer (2008), who identified four levels of listening:

- **Downloading:** This is listening in a way that confirms what we already know. This happens frequently. In this situation, we are attentive to the facts only to build our own case. But this only leads to short-term gains.
- **Factual listening:** Attention is paid mainly to facts and to information that is different from what we already know. Downloading and factual listening originate from within the boundaries of our own mental-cognitive or thought processes.
- **Empathic listening:** This is a deeper type of listening. When we engage in dialogue, we listen from the place that other persons are speaking from, and as a result our perception shifts. For example, we move from looking at figures and facts (as in downloading and factual listening) to seeing and truly hearing the person's story. Empathic listening is vital in dealing with conflict, particularly where there is high emotional stress. Scharmer (2008: 54) suggests empathic listening 'requires an open heart to really feel how another feels'.
- **Generative listening:** This is the highest level of listening far beyond downloading, factual and empathic listening. At this fourth level of listening, we are developing insights, not only about the current situation but also about future pathways. It is literally as if we are one, or in communion, with the situation and we see all sorts of possibilities ahead. Not surprisingly, Hanlon and Rigney (2011: 5) state that 'with generative listening, real transformation can take place between both the listener and speaker'. Managing for sustainable development impact means that we too need to engage in generative listening for transformational change to come about.

Giving feedback

Feedback is essential for learning, growth and development. And yet it can be an unnerving process. How well you give feedback affects people's morale, confidence and ability to learn and improve, so it is important to be careful when giving it. Providing effective feedback involves engaging people in dialogue and creating an atmosphere where people feel safe to speak as well as listen to each other.

BOX. 5.1 OVERCOMING OBSTACLES AND COMMUNICATING EFFECTIVELY

Overcoming obstacles

Although there are different ways of communicating across countries, cultures, sectors, organizations and age groups, there are a number of practical things that leaders and practitioners can use to overcome some of the communication obstacles.

Listen carefully to your staff and other stakeholders; make sure that discussions take place in an atmosphere where they can freely share their ideas.

Devise ways to communicate individually with people in the initiative/organization. For example, have brief informal chats with them from time to time.

Find ways to ensure that there is communication across programmes and projects, for example, by setting time aside for meetings and identifying areas of coordination and collaboration. Build coalitions of support inside and outside the organization to help you engage and influence people.
Create a common language
.

Establish some basic communication guidelines, such as protocol on the media, formats used and content. Email has become a well-established medium of communication within and among organizations, but it is often misused, not well targeted, or contains too much unclear information. In urgent situations or when you need to discuss sensitive issues; face-to-face meetings are often more appropriate than emails.

Don't make assumptions and draw conclusions too quickly, keep communication channels open and seek clarification where possible.

Communicating effectively during meetings

Do not have open-ended meetings: A productive meeting takes time to plan. It is worthwhile discussing beforehand the main objectives of the meeting so that you can develop a good agenda and circulate this prior to the meeting. Also indicate how long the meeting is expected to take.

Meetings can be formal or informal. In some settings, people prefer to have lengthy, formal meetings. What is essential is that those who attend are the "right" people and that everyone is clear about the objectives of the meeting.

Ensure presentations are concise and to the point.

Ensure there are adequate resources such as a meeting room, paper to write down ideas and action points, and flipcharts to capture ideas.

Ensure that at the end of the meeting concrete decisions are made with a list of action points and responsible persons. Good facilitation/chairing is needed to ensure an effective process, with adequate attention to engaging people.

If hostile situations develop during a meeting, avoid taking a defensive approach. Acknowledge that there is a problem by re-framing any comments made. For example, instead of saying that you hear a lot of anger or hostility in a person's voice, you could say: "I hear from your statements that you have concerns" or "You speak with a lot of passion".

For feedback to have the most impact, it should be timely, relevant and in some cases private. To get your message across, provide positive verbal and non-verbal feedback frequently. Everyone needs reassurance that they are reading nonverbal communication correctly, whether it's a smile that means you're doing great, you're doing better than most beginners, or you'll catch on eventually.

Another point to keep in mind when giving feedback is to focus on behaviour rather than on personality. For example, instead of calling a colleague inefficient, be specific in your complaint: "You don't return phone calls; this causes problems both in and outside the office". Further, provide feedback that is descriptive, rather than judgemental. Description tells us what happened. Judgment evaluates what happened. For example, in evaluating a report, don't say, "This is a lousy report!" Instead, try: "The report doesn't focus on the areas that need to be addressed", or "This report seems to have a lot of grammatical and spelling mistakes".

Limit feedback to specific issues rather than making general comments, so that the other person can really understand what it is you want done differently. For example, in an office situation, instead of saying "These folders are not arranged correctly", it's better feedback to say, "These should be arranged chronologically instead of alphabetically". Also, provide information the receiver can use and focus feedback on activities the receiver controls. Finally, check to see if the receiver of your message understood what you said. One way of doing this is to say, "I'm wondering if what I said was clear."

Non-violent communication (NVC)

NVC is a powerful tool based on the principles of non-violence. The vision of Rosenberg (2003) was to create a new value system where conflict and violence are resolved peacefully without the usual compromise. This is made possible through creating a space where people can listen and understand each other's needs free from prejudices, and develop mutual respect for each other. The NVC model (see Table 5.2) comprises two parts or roles - expressing honestly and listening emphatically - and each part has four components (i.e. observations, feelings, needs, requests) for communication, which ultimately lead to giving and receiving from the heart. The model works best when there is a mediator facilitating the process. The parties involved play both roles in the dialogue. An important part of the NVC model is understanding the questions asked and articulating your response to reflect your own feelings, needs and requests without any form of evaluation or judgement. NVC has wide application and is not just restricted to resolving conflicts and violence, but also extends to areas such as improving organizational effectiveness and strengthening relationships.

Table 5.2 The non-violent communication (NVC) model
Source: Adapted from PuddleDancer Press and Center for
Nonviolent Communication, 2009

HONESTLY EXPRESSING	EMPATHICALLY LISTENING
how I feel and what I would like. Do this without passing judgement or wanting to hold someone responsible or making any demands.	how the other person feels and what he/she would like. Do this without passing judgement or holding someone responsible or making any demands
Observations: What concrete actions do I see that affect my well-being? Feelings: Ask yourself how you feel about what is happening or has happened. I feel…	**Observations:** What do you see/hear? Feelings: How do you feel about what you have seen and heard? Try to empathize with what you hear.
Needs: Ask yourself what your needs, values, desires are. The way you express them must not contain any reference to how they will be fulfilled. They must not be expressed as a demand or criticism. The need expressed must be without reference to the other party. I have a need ….	**Needs:** What are the needs, values, desires of the person you listen to? Try to repeat the needs of the other person.
Requests: Ask concrete requests (i.e. doable action) and use clear action language. I would like you to…	**Requests:** What would you be willing to do about it? Try to give an emphatic response when you reply.

DEVELOPING A COMMUNICATION STRATEGY

In order to effectively communicate with stakeholders, we need to openly discuss issues in an atmosphere of trust, engage in dialogue, listen deeply to each other, and overcome obstacles to communication. Developing an effective communication strategy helps ensure that the areas we want addressed in M4SDI are covered. Implementing the communication strategy can support: building relationships; coordinated action; accountability to different stakeholders; dialogue and shared learning; continued motivation and engagement; avoiding or dealing with conflict (see Chapter 3); and decision-making processes.

Form a team to draw up and implement a communication strategy. The team members will need to have good interpersonal skills, possess tact, patience and commitment to the process. The team leader on the other hand has to have a good understanding of the initiative/organization as well as some background in communication. To ensure that communication is relevant and oriented towards managing an initiative/organization for sustainable development impact, it is crucial that staff and stakeholders are engaged in agreeing on what needs to be communicated, how and for what purpose.

When developing a communication strategy, keep in mind that the communication activities need to be in line with the objectives of the initiative/organization. Also, indicate how the communication strategy will support the achievement of its overall objectives. The main elements of a strategy include: executive summary; purpose of the communication strategy; description of the initiative/organization; communication issues to be addressed; tailoring communication; communication methods and processes; work plan; monitoring and evaluating the communication strategy.

Executive summary
This provides an overview of the communication strategy, outlining the key points from each section.

Purpose of the communication strategy
Indicate clearly and simply why the communication strategy is being developed and how it can support your initiative/organization to manage towards sustainable development impact. The strategy can have different purposes, e.g. to enhance engagement and commitment of staff and key stakeholders in the core M4SDI processes (Chapter 6-8) or promote the work and results of the organization/initiative to gain future support.

Description of the initiative/organization
Describe what the initiative/organization is about – the environment in which it operates, what it does, the information needs and challenges, and the people targeted.

Communication issues to be addressed
Describe what particular communication issues need to be addressed.
This requires understanding what staff and stakeholders need in terms of internal communication, and how this can support them in the development, implementation and monitoring and evaluation of the initiative. For example, staff and key stakeholders may feel left out of decision–making if they don't get any feedback or see any changes happening in relation to suggestions made. In terms of external communication – e.g. directed at the wider public – stakeholders may need to show more clearly the results of the initiative/organization in order to get support for the work they do. Feedback loops and regular meetings may help solve these issues.

*Table 5.3 Examples of messages
tailored to stakeholder groups*

STAKEHOLDERS	NEED TO KNOW	COMMUNICATION MESSAGE
Staff	What kind of working environment we provide	We care about creating a workplace where you can continually learn and enhance your capacity to serve stakeholders.
Users	What products and services we offer	We provide good, reliable information products and services; we value feedback.
Policy-makers	What we want to see changed	We have strong evidence and good knowledge of our work on the ground.

Tailoring communication

Agree on and describe who will be engaged in communication activities within the initiative/organization and who is to be targeted based on the communication objectives. For example, to improve internal communication, engage staff or relevant stakeholders in thinking through how this needs to be done. This can help secure buy-in for a particular change process. For external communication (e.g. to reach a wider public), only a few people need to be involved.

Agree on what messages you would want to get across and for what purpose, and ensure they are clear, simple, timely and regularly enforced. The messages also need to be appropriate and relevant to the needs of the targeted stakeholders (see Table 5.3). When tailoring communication, bear in mind the four levels of listening (Scharmer, 2008) as discussed earlier.

When you really want to enhance learning and change, it is necessary to work towards a deeper level of listening, generative listening, by creating space for dialogue. This can be done, for example, during staff or stakeholder meetings so as to agree upon shared objectives and ideas or messages to communicate to a wider audience, and how this can be done in collaboration.

Communication methods and processes

There are many ways of communication. These include reports, books, brochures, emails, website information, as well as more interactive methods like face-to-face meetings and dialogue (see Table 5.4). Interactive methods and processes for communication are more effective and useful when engaging with smaller groups of people, and when working with key staff and stakeholders. When you want to reach a wider audience, use less interactive communication methods. Communicate with staff and stakeholders on a regular basis by actively going out and engaging in dialogue with them to better understand the situation, and what is needed in terms of communication to support situation analysis, planning, implementation and M&E.

You also need to make strategic choices about the communication channel. For example, you might want to use social media to reach young people on a particular topic. In another instance you might want to use radio to reach farmers. Some methods are more expensive than others, so consider the cost implications. Developing a table showing the targeted audience, purpose of communication, and communication methods, channels and processes, can be useful. For communication to be effective, a mix of methods may be useful.

Table 5.4 Key communication methods and processes
Source: Based on Better Evaluation, 2013 and Torres et al., 2005

LEAST INTERACTIVE
mainly written

- Short written communications
- Memos and email
- Postcards
- Interim Reports
- Final reports
- Executive summaries
- Newsletters, bulletins, briefs (e.g. policy briefs), brochures
- News media communications
- Website communications
- Mobile data technology: sms
- Postcards
- Web 2.0 e.g. online mapping; alerts and RSS (Rich Site Summary) feeds

POTENTIALLY INTERACTIVE
often a combination of (creative) presentations and interactions

- Verbal presentations
- PowerPoint presentations
- Flip charts
- Video Presentations
- Posters
- Displays and exhibits
- Photography
- Cartoons
- Images
- Pictures/drawings
- Infographics
- Poetry
- Drama/theatre
- Storytelling
- Mobile data technology using smart phones
- Open data
- Web 2.0 and social media (e.g. Google Docs; voice over the internet; LinkedIn; Facebook)

MOST INTERACTIVE
high interaction with users

- Working sessions
- Synchronous electronic communications
- Chat rooms
- Teleconferencing
- Video conferencing
- Web conferencing
- Personal discussions
- Communities of practice (online and/or face-to-face)
- Verbal briefings

Examples of communication methods that people use to stay informed about technical and organizational issues include meetings (face-to-face, teleconferencing), memos and emails. In communicating M&E findings, reports (preferably supported by visuals) can be used, but also think of (policy) briefs, social media or presentations, and engaging people in dialogue to critically reflect on the findings and think through implications for action in their context.

Work plan

To implement the communication strategy, draw up a work plan indicating key communication activities and milestones, timeline, roles and responsibilities, and budget.

Monitoring and evaluating the communication strategy

Allocate time and resources to determine whether your communication strategy is working. Identify the indicators you will use to measure the success of your strategy. This can be done using readily available data such as the number of hits to your website, and generating statistics from your management information system (MIS) on things like the number of newsletters distributed, and feedback from dialogue sessions with stakeholders. Get feedback from those directly involved in the initiative/organization to find out whether the strategy is working, what needs to be improved and how. Additionally, share and reflect on findings from monitoring external communication (e.g. from websites). This can be done during planning and review sessions.

SUMMARY

Effective communication is vital for M4SDI. It is the thread that binds everything together, not only during the planning phases of an initiative/organization, but also during implementation and M&E. Investing in communication can prevent or help deal with conflict, build relationships and trust, and commitment and support. During planning, communication helps identify issues and options for change. And it supports coordination and collaboration during the implementation process. Communication supports M&E processes and helps make sense of findings.

In order to effect change, leadership/development practitioners need to have good communication skills. For communication to be effective, active engagement in dialogue is important to better understand each other's views and construct together the communication processes necessary to support change processes. Developing and implementing a shared communication strategy is useful for identifying why and how communication can support change processes, and how to tailor it to different audiences. Different communication methods and processes can be used, ranging from written materials involving little or no interaction, to highly interactive methods and processes where dialogue and engagement can lead to a deeper understanding of each other, the context, and what is needed to effect change. Asking powerful questions, giving feedback and using the non-violent communication model can support us in our communication. Moving from downloading and factual listening to empathic and generative listening can truly support transformational change in the way we communicate with each other and manage for sustainable development impact.

PART 2

CORE
M4SDI
PROCESSES

CORE M4SDI PROCESSES

In Part 1, we delved into the more theoretical issues and perspectives and their implications for managing for sustainable development impact. We showed why and how key orientations, capacities and conditions and communication need to be considered within the context of a development initiative/ organization. A number of useful tools, methods and approaches were suggested to help assess relevant (context) dimensions and dynamics of initiatives/organizations. These elements form the basis for effectively managing for sustainable development impact (M4SDI). Part 2 builds on this, considering core processes that are important to managing an initiative/ organization within the context of a dynamic and unpredictable environment and practical ways of carrying out these processes. Stories on how the M4SDI approach works out in practice are shared at the end of the book.

Strategic guidance: This process involves being well-informed about the context in which the initiative/organization is operating, and responding accordingly. It is about thinking and planning strategically, which involves knowledge, information and (practical) wisdom: understanding what is relevant and important in a particular situation. This, of course, takes into consideration stakeholders' ideas of what they would like to see the initiative/organization achieve, how they think this change will happen (preferably based on evidence), what assumptions underpin the envisaged change process (their 'Theories of Change'), and keeping an eye on developments in the internal and external contexts. Strategic guidance also includes managing in a coherent way based on a good situation analysis, a well-developed Theory of Change and a change management process to help keep the initiative/organization focused on its goals.

Effective operations: Strategic guidance needs to guide action, which relates to operations. Ensuring effective operations involves turning strategic plans and ideas into practical implementation procedures and measures that relate to every aspect of the initiative/organization (i.e. project management, finance management, human resource management, operational planning, procurement and contract management, maintenance management, information management, and coordination and communication).

Monitoring and evaluation (M&E): Although monitoring and evaluation are different processes, they are intricately linked and go hand in hand. M&E supports strategic guidance and effective operations by providing valuable information about how the initiative/organization is faring to support decision-making processes. M&E is much more than merely checking the extent to which targets have been met. It also implies monitoring what emerges in a complex context for adaptive management. If carried out properly and responsibly, not only will it provide useful information for primary stakeholders, funders and partner organizations, it can also promote understanding and partnership with stakeholders. Furthermore, M&E can be used to inform policies, generate new knowledge and empower people.

The figure below shows the relationship between the core processes, key orientations, capacities and conditions, and communication.

In the following chapters, the three core M4SDI processes are discussed within the context of underlying theory and in relation to key orientations, capacities and conditions, and communication. Selected methods and tools to carry out the processes are provided. In the final chapter, stories of how the M4SDI approach has been successfully integrated into initiatives/organizations are presented.

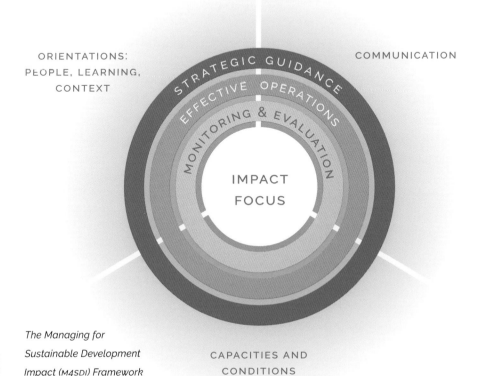

ORIENTATIONS:
PEOPLE, LEARNING,
CONTEXT

COMMUNICATION

STRATEGIC GUIDANCE

EFFECTIVE OPERATIONS

MONITORING & EVALUATION

IMPACT
FOCUS

The Managing for Sustainable Development Impact (M4SDI) Framework

CAPACITIES AND
CONDITIONS

CHAPTER 6

WHAT STRATEGIC GUIDANCE INVOLVES

MAIN BUILDING BLOCKS IN STRATEGIC GUIDANCE

SITUATION ANALYSIS

THEORY OF CHANGE
What are Theories of Change
About assumptions
Developing a Theory of Change

LOGICAL FRAMEWORK MATRIX (LOGFRAME)

SUMMARY

STRATEGIC GUIDANCE

LEARNING OBJECTIVES

LEARNING OBJECTIVES

- Understand the key role strategic guidance plays in M4SDI
- Understand what is involved in strategic guidance

This chapter explains what strategic guidance entails and how it relates to the other core M4SDI processes and key orientations. The competencies that support the process are also mentioned. In addition, the three main building blocks that shape strategic guidance are outlined in some detail – situation analysis, articulating a Theory of Change (ToC) and/or Theory of Action (ToA) and developing a logical framework matrix (logframe). A selection of useful methods and tools is also included.

WHAT STRATEGIC GUIDANCE INVOLVES

Strategic formation is a complex space... Strategy formation is judgmental designing, intuitive visioning, and emergent learning; it is about transformation as well as perpetuation; it must involve individual cognition and social interaction, cooperation as well as conflict; it has to include analyzing before and programming after as well as negotiating during; and all of this must be in response to what can be a demanding environment. Just try to leave any of this out and watch what happens!

Mintzberg et al., 1998: 372–373

As the quote suggests, strategic guidance is a dynamic process that involves being able to strategically guide your initiative/organization in an often complex context. It is based on an in-depth understanding of the context (situation analysis), making explicit your assumptions on how change happens (Theories of Change) and laying the basis for strategic planning. Strategies (see Box 6.1) or strategic plans can be made explicit in a ToC/ToA, or summarized in a logframe. This process requires active engagement of stakeholders (people orientation) in a process of learning (learning orientation), while monitoring and responding to a changing context (context orientation). For this, technical and strategic competencies (see Chapter 4) are required: strategic thinking, systems thinking, strategic foresight, facilitating learning and engagement, managing change, and communication competencies, see Chapters 2 and 4. Strategic guidance provides the basis for effective operations, especially the development of an annual work plan and budget (AWPB) and M&E, which in turn informs strategic guidance.

BOX 6.1 WHAT IS A STRATEGY?

Much work has been done on strategy, particularly in the realm of business and the military, and as a result there are a range of definitions out there. For example, Benjamin Tregoe and John Zimmermann (1980), in their book on *Top Management Strategy: What it is and how to make it work*, define strategy as 'the **framework** which guides those choices that determine the nature and direction of an organization'. Henry Mintzberg (2000), a well-known expert on strategy and organizational development, indicates that strategy is a **plan**, a path from here to a future (an intended strategy), as well as a **pattern**, where actions and behaviour are consistent over time (a realized strategy). Given these two definitions, Mintzberg thought that a distinction ought to be made between different types of strategies. His work shows that successful organizations do not implement all of the strategies they initially develop (the **intended strategy**). And so strategy development must be seen as a learning process. As an initiative is implemented, the **strategies realized** may be a combination of what was intended, left behind, and picked up, depending on the situation on the ground. An **emergent strategy** comes about when the patterns that emerge were not intended, see figure below.

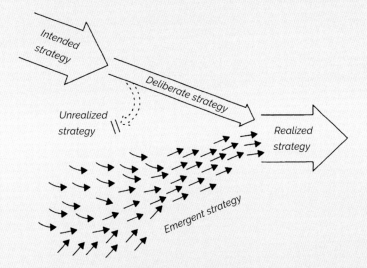

Forms of strategy
Source: Mintzberg, 2000: 24

Intended strategy

Deliberate strategy

Unrealized strategy

Realized strategy

Emergent strategy

Fred Nickols (2016) in his review of various definitions and meanings on strategy, including those outlined above, summarizes that a strategy is many things: a plan, pattern, position, ploy and perspective. It is the bridge between policy or high-order goals on the one hand and tactics or concrete actions on the other. He concludes by saying that strategy is execution. And as we adapt to changing circumstances, we need to adapt our strategy. A sound strategy and a sound execution are therefore essential for the success of any initiative/organization.

MAIN BUILDING BLOCKS IN STRATEGIC GUIDANCE

In this section, the main building blocks in strategic guidance – situation analysis, Theory of Change (ToC) and the logical framework matrix (logframe) – are presented in detail. Situation analysis provides the basis for developing a ToC, which in turn can provide the basis for a strategic plan that can be summarized in a logframe.

In M4SDI, the situation analysis, which is part of the ToC process, is considered a distinct process which helps leaders and practitioners understand the internal and external environments in which their initiative/organization operates. In M4SDI we advocate the use of ToC whilst recognizing that the logframe is still used by many organizations, despite its limitations (see section 'Logical framework matrix').

SITUATION ANALYSIS

Situation analysis is an important way of understanding the context in which the initiative/organization operates (see Box 6.2). Conducting a situation analysis involves activating strategic competencies such as strategic thinking, systems thinking and foresight in order to determine what you need to know and who to engage. This will inform choices for situation-specific processes and tools. Making maximum use of existing sources of information is good practice. Key themes for a thorough situation analysis include looking at: stakeholders (i.e. power relations, networks, interests, stakes (see Box 6.3); issues and problems; biophysical setting (i.e. geographical characteristics such as climatic conditions, main forms of land use, environmental problems or risks); infrastructure; and formal and informal institutions (see box 6.4).

BOX 6.2
WHAT IS SITUATION ANALYSIS?

Funnell and Rogers (2011: 151, 154) indicate that 'a situation analysis identifies the nature and extent of the problems or opportunities to be addressed by the program… The situation analysis also identifies the known causes of or causal pathways to the problem and the known consequences of the problem (why the situation is problematic and worth addressing). A program may be trying to address all three types of the situation: the problem, its causes, and its consequences… A good situation analysis goes beyond a focus on problems and deficits to identify strengths or opportunities and may reframe perceived problems as opportunities'.

BOX 6.3
STAKEHOLDER ANALYSIS

The success of your initiative/organization depends, to a large extent, on your stakeholders, so it is important to know who they are. You will need to know whether they can complement your efforts or whether they have conflicting interests.

Stakeholder analysis can help to:
- identify stakeholders who might be affected by an initiative and those who can affect its outcome;
- identify local institutions and processes upon which to build;
- empirically understand existing patterns of interactions;
- understand the needs and interests of key stakeholders and assess their possible involvement;
- provide a foundation and strategy for engagement in planning, monitoring and evaluation (PME) processes: mobilization of key stakeholders, building common awareness, creating ownership;
- better target interventions and approaches;
- help with policy-making (as a management tool);
- predict and/or manage conflicts.

In applying stakeholder analysis tools, first consider what the information needs are, and then decide which tools would be appropriate. Always keep in mind that stakeholders may have different stakes, even within the same stakeholder group, and that stakes evolve every day.

BOX 6.4 INSTITUTIONS AND INSTITUTIONAL ANALYSIS

According to Brouwer et al. (2015) institutions are 'the "rules" that help society to function. These can be formal or informal; they can be political, legal, social, cultural, economic, or religious. In the widest sense, institutions include language, currency, marriage, property rights, taxation, education, and laws. Institutions help us know how to behave in given situations, such as driving in traffic, bargaining at a market, or attending a wedding. Institutions are critical for establishing trust in society. By definition, institutions are stable, long lasting, and resist change'. Vermeulen et al. (2008) state that institutions can be best viewed in terms of: giving meaning to our lives and the social and natural world we inhabit; the associations we make to work together to achieve social, economic and political objectives; the basis for control over what individuals and organizations should or can do; reoccurring action carried out by individuals or organizations in social, economic and political life.

Questions for institutional analysis include:

Meaning:
- What are the general beliefs in the government and society about the emerging issue?
- What are the norms and values in the community and the society at large?
- What are the main theories, conceptual frameworks and bodies of knowledge used to set policies and design interventions?
- How much alignment or contradiction is there between the different theories and between theory, cultural values and practices?

Association:
- Which organized stakeholders are important to the emerging issue (government agencies, donors, NGOs, community-based organizations, etc.)?
- What contractual, formal or informal relationships exist among these different stakeholders?

Control:
- What is the national policy on the emerging issue? How is the emerging issue being dealt with in relation to other national strategies and policies (e.g. Poverty Reduction Strategy Papers)?
- What are the specific mandates of the different organizations?
- What are the rules and regulations governing the institutions?
- What are the private-sector policies and strategies?
- What are the informal rules governing established practices?
- What are the reasons behind these informal systems?

Action:
- As a result of the above, what services are actually operating?
- Who is using them and what are the patterns of behaviour?
- How significant is the informal sector and how would you characterize its behaviour?
- How do service providers behave towards their clients?
- What type of corrupt behaviour exists in the sector?
- What is the level?

Table 6.1 provides an overview of key questions to ask in a situation analysis and some related tools. See also the elaborate list of tools in the Annexes and Wageningen University & Research's M4SDI portal for an expanded list of tools and the MSP portal for other tools. It is important to first think about what you want to know before choosing or adapting a methodology or (mix of) tools. Methodologies and tools all have advantages and disadvantages, so review them before making a choice. For example, when using stakeholder analysis tools, the matrices developed do not necessarily reflect complex situations. Also power balance changes, so don't neglect stakeholders with low interests and low power, but maintain regular contact with them. Furthermore, remember that the views obtained are subjective, so try to get opinions from a variety of sources.

Table 6.1 Selected situation analysis questions and methodological options

Key problem/issue analysis questions

What are the main problems or issues the initiative/organization aims to address? How have these problems or issues come about? What are possible opportunities? What are the trends and possible future scenarios?

Key stakeholder analysis questions

Who are the main (potential) stakeholders? How do they relate to each other? What are their views, perceptions, interests, power relations, problems and potential contributions?

Methodological options

- Community resources mapping
- Drivers and constrainers of change
- Force field analysis
- Institutional analysis (see Box 6.4)
- Problem tree
- Rich picture
- Scenario analysis
- Supply chain analysis
- Sustainable livelihoods framework
- SWOT (strengths, weaknesses, opportunities, threats) analysis
- Tools for institutional, political and social analysis of policy reform (also, for stakeholder analysis)
- Value chain mapping

Methodological options

- Alignment, influence and interest matrix
- Fast arrangement mapping
- Network mapping or net-mapping
- Political analytical tool
- Power analysis tools (e.g. power cube, stakeholder power analysis, power ranking)
- Social network analysis
- Stakeholder analysis matrix
- Stakeholder characteristics and roles matrix

Source: Adapted from Vermeulen et al., 2008 and Brouwer et al., 2015

The basic concept of Theories of Change is not new. There has been growing recognition that we need more than linear and reductionist models of how change is expected to happen since reality is often complex. For example, logic models (e.g. logframe) tend to leave out important aspects of change processes and have little focus on in-depth reflection. Notwithstanding this, they are still requested by many funding agencies and can present an initiative in summary format. Exploring and articulating existing Theories of Change together with your stakeholders will, in part, lead to a shared understanding of the initiative/organization, its purpose, core values and strategic choices. This lays the foundation for a more coherent programme strategy and implementation throughout the initiative and on the ground (van Es et al., 2015).

BOX 6.5 THEORY OF CHANGE, THEORY OF ACTION, PROGRAMME THEORY, LOGFRAME: WHAT'S THE DIFFERENCE?

Theory of Change (ToC) is concerned with the dynamics of change within a particular context and the causes of change, regardless of any planned intervention. ToC discussions may touch on areas such as how changes in behaviour happen (individually and in groups), how shifts in the balance of power occur, and the role of the state and civil society. At the heart of a good ToC is the explicit inclusion of values underlying views or perspectives on how change happens, and the assumptions around change and the drivers of change.

A **Theory of Action (ToA)** is an operational ToC or strategy for a particular initiative. It shows how an initiative is designed to bring about the desired change. Combined, the ToC and ToA provide the **programme theory**.

The **logframe** is a summarized ToA that reflects the underlying ToC. It is often used as a summary and to communicate how change is expected to happen. The logframe is a planning tool that assumes a linear cause-and-effect relationship. Most logframes only deal superficially with assumptions and do not make values explicit. See section 'Logical framework matrix (logframe)'.

Different organizations use different terms. What is important is to be clear about these terms. In this document, we use the term 'Theory of Change' to capture all of these terms, depending on how much detail is required in terms of making assumptions and strategies explicit.

Source: Adapted from Wageningen University & Research, 2015

What are Theories of Change?

'Theories of Change are the ideas and hypotheses ("theories") people and organizations have about how change happens. These theories can be conscious or unconscious and are based on personal beliefs, assumptions and a necessarily limited, personal perception of reality' (van Es et al., 2015: 12).

Theory of Change (ToC)[1] is referred to in various ways – 'theory of action', 'programme theory' or even the 'theory of assumptions' (see Box 6.5). Theories of Change are about how people think economic, political, social or cultural change happens and their contribution to the change process. The way that people understand change and their environment is influenced by their underlying beliefs or assumptions about life and society as a whole. Theories of Change processes are about making explicit these underlying assumptions.

Articulating your ToC will help you to understand the challenges and opportunities available to your initiative/organization, and forms a good basis for your strategic and operational plans and M&E. According to Rogers (2014: 2), 'a theory of change can be used for strategic planning or programme/policy planning to identify the current situation (in terms of needs and opportunities), the intended situation and what needs to be done to move from one to the other. This can help to design more realistic goals, clarify accountabilities and establish a common understanding of the strategies to be used to achieve the goals'.

While situation analysis can be part of the ToC process, in M4SDI we describe it as a specific building block of strategic guidance. Making the ToC explicit and adapting it over time towards sustainable development impact, in response to a changing context, is also part of the strategic guidance process. Here we use ToC for strategic planning and management. Strategic thinking is an important competency in ToC.

Theories of Change can be used for management and decision-making as the initiative/organization develops and progresses, for instance by adding a Theory of Scaling, which '…is meant to enhance readiness to engage effectively and responsibly with scaling processes by supporting four core functions of scaling initiatives: anticipation, inclusiveness, responsiveness, and reflexivity' (Wigboldus et al., 2016: 93-94). See also Chapter 1 on scaling. To help articulate a Theory of Scaling some of the following questions could be asked, so that assumptions become explicit: Why would this go to scale? Why would it be a good idea if this went to scale anyway? What if this goes to scale? Who drives the scaling agenda and who will ultimately benefit?

1/ A useful website on ToC is: www.theoryofchange.nl

Like with Theories of Scaling, certain issues or situations are dynamic and unpredictable, and thus complex. In such situations a more flexible and emergent planning is needed. Collaborating with stakeholders on agreeing on a range of strategies to work with, and monitoring these closely to see what works and what emerges and responding to this, is critical here.

Further, Theories of Change can be helpful in identifying the way people, organizations and situations change as a result of the activities carried out by the initiative/organization and in creating models of good practice. It is important that your key stakeholders are closely involved in developing the ToC as this creates ownership of the process and ensures that the initiative/organization is relevant and useful to the end-users or target populations.

In this guide we refer to the ToC in different ways. **It is a way of thinking** – by this we mean the overall approach we take when viewing the world and tackling problems. This entails asking critical questions, critically reflecting on and making sense of issues that have a bearing on the initiative/organization, taking on board uncertainty and the multiple perspectives of stakeholders. We also refer to the ToC as a **process** of critical analysis and reflection with staff and stakeholders, which provokes thought and discussion with the ultimate goal of agreeing on the type of change needed. The change needs to be based on what is possible, the assumptions, given time and financial resources. The ToC is also regarded as a **product** – the outcome of the ToC process – which can be represented visually (e.g. as a map, rich picture, or infographic) and/or as a narrative. Often both are needed – the description allows for in-depth discussion and analysis of power, politics of change, needs and choices, and actors involved. When developing your ToC try to be as creative as possible. The most important criteria are that it should make sense to stakeholders, facilitate a deeper understanding about what and who will be involved in the change processes, how the change process is expected to be influenced by external factors and actors, and be evaluable.

Developing a plausible ToC clearly outlining the kind of assumptions and choices made, helps initiatives/organizations and other change actors to understand how their work and their relationships contribute to complex, long-term social change. It provides a framework which can be used to plan and update activities, conduct stakeholder dialogues, learn from experiences, and communicate the extent of, and reasons for, success and failure. To carry out a ToC process, competencies in systems thinking, strategic thinking, critical reflection and creative thinking, strategic foresight, facilitating learning and engagement, managing change and communication are important (see Chapter 4). Box 6.6 outlines some key points on enhancing the ToC process.

BOX 6.6 KEY POINTS ON WHAT MAKES FOR A GOOD THEORY OF CHANGE

The quality of a Theory of Change (ToC) process rests on 'making assumptions explicit' and making strategic thinking realistic and transparent.

Allot sufficient time and resources to support ToC thinking. This involves conducting analyses and consulting stakeholders. People also need to take time away from their everyday tasks to discuss and critically reflect during the ToC process.

Create an open learning environment where people can share and discuss their personal, organizational and analytical assumptions, and challenge beliefs and learn from each other.

Use ToC thinking to understand how change happens and to challenge dominant narratives.

Cross-check critical thinking with evidence from research (qualitative and quantitative) and learning from other analytical perspectives. Make sure that risks and uncertainties and unintended effects (both negative and positive) are captured.

Use documented ToC and visual diagrams to understand change processes and guide implementation, evaluation and change management. It is important that the ToC should not be rigidly used as a pathway for change.

Use ToC frameworks and visuals to support a more dynamic exchange between different stakeholders to help open up new ideas and challenge old ones.

Identify a number of pathways to impact, as issues are often non-linear and emergent.

Develop a ToC (more explicitly, the Theory of Action or the Programme Theory) that is evaluable, i.e. that has a meaning that is consistent to all readers and which can be verified to be happening or not happening as planned, preferably not only at the end of a particular initiative, but also during the process of implementation.

Source: Adapted from Vogel, 2012

About assumptions

In Chapter 2 we saw how assumptions form the basis of our Theory of Change (ToC) – they explain our thought processes, reasoning and how we arrive at certain conclusions. Assumptions are the 'theories' in ToC thinking – they are hard to articulate because they are deeply held perceptions that have become 'rules of thumb' that are taken for granted. Assumptions are statements about how and why we expect a set of changes to come about as depicted in the pathways of change. These statements can reflect understandings of the change process taken from research, or they can be taken from practical experience and reflection. They also reflect an understanding of the context within which an initiative/organization operates. Practical experience has taught us that it is not easy to clearly articulate these assumptions. It takes time and dialogue, with, where possible generative listening (see Chapter 5), so as to better understand each other and generate new ideas for addressing particular situations.

Often assumptions raise questions about the extent to which we can bring about the change we expect. This is particularly relevant in scenario planning where assumptions are made to determine possible future developments. The ToC therefore offers a framework for more focused learning about these assumptions. By spending time to check and test assumptions, you will be able to find new ways of addressing issues of concern. This, however, calls for a great deal of openness

BOX 6.7 TYPES OF ASSUMPTIONS

There are types of assumptions about:

- **Causal links:** These are links between changes at different levels in the change pathway (more related to the internal logic input–activities–output–outcome–impact pathway). They are fairly obvious and easy to make explicit. Example: Providing agricultural extension will lead to improved agricultural production.
- **Operations and the external context:** For example, there may be assumptions about (lack of) political stability or freedom of expression and what might happen in the future based on trends and developments.
- **Paradigm or world view:** This is about assumptions at a much higher (macro) level, e.g. social change best occurs by civil society demanding and building responsive government.
- **Dominant belief systems in society:** Dominant beliefs inform judgments about what is appropriate and feasible in a specific context e.g. in relation to the different roles men and women play in society.

Source: Adapted from Guijt, 2013

and critical reflection. We also need to be alert to any new knowledge that calls into question our assumptions and be willing to revise them if need be. Box 6.7 gives a good overview of the types of assumptions we can make in developing our ToC.

Developing a Theory of Change (ToC)

Distinct methodological steps (see Figure 6.1) can be singled out to develop a ToC (product). These are: identify the purpose of the ToC; develop the vision and define the desired change; identify domains of change; identify strategic priorities; develop pathways of change; and review and adapt the ToC. The situation analysis outlined earlier in this chapter informs this process. The ToC has the most chance of succeeding if it is carried out in collaboration with stakeholders to engage them in dialogue and get a deeper understanding of issues and assumptions. It is also the basis for implementation and (collaborative) M&E, and can be regularly revised and adapted. For more complex issues, it is important to closely and collaboratively monitor the strategic areas and check if assumptions hold or are refuted, since cause-and-effect relationships are often not known beforehand but discovered over time.

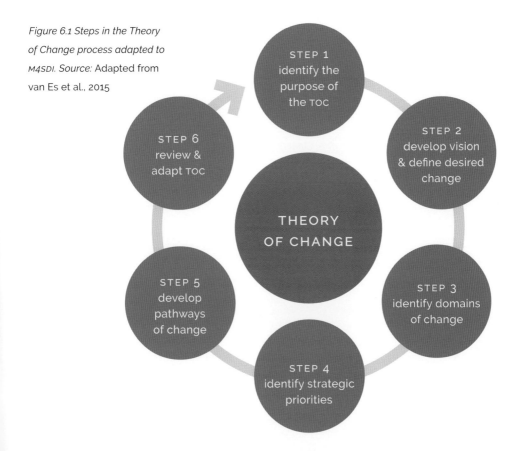

Figure 6.1 Steps in the Theory of Change process adapted to M4SDI. Source: Adapted from van Es et al., 2015

STEP 1 identify the purpose of the TOC

STEP 2 develop vision & define desired change

STEP 3 identify domains of change

STEP 4 identify strategic priorities

STEP 5 develop pathways of change

STEP 6 review & adapt TOC

THEORY OF CHANGE

Step 1. Identify the purpose of the Theory of Change

Ideally, the purpose of your ToC is determined by you and key stakeholders before carrying out the situation analysis. Identifying the purpose will enable you to decide who to involve in the process, the level of detail of the ToC, and the questions you need to ask at each step of the process. According to van Es et al. (2015), a ToC process can be aimed at different levels (see Figure 6.2) and used for different purposes, including: for programme and project design; to review and improve an existing initiative and underlying assumptions in response to internal and external changes; as a basis for (collaborative) monitoring, evaluation and (related) learning; to review the suitability of scaling initiatives; for strategic learning design and knowledge generation. An important part of identifying the purpose is to remain focussed and realistic in what you set out to achieve.

Step 2. Develop the vision and define the desired change

After the situation analysis, try to visualize, along with your stakeholders, the desired change you want to see in the future, taking into consideration the findings from the various analyses done earlier (e.g. problems/issues analysis, institutional and stakeholder analyses, identification of future trends and opportunities). The vision you create must be within the bounds of possibility, reflecting the

Figure 6.2 Theory of Change at different levels
Source: van Es et al., 2015: 18

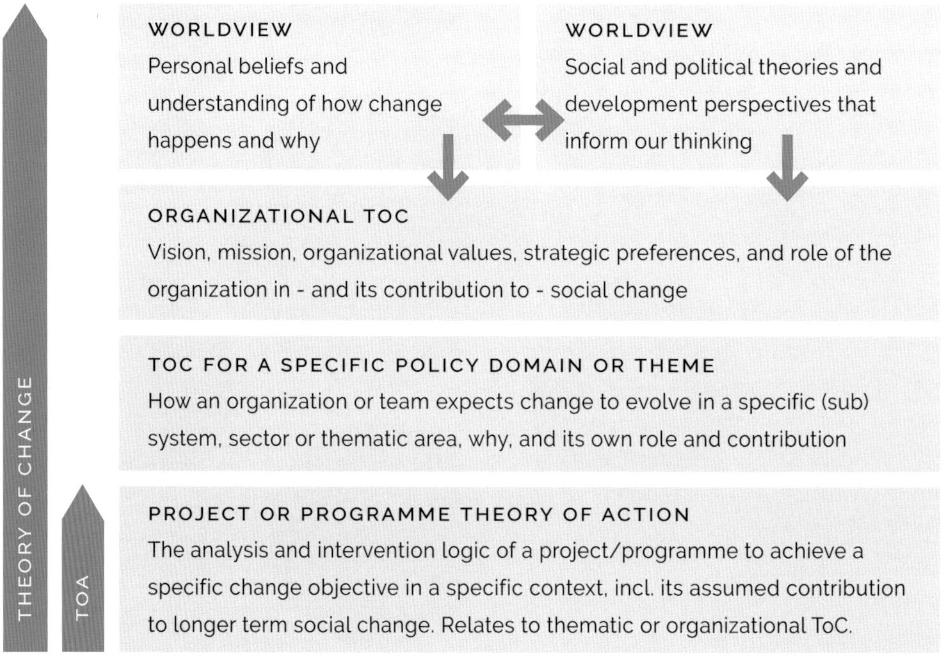

WORLDVIEW
Personal beliefs and understanding of how change happens and why

WORLDVIEW
Social and political theories and development perspectives that inform our thinking

ORGANIZATIONAL TOC
Vision, mission, organizational values, strategic preferences, and role of the organization in - and its contribution to - social change

TOC FOR A SPECIFIC POLICY DOMAIN OR THEME
How an organization or team expects change to evolve in a specific (sub) system, sector or thematic area, why, and its own role and contribution

PROJECT OR PROGRAMME THEORY OF ACTION
The analysis and intervention logic of a project/programme to achieve a specific change objective in a specific context, incl. its assumed contribution to longer term social change. Relates to thematic or organizational ToC.

THEORY OF CHANGE

TOA

complex and dynamic nature of the
environment in which the initiative/
organization operates. Visioning, a
tool used to create a shared vision, is
particularly helpful (see Box 6.8).

Step 3. Identify domains of change
After having defined the desired
change, try to identify domains
of change, where you and your
stakeholders believe change is most
needed. These include medium- to
long-term changes such as a change in
behaviour, relationships, capabilities,
formal and informal institutions. A
key guiding question could be: Who
and/or what needs to change for the
envisaged change to come about?
One way of going about this is to
pick out for each domain the main
factors that keep coming up in your
discussions with stakeholders and see
if they are in line with the capabilities
and competencies of the initiative/
organization.

Step 4. Identify strategic priorities
This step is about strategically analysing and deciding on priorities and the
domains of change where you can have the most influence. It is about answering
the question: What changes can we best influence within the next few (say, three
to five) years? Ritual dissent is an effective tool to help you explore and identify
which strategic options will be most effective and how they can be improved (see
Box 6.9).

Step 5. Develop pathways of change
Once the strategic priorities have been identified, develop pathways of change
that make explicit your assumptions about how change happens. The pathways
developed should show the relationship between the activities, and intermediate
and long-term changes. To develop pathways, you need to work backwards from
your desired future to what needs to be done to change your current reality. It
means envisaging how the change process will develop over time. The change

Ritual dissent is a workshop method designed by David Snowden (Cognitive Edge) to test and enhance ideas or proposals by subjecting them to ritualized dissent (challenge) or assent (positive alternatives). Ritual dissent is used by leaders/development practitioners (in our case) to stimulate the process of generating new ideas. It is essentially a forced listening technique that does not involve dialogue or discourse.

The approach involves a spokesperson presenting a series of ideas to a group; this group listens to the ideas in silence. The spokesperson then sits with his/her back facing the audience and listens in silence while the group either attacks (dissent) or provides alternative proposals (assent) to the ideas presented. The 'ritualization' of not facing the audience de-personalizes the process and the group-setting in such a way that the attacks or different ideas or proposals are not considered personal, but helpful.

Listening in silence without eye contact strengthens our listening skills. The overall plans that emerge from the process tend to be more resilient than those from consensus-based techniques.

Source: Cognitive Edge, 2017

---

management model, developed by Kotter (2007) can be used to identify pathways of change areas to implement organizational change (see Chapter 4 section 'Managing change competency'). The Cynefin framework, as explained in Chapter 2, is also useful to identify the level of complexity and related strategies. Particularly for complex issues, where cause and effect relationships cannot yet be identified, it is important to prioritize a range of strategies or safe fail experiments, and monitor these closely in collaboration with stakeholders, so as to be able to adapt in response to what works and what emerges.

As mentioned earlier, you also need to check your assumptions regularly. Some questions to ask include:
• Are the strategic priorities identified the right ones?
• Do we need to revisit our expected changes?
• Do we need to include other stakeholders?
• What kind of conditions and capacities do we need for the pathways of change to take hold?

After answering these questions, develop pathways for each strategic priority identified. Try to include text explanations to show the richness of the complexity.

Step 6. Review and adapt the Theory of Change (ToC)

Each step in the process so far has most likely resulted in changes in the overall picture. It is typical for a ToC that is being mapped to be revised several times before it provides a complete and clear picture of your change effort. Test whether the most relevant changes and strategies are included, that there are linkages between the strategies, short-term and longer-term changes are logical, and important assumptions are clear. If you didn't get the chance to develop the map along with (all) stakeholders directly involved in the change process, try to share the latest version of your ToC with them. It is also worthwhile consulting experts in the field. Discuss whether your key stakeholders share your vision and main assumptions about the change process, the logic of linkages between strategies and results/outcomes, and the choice of strategies. Based on the discussions, you might need to revise your ToC.

For the ToC to be truly effective, it has to be firmly anchored into the strategic guidance process. This also entails using it as the basis for M&E as discussed in Chapter 8. In this way, the ToC can be used in learning and decision-making, revised regularly and adapted to reflect change. Engaging stakeholders in this process is crucial for enhancing impact.

LOGICAL FRAMEWORK MATRIX (LOGFRAME)

After mapping the ToC for your initiative/organization, it is important to consolidate it into a ToA (strategy or strategic plan), which can be summarized (1-2 pages) in a logframe. This can support requests for funding, communication and shared understanding.

The logframe is commonly used by many agencies engaged in international development and is a useful tool in consolidating and summarizing the ToC. For example, an important aspect of the logframe is that it is often used as a basis for AWPBs. This is because it provides a good framework for setting out objectives, indicators, sources of information and assumptions used to develop and carry out monitoring, analysis and reporting. The matrix also provides a reference point and structure from which to develop progress reports. However, we need to be aware of the limitations such a matrix presents. In terms of management, we cannot capture all that is important in a set of boxes, and there is the danger that the matrix developed might be turned into a blueprint for the initiative/organization, which is often not realistic given the complex contexts in which many initiatives/organizations operate. For example, there are areas that practitioners have direct control over (e.g. activities and outputs), as well as areas where they have limited or no control (e.g. outcome and goal), but are often still held accountable. A common advice therefore is to regularly revise the matrix, for example, during annual review processes and events, and whenever the underlying Theory of Change is reviewed. Leadership has a crucial role to play here as well.

The logframe has four columns and three or four rows, as shown in Tables 6.2 and 6.3. The matrix implies a linear process, but in fact it is developed through an iterative process, in the form of a series of connected propositions (or hierarchy of hypotheses), and based on the ToC:
- *If these Activities are implemented, and these Assumptions hold, then these Outputs will be delivered*
- *If these Outputs are delivered, and these Assumptions hold, then this Purpose will be achieved.*
- *If this Purpose is achieved, and these Assumptions hold, then this Goal will be achieved.*

To construct your own logframe, it is worthwhile to look at the main elements of the matrix.

The first column is the intervention logic/overall objective/narrative summary: This is an umbrella term for the 'means-end' logic of the initiative that includes goal, purpose, outputs and activities. It is also called 'objective hierarchy' or 'narrative summary'.

- **Goal/overall objective:** This refers to broad (sustainable development) issues to which the initiative/organization seeks to contribute. An example in Table 6.3 is 'Improved food security for 10,000 farmers in the Upper East Region (UER), Ghana, in 10 years'.
- **Purpose/outcome/strategic objective:** This is the intended benefit – what an initiative/organization hopes to achieve. The initiative/organization will achieve its purpose if the outputs are achieved and the assumptions in place hold. An example of a purpose is 'Improved agricultural production', while an assumption made towards the goal of improved food security is that the project on nutrition and health is successful (see Table 6.3).
- **Outputs:** The outputs of the initiative/organization are the products of its activities – they are those observable, measurable changes and tangible products/ services. Outputs contribute to achieving the above-mentioned purpose. An example could be 'Farmers trained in good agricultural practices'.
- **Activities:** These are the means through which outputs are produced. An example could be 'To commision a team of experts to conduct workshops to train farmers in good agricultural practices in the region'.
- **Inputs/means:** These concern what is actually needed to run the activities,

including the budget. For example, you will need experts, training materials, accommodation, etc. Costs (similar level to inputs) are about the costs of these inputs.

- **Indicators or objectively verifiable indicators (OVIs):** OVIs provide a means of measuring the performance of the initiative/organization. The indicators can be quantitative and qualitative in nature (see Chapter 8). It is not easy to develop indicators e.g. a farming community's idea of improvement of life may be totally different from that of an outsider. You will need to be clear about what you need to know and how to get the information. Only core indicators are described in a logframe (see also Chapter 8).

- **Means of verification (MOV) or source of verification (SOV):** This refers to how you collect the information, including the methods and sources of data (see Chapter 8).

- **Assumptions:** These are external factors which may positively or negatively influence the events described by the narrative summary, including any external phenomena beyond the control of the initiative/organization. Only those concerns or anticipated opportunities which can actually be substantiated should be included. The ToC process can help to make explicit some of these external conditions and help you think through how to minimize the negative effects by redesigning the initiative. For example, if a project area is drought-prone, then the risk of drought can be minimized by introducing drought-prone seeds and irrigation schemes.

Table 6.2 Example of a logframe matrix

Intervention logic	Indicators (OVIs)	Means of verification (MOV)	Assumptions
Goal			
Purpose			
Outputs			
Activities			

Table 6.3 Partial logframe matrix for an agricultural project in North Ghana

GOAL	OVIs	MOV/SOV	ASSUMPTIONS
Improved food security for 10,000 farmers in UER, Ghana, in 10 years			

PURPOSE	OVIs	MOV/SOV	ASSUMPTIONS
Improved agricultural production	Number of bags of crops produced per acre	Farmer records	Other project on nutrition and health is successful

OUTPUTS	OVIs	MOV/SOV	ASSUMPTIONS
Farmers trained in good agricultural practices (GAP)	Number of male and female farmers trained in GAP	Training assessments	Agricultural knowledge applied
Irrigation systems improved or built	Type of irrigation systems improved or provided Number of male and female farmers accessing irrigation systems	Irrigation reports and interviews	Market prices for inputs remain fairly stable
Drought-resistant seeds produced and provided	Amount and type of improved seed varieties produced	Farm records and seed supplier reports	
Loans provided and farmers linked with financial institutions	Number of male and female farmers receiving a loan for agricultural production	Financial institution reports	

SUMMARY

Strategic guidance is a critical strategic process in the M4SDI approach. It is during this process that efforts are made to understand the context in which the initiative/organization operates and to strategically plan and steer it towards sustainable development impact. Strategic guidance comprises undertaking situation analysis, developing and adapting your Theory of Change (ToC), and based on this, developing a strategic plan that can be summarized in a logical framework (logframe). The ToC and logframe are regularly revised during M&E to support strategic choices for change. For strategic guidance to work, the initiative/organization must be people-, learning-, and context-oriented. Key strategic competencies which underpin the strategic guidance process include systems thinking, strategic thinking, strategic foresight, facilitating learning and engagement, managing change and communication.

Situation analysis is important in exploring problems and issues, their causes, options for change, key stakeholders (and interrelationships e.g. in terms of power), and in identifying possible future trends and opportunities. This provides the basis for the development of the ToC, which is essential in thinking through and making explicit our assumptions on how change happens. Preferably, this is done in collaboration with stakeholders, particularly for issues that are complex, and where cause-and-effect relationships are not yet known. Here multiple strategies or field experiments can be designed and closely monitored so as to respond to what works and what emerges. Having a well-thought-out ToC provides the basis for M&E, the logframe and adaptive management.

CHAPTER 6

CHAPTER 7

EFFECTIVE OPERATIONS

- Understand the key role effective operations play in M4SDI
- Learn which areas of operations are important to focus on in M4SDI

Every organization or development initiative has an operations side to it even if it is not called 'operations'. The main purpose of effective operations is to turn strategies or strategic plans and thinking into practical implementation procedures and measures. This includes developing detailed operational plans that touch on every aspect of the initiative/organization (i.e. work plans, human resources, finance, procurement and contracts, maintenance of equipment and office buildings, and managing information).

For strategies to be successfully implemented when managing for sustainable development impact (M4SDI), effective operations need to be in place and this will depend on the people involved in the operations process. For example, it is essential that leaders, managers and other development practitioners ensure that operations are in line with the strategic plan. Often, this will include reinforcing and rewarding desired new behaviours and attitudes of those directly involved with the initiative/organization (see section 'Human resource management').

In the following sections, we look at effective operations in relation to the other core processes (strategic guidance and M&E) and key orientations. We also explore the role of leadership and the strategic and technical competencies that are essential for effective operations. Furthermore, key areas of focus in managing effective operations are highlighted. It is worth remembering that initiatives often operate within the framework of an organization. Given that the latter has its own rules and regulations, there may be limitations on actions you can take, especially in relation to managing human resources and financial management. Effective operations are therefore a balance between the organizational setting, the envisaged strategies and the realities on the ground.

Managing financial and other operational issues can be quite demanding and time-consuming, especially if a new strategy calls for drastic changes in the way the initiative/organization is run. To respond quickly to a change in direction, systems need to be in place (or developed) to support the change process. Special attention should be paid to ensuring that the more strategic, learning and impact-oriented M&E work plays a crucial role in informing decision-making in the strategic guidance process. Building M&E into your operations processes will also help you determine whether you have been effective in your operations and identify areas of weakness that need addressing (see Chapters 6 and 8).

The strategy is an important guide for the operations process. It is where strategic planning becomes strategic action. This involves revisiting the objectives of the initiative/organization, developing annual work plans and budgets (AWPBs) and aligning strategies and policies with operational systems, procedures, processes and culture.

Much of operations planning and management involves interacting and dealing with people. Having some insight into how people are as individuals, how they behave in groups, what their motivations are, and being able to manage conflict (see Chapter 3 section 'People orientation'), will impact on the overall performance of the initiative/organization. This means that operations planning and management has to be people-oriented. It also entails facilitating organizational change processes (e.g. how information is exchanged, interaction with management and staff and with key stakeholders, setting up systems, changing culture) that support the work of the initiative/organization. Identifying these processes, ensuring that they run smoothly and improving them over time requires some measure of learning (see Chapter 3 section 'Learning orientation').

KEY COMPETENCIES FOR EFFECTIVE OPERATIONS

To implement operations effectively, the operations leader/manager needs strategic competencies in systems thinking and managing change. It is also essential to have appropriate conditions and technical competencies in place to support operational planning and management (see Figure 7.1). Although effective operations are important, the focus on operational matters should not take attention away from learning, especially where an initiative/organization needs to adapt to deal with changes in its external environment.

Key competencies needed for operational planning and management include the following:

Project management: This is critical and ensures that overall operations are consistent with the strategy. It also involves keeping a close eye on processes and ensuring that they are in line with the needs of staff and stakeholders, and performance measurement for strategic and operational decision-making.

Financial management: This refers to the effective management of financial resources and includes analysing financial flows, actively encouraging staff to seek funding from diverse sources and developing clear policies and procedures on accounting and fund acquisition.

Figure 7.1 Key competencies for operational planning and management

Human resource management: Literally this means managing people in order to achieve the objectives of the initiative/organization. It involves having a good understanding of: what the initiative/organization is about; people issues with respect to staffing (i.e. people with the appropriate knowledge, skills and competencies); incentives; well-functioning teams; training; and performance and conflict management. Being able to manage people processes and communicate effectively is essential.

Operational planning: This is important when turning your strategic plan (as described in your Theory of Change/Theory of Action or summarised in your logframe) into an operational plan and entails having detailed information about roles and responsibilities, day-to-day tasks needed for strategy implementation, timelines, and required financial resources. It also involves setting out milestones and conditions for success within specific timeframes, and identifying ways to improve processes.

Procurement and contract management: These form an important part of operations. Resources and expertise (i.e. goods, services, works) are often required to support the running of the initiative/organization. Developing guidelines for acquiring these goods, services and works in line with national laws and regulations, and in some cases with the requirements of funders, is a key consideration. Expertise in procurement and contract management is important for developing a sound framework that can be used to support the needs of the initiative/organization.

Maintenance management: The assets of an initiative/organization, such as equipment and office buildings, must be in good condition and operate properly. Maintenance management is an ongoing process. To manage maintenance operations, it is useful to develop a plan in line with the overall strategy of the initiative/organization.

Information management: This is about how information is used, managed and who has access to it. The development of an information system to support operations and the technical work of the organization is critical to the proper functioning of any initiative/organization.

Coordination and communication (internal/external): Both need to be effective for operations to meet the needs of management, staff and external stakeholders and involve having a good overview of the initiative/organization and its operations. Changes in policies, systems, structures and procedures need to be communicated in a way that avoids confusion and supports a culture change where needed. It is also important that leaders and other change agents, or members of the change guide team, use clear, simple language and present information in an attractive way as well as engage people in dialogue so that they can become actively involved and support the change process. Keeping the lines of communication open will make it easier for people to share ideas, provide feedback, discuss concerns and generate ideas together for a shared vision. Developing a communication strategy with leaders and development practitioners is key to ensuring that the communication process is integrated into the work of the organization (see Chapter 5).

KEY AREAS OF FOCUS FOR EFFECTIVE OPERATIONS

This section focuses on the key areas of operational planning and management where these competencies are critical.

Operational planning

Operations are usually guided by the annual work plan and budget (AWPB) and feedback from having regular meetings with implementers and primary stakeholders. The strategic plan forms the basis of the AWPB, which guides the implementation of the development initiative. The AWPB lays the groundwork for developing more detailed work plans (e.g. on a quarterly or monthly basis). This can be in the form of matrices which come in many shapes and forms, including the commonly-used Gantt chart describing the activities, outputs, milestones and indicators/targets. Work plans are developed for different components of the initiative/organization with related responsibilities. The AWPB also includes a time plan indicating when activities should take place and a budget specifying the cost of each component and its activities. To implement the work plan, develop a personnel plan with roles and responsibilities of staff and partner agencies and their needs (e.g. resources, training, and access to expertise) and a procurement plan for material/equipment and services detailing the requirements for each activity.

Use the AWPB periodically (e.g. quarterly) to measure performance against benchmarks, to serve as a mechanism for review and adjustment, and to plan future operations. Actively seek the input of those involved in the implementation of the organization's initiatives. Flexibility and adaptability in management are crucial in M4SDI as this enables the initiative/organization to take advantage of opportunities and adjust to changes in the environment.

Table 7.1 Example of an AWPB outline

Source: Adapted from Guijt and Woodhill, 2002: 3–28

1 **Introduction** Describe the initiative/organization, its objectives, the various components of the strategy (as indicated in the Theory of Change/Theory of Action or logframe). Include critical issues that affect the initiative/organization such as external factors and assumptions. Refer to the Theory of Change (see Chapter 6 section 'Theory of Change').

2 **Current status of implementation** Update the status of the initiative/organization, mentioning any problems encountered, lessons learned and new developments and opportunities.

3 **Overall work plan and budget** Give an explanation of each component, including the rationale, strategy, expected outputs, resources needed, funding and changes in the current AWPB vis-à-vis the previous year.

4 **Output/activity and budget plans** Develop detailed work plans for each component. Identify the resources needed to carry out each activity (along with an Output column), and indicate who is responsible and how the plan will be monitored. Develop an accompanying budget plan that shows the financing for each component and activity.

5 **Personnel plan** Outline the roles and responsibilities of staff and partner organizations. Identify the needs of staff and partners, including whether additional staff will be required, and the level of coaching and training needed.

6 **Procurement plan relating to goods, services and works** This includes the goods, services and works required, the purpose and costs involved, whether the procurement method will be open or restricted, the schedule of planned calls for tenders and approval dates, and indicators used.

7 **Overall work plan for a given time period (Gantt chart)** Develop a Gantt chart to show the timeline of activities as well as the expected outputs.

8 **Annexes** Templates for output/activity plan, budget, indicators and monitoring schedule, contracted services monitoring, training activities.

To develop your AWPB, take the activities from the logframe (or from the Theory of Change/Theory of Action, see Chapter 6) and insert them into the first column of the work plan. Add some detail on each specific activity and add sub-activities where necessary. Indicate what is to be done, by whom and when. Check that the people you assign tasks are not over-burdened and that the timing is realistic. Also, mention the budget, specifying what it should be used for, and where the funds should come from. Make sure that at crucial stages in the process staff and stakeholders are consulted to promote ownership and effectiveness.

It is important to note that every AWPB should be tailored to meet the needs of each initiative/organization. Developing an overall financial strategy to support the work plan is also essential. Table 7.1 shows an outline for an AWPB.

Armed with a good idea of what your development initiative/organization should be doing, you will be able to identify and manage the resources to facilitate the change process. To assist you even further, make a list of the resources – these include staff, partners and other stakeholders, consultants, and their competencies/skills, finance, equipment, goods, services and works, time and information – and the systems needed to support each activity.

Human resource management

One of the most valuable assets of any initiative/organization is its human resources. However, managing people and their development, and motivating them, can be quite challenging as this involves dealing with diversity, power and conflict (see Chapter 3). In determining the human resources required for an initiative/organization, consider whether you have sufficient staff with the 'right' competencies and whether conditions are in place to motivate them to do the work. This includes developing policies, guidelines and procedures, securing finances, and strengthening M&E and human resource management systems. It also involves engaging people in the (planning of) implementation and ensuring effective communication (see Chapter 5). To do this, it is essential to have people with technical competencies in operational planning and management, resource management, strategic planning, M&E design, and strategic leadership competencies such as strategic thinking and foresight, managing change, facilitating learning and engagement, and strategic communication (see Chapter 4). They will need to be recruited/hired, trained, motivated, and supported. Human resources management also involves identifying core functions to be performed in support of the strategy, carrying out staff performance assessments and development, assessing the level of responsibilities, developing clear job descriptions, and determining measures to motivate staff (i.e. incentives such as benefits, salaries, staff development). This also applies to partners engaged in the initiative, especially in terms of developing their competencies.

To further facilitate change processes, find ways to reinforce change among staff and stakeholders and involve them in the development of new ideas. This includes recognizing people's progress in adopting new behaviours and rewarding them, e.g. awarding honoraria or taking the department or unit out to lunch. Allocating adequate time and resources for members of the change guide team to meet and engage in change activities, coaching and training are important considerations. Time and funding also have to be made available for communication processes within and outside the initiative/organization. Another way to bring about change is to avoid doing things the old way, which often involves a change in organizational culture. Also, look for opportunities to embed change in daily work processes. For example, an NGO introduced 'brown-bag' lunches on Tuesdays where staff could come together informally to discuss their work. This exchange, which was strongly supported by senior management, led to increased efficiency within the organization and better collaboration among staff.

Financial planning and management

Development activities have associated costs, so a budget is needed to cover them. Check to see whether total costs are within budget and make adjustments where necessary. Prioritize activities that contribute the most to agreed targets and desired changes.

To facilitate the process, develop a financial strategy and a plan to access funding for operations. The plan needs to take into account unforeseen expenses and include funding for research and development (R&D i.e. innovation), M&E (e.g. impact evaluation) and communication processes. Making funding available for R&D is crucial to stay ahead of the game, build knowledge and consolidate and share learning. R&D is particularly important when dealing with complex issues, especially where innovation, adaptability, flexibility and cost-effective solutions are required. The Ebola outbreak in some parts of West Africa in 2014, for example, highlighted how vulnerable many countries were to health risks and pointed to the importance of R&D locally, regionally and internationally in treating infected patients and improving systems to reduce the threat of the disease.

Establishing good accounting guidelines, policies and procedures helps support daily operations and processes, including how to access project funds. Having guidelines in place saves time, and more importantly, facilitates the delegation of authority and increases transparency. Guidelines also help to build institutional memory, clarify roles and responsibilities and ensure that good quality financial data are collected for decision-making on a consistent basis. Good financial management practices require staff and key stakeholders to keep proper documentation on expenditures. Being clear about who is responsible for making key decisions, such as where to make budget cuts when funds are insufficient to cover planned expenses, is also crucial. Further, applying the 'four-eye principle', which means that any decision, transaction, payment, etc., must be approved by a minimum of two people, and separating job functions will make systems less vulnerable to fraud and corruption.

Many organizations find it easier to monitor and manage their finances if they have a general budget for the organization and separate budgets for projects. When drawing up a budget, consider each project's share of the fixed costs (e.g. rent, insurance, utilities, and capital assets).

Most initiatives/organizations have a special management (disbursement) unit to help:
· make disbursements for authorized payments;
· ensure that authorized payments are made in accordance with the annual work plan and budget and are in line with the disbursement category provided in the credit/loan agreement;
· keep track of expenditure (bookkeeping);
· produce periodic financial reports (monthly, quarterly and annual monitoring reports);
· produce and submit requests for replenishments;
· make the necessary arrangements for year-end closing of accounts, and prepare and submit financial statements for external audit; and
· submit audit reports by independent auditors to financing organizations.

Other aspects of financial planning include the need to secure funding from multiple sources to increase sustainability of the initiative, and coping with different rules associated with managing funds from various sources. Keeping track of funds with the aid of a computerized system is important to help facilitate audits and give a good overview of the financial situation. The system should also be used to maintain, monitor and analyse financial data.

Staff need to have the right technical expertise to ensure that the processes and requisite resources are in place to carry out the financial management of the initiative/organization. Where necessary, strengthen this capacity either through training or on the job coaching, or recruit staff with the relevant expertise.

Procurement and contract management

Procurement is one of the most critical operations in the implementation of initiatives, since this generally involves the public procurement of goods, (e.g. materials and equipment), services (e.g. administrative and technical assistance) and works (e.g. building a school). It is also an area where major drawbacks in project implementation can occur. But what do we mean by public procurement? The European Commission (2017) refers to public procurement as 'the process by which public authorities, such as government departments or local authorities, purchase work, goods or services from companies'. In this guide, the procuring entity is the initiative/organization interested in acquiring the goods, services or works to support its activities.

Delays in the implementation of initiatives are often attributed to delays in procurement of the inputs. Also, the procurement process may be prone to corruption and fraud and can be a risky and delicate business. Getting procurement right is therefore a prerequisite for proper project implementation. It also means that you get the best value for money and that you function with economy and efficiency. Economy refers to the procurement of the right type of goods, services and works at the lowest price. Efficiency, on the other hand, refers to obtaining the right type of goods, services and works at the right time and place. Box 7.1 highlights some important points that are universally considered good practice in the procurement field. Developing your own guidelines based on national law and regulation is a strategic move that will save much time and inconvenience.

Usually, an important part of procurement is the tendering process which involves 'choosing the best or cheapest contractor to supply goods or do a job by asking several companies to make offers for supplying the goods or doing the work' (Cambridge Dictionary, 2017). If public money is used to purchase goods, services, or works, the public entity may not allow the procuring entity to select a sole contractor without comparing their offer with that of other potential contractors. In this case, tendering has to be done. There are different procurement procedures within of the tendering process. The European Commission (2016), for example, makes a distinction between competitive negotiated, restricted or open procedures:

Competitive negotiated: The contracting party invites candidates of its choice to submit tenders. From these tenderers it selects the one that offers the most economically advantageous offer. The tender is not advertised, so contractors who have not been invited to participate generally do not know about it.

Restricted: In 'restricted' calls, the tender is published in newspapers, journals or online. In the first phase of a two-stage process, contractors are invited to send an 'Expression of Interest' to show that they are qualified. A small number of contractors are shortlisted based on pre-set selection criteria. The contractors shortlisted are invited to submit a full tender in the second phase of the process. The contractor with the best price, who meets all the technical requirements, wins the tender.

Open (international or local): An advertisement is placed in local newspapers, trade journals, or websites inviting contractors to apply for tender documents. All contractors may submit a tender. Open tendering is a transparent process which ensures that only the contractor with the best price and meeting all the technical requirements will win the tender.

Procedures will also vary according to the value of the contract and the financial thresholds (see Box 7.2) set by the organization undertaking the tendering process. For EU-funded projects, a competitive negotiated procedure is allowed for lower value contracts. Large contracts require open or restricted procedures. Always check which procurement and tender rules apply, as different countries and funders may have different rules.

According to the European Commission (2015) there are six stages in the tendering process:

1. Preparation and planning: This involves consulting management and stakeholders to identify needs, budget and funding. It also involves the preparation of specifications or terms of reference (ToRs), tender documents, request for proposals (RFPs), solicitation letters and other documents. For example, it is important to determine whether the tender is open or restricted or if there is any conflict of interest. Also determine the nature of the contract – the subject matter to be addressed and whether it will be a single contract or done in lots. This preparation and planning stage is crucial because if it goes wrong then problems are likely to persist.
2. Publication of contract notice: The tender is advertised to get competitively priced bids.
3. Submission of tenders: Prospective tenderers must follow the procedures stipulated in the advertisement and submit their bids on time.
4. Bid evaluation to select the tenderer(s): This must be based on the published criteria for award. These criteria should not be changed half-way through the process.
5. Awarding of the contract: It is important to notify the service providers selected. The process also includes: formally awarding the tender; preparation of contract agreements; signing of contracts.
6. Implementation of the contract: This means ensuring that the contract is implemented according to the stipulated conditions. Sometimes additional work is needed, and organizations make the mistake of asking the same contractor to do it instead of going through another round of tendering.

To develop and implement procurement procedures, competent staff, structure and processes are essential. Some organizations have a procurement unit with qualified procurement personnel and a functioning training programme for staff. They also have in place procurement policies and procedures which outline processes related to purchasing, receiving and contracting.

Maintenance management

Throughout the lifetime of a development initiative/organization, various types of goods, services and works will have to be procured to support operations. These might include vehicles, construction equipment, farm equipment, office buildings/space, office supplies and consumables, office furniture and equipment, insurance, etc. The proper functioning of buildings and equipment is also critical for the smooth implementation of operations. Maintenance management is therefore an important aspect of the operations process, and it is crucial that systems and resources are put in place to ensure that equipment and office buildings are well maintained.

Kobbacy and Murthy (2008) state that maintenance management can be done at three levels – strategic, tactical and operational. The strategic level is where a maintenance strategy or plan is developed in line with the overall strategy of the organization. This strategy also ensures that maintenance activities are carried out in an efficient and cost-effective way taking safety into consideration. At the tactical level, much of the planning and scheduling of maintenance activities is done for both long- and short-term activities. The operational level is concerned with the actual carrying out of maintenance activities, which involves preparing work orders, implementing the activities and documenting data which can be analysed to determine if there are any areas where improvements can be made.

Information management

Good information is essential to the proper functioning of an initiative/organization at all levels. Information is data presented in a form that is meaningful to the recipient. Data becomes information when it is transformed to communicate meaning, knowledge or ideas and the quality of information relates to accuracy, completeness, relevance and timeliness. Leaders and development practitioners need to have access to quality information if they are to communicate their ideas effectively and manage their projects well. Information also has a cost component to it. For example, information will need to be collected for performance indicators and to support daily operations and strategic decisions. The amount of information you will be able to collect and store will very much depend on the funds available.

So, information collected needs to be cost-effective and well managed.

There are other important terms relating to the management of information that can be quite confusing and it is important to understand the differences – they are information management, managing information and management information system (MIS). Information management refers to the people, processes, and technologies involved in creating, collating, organizing and storing information to support the work of leaders, managers, and other development practitioners, and to help with the monitoring of activities, results and resource use. Managing information, on the other hand, involves determining what information is needed, collecting and analysing this information, storing and retrieving it when needed, and using and communicating the information.

Gupta (2011) defines a management information system (MIS) as one that:
- provides information to support managerial functions like planning, organizing, staffing, directing, controlling;
- collects information in a systematic and routine manner in accordance with a well-defined set of rules;
- includes files, hardware, software and operations research models of processing, storing, retrieving and transmitting information to users.

What we are primarily concerned with at the operational level is the development of an MIS to support decision-making processes within the initiative/organization.

Developing a management information system (MIS)
Setting up an MIS for an initiative/organization allows you to manage information and improves access to data so that you can make informed decisions and become more effective in your operations internally and on the ground. To get an overview of what is required to set up an MIS, try drawing an information flow map for your initiative/organization. Although an information flow map is not easy to draw, it is useful in creating a good overview of information exchange processes. It also enhances shared understanding about who is responsible for what information.

Developing an effective MIS takes time and money to design it, so start thinking about it fairly early on. It has to support the information needs of the initiative/ organization so that you are in a position to make strategic, tactical and operational decisions. However, before embarking on the development of a new system and investing a lot of funds, it is important to develop your M&E framework (see Chapter 8), so that it is clear what kind of information will be required for strategic and operational decision-making, and how this is to be collected, processed, analysed and used.

Some issues to consider when developing an MIS are:
· What key data will the system handle (e.g. text only, or multi-media content as well)?
· Who will use the system and what information will the system produce?
· How will the MIS support M&E?
· How can procedures for input (uniformity, coding, standardization) be developed?
· How can accessibility, flexibility and adaptability of the system be sustained?
· How can the system be made robust enough so that mistakes do not lead to chaos?
· How do you avoid the garbage in garbage out principle? How will you be able to check the quality and accuracy of information?
· How do you ensure compatibility with other management systems?
· How can the future be anticipated, to avoid changing systems every few years?
· How do you regularly review whether the MIS is meeting the needs of staff and other stakeholders?

Other considerations that we have found useful include the importance of designing simple and manageable systems by customizing off-the-shelf software, as well as adopting a modular approach to software development (not one huge system, but connected components), and exploring opportunities for harnessing the internet. Also, take time to develop a common understanding between consultant(s) and the organization and involve programmers and users alike in the needs assessment and in the development of the MIS.

SUMMARY

For a strategy to be successfully implemented, it needs to be operationalized. Annual work plans and budgets developed in the operations process are important in guiding the implementation of the strategy. Leaders and development practitioners have an important role to play in supporting effective operations by engaging and motivating people involved in change processes and in ensuring that operations are in line with the strategy. Apart from operational planning, project management, financial management, human resource management, procurement and contract management, maintenance management, information management (including MIS) and coordination and communication are crucial areas in ensuring effective operations. This focus on operational issues, however, should not take attention away from the need to reflect on and learn from strategic issues and how the initiative/organization can successfully adapt to changes in the environment.

CHAPTER 8

MONITORING AND EVALUATION (M&E)

Evaluation is an essential characteristic of the human condition, and perhaps the single most important and sophisticated cognitive process in the repertoire of human reasoning and logic. Evaluation serves society by providing affirmations of worth, value and improvement to name just a few, and is a process which permeates all areas of human activity, scholarship and production.

Coryn and Westine, 2015: 1

LEARNING OBJECTIVES

- Understand the role M&E can play in managing for sustainable development impact
- Learn how to develop an M&E framework for a well-functioning M&E system

Over the years, monitoring and evaluation (M&E) have become key features of many initiatives/organizations oriented towards the Sustainable Development Goals (SDGs). According to the UN (2017) 'a robust follow-up and review mechanism for the implementation of the new 2030 Agenda for Sustainable Development will require a solid framework of indicators and statistical data to monitor progress, inform policy and ensure accountability of all stakeholders'. To support this process, EvalPartners, a global movement to strengthen national evaluation capacities, has been active in promoting the pivotal role evaluation can play in helping governments, civil society and the private sector design and implement initiatives to improve the lives and conditions of people. The Global Evaluation Agenda (GEA) 2016-2020, which is the first-ever global vision for evaluation, is part of that effort, and is the outcome of a highly participatory process aimed at addressing evaluation priorities around the SDGs.

With increasing interest in evaluation, capacity has also grown, as indicated by the number of Voluntary Organizations for Professional Evaluations (VOPE). Of the 158 VOPEs, 135 are at the national level, and 23 at regional and international levels (EvalPartners, 2017). But more needs to be done in terms of enhancing M&E capacity to support managing for sustainable development impact (M4SDI). This chapter aims to provide insight into the role M&E can play in M4SDI, and how to go about developing a framework for a well-functioning M&E system. We start by defining M&E and explaining current trends and how they affect M&E. Further, we explain how M&E supports M4SDI. We then move on to explain how an M&E framework can be developed and used to generate information for strategic and operational management. The steps to develop an M&E framework are based on much of the theory introduced throughout the guide and our practical experiences.

BOX 8.1 DISCOURSE ON M&E

Monitoring: This is a continuous process of data collection and analysis of performance indicators and enables you to compare a development initiative's progress with its intended results.

Evaluation: There are numerous definitions of evaluation. Many of them refer to programme evaluation, so it is important to understand the differences. For example, according to Michael Scriven (1991: 1) 'evaluation is the process of determining the merit, worth and value of things, and evaluations are the product of that process'. He also distinguishes between different types of evaluation e.g. formative (or process) and summative evaluation. Formative evaluation is often associated with a mid-term evaluation (for performance improvement), while summative evaluation has more to do with an end-of-initiative review (for issues like accountability, policy- and decision-making). Other evaluation definitions include the idea of improvement. For example, Kahan and Goodstadt (2005) describe evaluation as a 'set of research questions and methods geared to reviewing process, activities and strategies for the purpose of improving them in order to achieve better results'. In these two examples, the evaluator plays more of an external, independent and objective role.

At the other end of the spectrum, we have evaluators who recognize that under conditions of complexity, the approach to evaluation has to be different. This has given rise to the term developmental evaluation coined by Michael Quinn Patton

(2011: 1) who describes it as 'developmental evaluation supports innovation development to guide adaptation to emergent and dynamic realities in complex environments. Innovations can take the form of new projects, programs, products, organizational changes, policy reforms and systems interventions'. Here the developmental evaluator is more involved in the evaluation process and assists in data gathering and interpretation, helps to frame issues and test models, monitors developments and engages stakeholders in evaluative thinking (see Box 8.3). The definition of programme evaluation put forward by Patton (2008: 39) is 'the systematic collection of information about the activities, characteristics, and results of programs to make judgments about the program, improve or further develop program effectiveness, inform decisions about future programming, and/or increase understanding'.

Monitoring and evaluation (M&E): Notwithstanding the above, it is important to note that although many development experts and evaluators make a clear distinction between monitoring and evaluation, in reality, we tend to use them together because of the way they are intricately linked and this is strongly reflected in the guide. For us, M&E is a continuous process of gathering and assessing information, the findings of which are used to support development initiatives/organizations in various ways. For example, the findings could be used: to support strategic decision-making processes to steer and improve an initiative/ organization for impact; to influence policy; and to get stakeholder support to implement change.

We also look at the competencies (see Chapter 4) and key orientations (see Chapter 3) that support M&E processes. The importance of developing a communication and reporting strategy to promote learning, use and influence of the M&E findings, is also discussed. Finally, we look at how you can bring your M&E framework together and evaluate and adapt it in response to changing contexts and strategies.

DEFINITIONS

A number of definitions exist on (monitoring and) evaluation (M&E) and a brief overview of the discourse on M&E is given in Box 8.1. Other important terms on M&E are defined in Box 8.2. We also look at what evaluative thinking is and the importance of developing an evaluative culture within initiatives/organizations (see Box 8.3).

BOX 8.2 DEFINITIONS OF KEY M&E TERMS

M&E policy outlines the definition, concept, role and use of monitoring and evaluation within an initiative/organization.

M&E framework relates to the strategic plan for M&E. The framework is important for guiding monitoring and evaluation within a programme, or across programmes in an initiative/organization. It is based on the M&E policy.

M&E plan relates to the operational plan for M&E, and is based on the M&E framework.

M&E system is an integrated system of reflection and communication that supports project implementation. A well-functioning M&E system manages to integrate the more formal, data-oriented side commonly associated with the task of M&E, with informal monitoring and communication.

M&E matrix is part of the M&E plan and provides detailed information about how the initiative's strategy (e.g. Theory of Change) and operational plan will be monitored and evaluated. An M&E plan will include other events that make it possible to understand the project context, to reflect and learn lessons.

Source: Adapted from BetterEvaluation (no date: e–h) and Guijt and Woodhill, 2002

Patton (2014: 1) refers to evaluative thinking as systematic results-oriented thinking about what results are expected, how results can be achieved, what evidence is needed to inform future actions and judgments, and how results can be improved in the future. Buckley et al. (2015: 378), on the other hand, define it as 'critical thinking applied in the context of evaluation, motivated by an attitude of inquisitiveness and a belief in the value of evidence, that involves identifying assumptions, posing thoughtful questions, pursuing deeper understanding through reflection and perspective taking, and informing decisions in preparation for action'.

An organization with a strong evaluative culture therefore:
- Engages in critical self-reflection that is regular and systematic, and which challenges and improves the work being done by an initiative/organization;
- Engages in evidence-based learning done in a structured manner. Lessons are learned not only from successes, but also from mistakes. Knowledge-sharing is stimulated among staff and partners/ key stakeholders;
- Encourages innovation, risk-taking and change, so that new ways of doing things are developed and leveraged.

Source: Adapted from Mayne, 2008: 4

TRENDS IN M&E

Debates on the role, design and application of (monitoring and) evaluation have been ongoing. And debates have emerged around different topics. We highlight a few of them below.

Focus on impact

Over the years, the focus on impact has increased, due partly to the growing demand to demonstrate impact. With this, perspectives on M&E have changed, as indicated in Table 8.1.

Dealing with complexity

Evaluation has explored merit and worth, processes and outcomes, formative and summative evaluation; we have a good sense of the lay of the land. The great unexplored frontier is evaluation under conditions of complexity. Michael Quinn Patton, 2011: 1

The quote above echoes the debate around using linear approaches (like the logical framework) in planning and M&E, even though the reality in which initiatives/ organizations operate and the issues they address are complex (see Chapter 2). Evaluators have sought various ways to confront and deal with these realities.

For example, Patton developed the concept of developmental evaluation (defined earlier) which falls very much in line with the ideas expressed in Chapter 2, such as: close monitoring of (safe fail) experiments; looking at what works (or not) and how; what emerges; the unintended effects, and how to respond. Close collaboration with stakeholders, including engaging in processes of dialogue and learning, is key in complex contexts since cause-effect relationships can only be known in hindsight. Systems thinking is a key competency here as well.

(The politics of) evidence

Eyben (2013: 3) states that 'hard evidence, rigorous data, tangible results, value for money – all are tantalizing terms promising clarity for the international development sector. Yet, behind these terms lie definitional tussles, vested interests and contested world views'. Here Eyben draws our attention to the need for critical awareness of how power sustains and reinforces the development sector's results-and-evidence discourses. She further goes on to say that the 'tools and methods can have perverse consequences because of their hidden and invisible power to determine what knowledge counts when hierarchical ways of working block communications and dialogue', (ibid: 3). This implies the need to be cognizant of some of the consequences of using the resulting tools and methods, such as logical framework analyses and Theories of Change that shape working practices.

We also need to be aware of who decides the M&E agenda, including: Who decides what information is needed, and for what purpose? What and who's knowledge counts? What approaches count? Who is involved in data collection, analysis and sense-making of findings? Who makes decisions based on these findings and to what extent do emotions play a role in decision-making? These are important issues to be aware of and make explicit when engaging in M&E. Throughout the M&E process, collaborating with a range of stakeholders, not only 'experts', is crucial, as is being aware of power dynamics.

But how much does evidence really matter? Does it matter more than feelings? In an era of post-truth politics, partnerships searching for the truth are needed. Jonathan Breckon (2016) indicates that we need to understand the demand for evidence. In relation to evidence-based policymaking, he indicates that 'we must listen to governments, and shift the focus to improving the demand and capacity for using the best available evidence... we also need to look at the research on what works in evidence-use. Above all, we need to be really looking hard at what politicians or frontline staff actually need from research [or evaluation for that matter]. What governments want may not just be "what works" in policymaking, but wider evidence - data analytics, behavioural insights, horizon-scanning, or research from the "hard" sciences. All these types of evidence are valid as long as

From:	To:
Focused on activities and outputs	Including a focus on outcomes and impact.
M&E mainly for projects	M&E also for organizations, sectors, value chains, across sectors. Harmonizing M&E for different funding agencies.
Design of M&E focused on accuracy	Design of M&E focused mainly on utility for primary stakeholders, and even influence. Alkin and King (2016) mention different types of evaluation use: instrumental use, conceptual use or enlightenment, and symbolic use. 'The additional category of process use, added years later, highlighted the potential utility of people's participation in the evaluation process' (*ibid*: 1). Linking M&E to internal planning and decision-making processes.
Dominated by linear cause-effect thinking and the use of logic models (CDI, 2012)	Evaluation inspired by systems and complexity thinking in view of rapidly changing environments and increasing interdependencies.
M&E considered only as compliance with external reporting requirements, and therefore viewed as a burden	M&E recognized and appreciated as an integral part of management and organizational learning.
M&E driven by external directions and assessment	M&E co-designed and owned by those directly responsible for implementation
Randomized control trials (RCTs) as the gold standard for impact evaluation; quantitative information valued more than qualitative information	Impact evaluation to draw on a wider range of designs and methods (Stern et al., 2012).

Table 8.1 Changing perspectives on M&E

From:	To:
Evidence as a neutral input for decision-making	Realization about the politics of evidence: understanding power dynamics in terms of whose and what knowledge counts and which results matter as evidence and learning to strategize within this area to create your space and your own brand of transformation.
M&E based on a fixed set of indicators	M&E based on agreed information needs, based on input from key partners/stakeholders, and a complex and changing context.
Primary focus on identifying indicators	Focus on clarifying performance and evaluation questions and from there only defining appropriate indicators
Generating lots of unused data	The anticipated use of data (by different stakeholders) is one of the key determinants in defining what data will be collected.
Data analysis and sense-making only by (M&E) expert	Stakeholders engaged in data analysis and sense-making.
Studies leading to long reports	Rist and Stame (2011) write about the move away from producing lengthy studies towards using streams – ongoing data, real-time data, harvesting data from many different official and unofficial sources facilitated by ICTs.
Preparing only one generic evaluation report	Multiple forms of reporting aimed at various audiences. Increased attention to visualization draws attention to key messages, for example, the use of documentary/dramas, mapping, photos, poems, streaming, and video.
Limited capacity and competency in M&E; 'expert' evaluators often based in the North. Evaluators play a key role in M&E and are responsible for evaluation even though stakeholders may be involved	Increasing M&E capacity. Expanding number of national evaluation associations in different parts of the world. M&E is not just the sole responsibility of evaluators; everyone has a role to play.

they are trustworthy and useful for governments' (*ibid*: 1–2). This also holds true for others. It is crucial to understand what evidence people need and help them in thinking through what is really needed to bring about change.

Another important issue is the increasing emphasis on M&E to show evidence (accountability) and results (impact) to justify investments in development initiatives and the implementation of policies. Whilst there has been a strong focus on impact, we need to bear in mind that this is only one of the DAC evaluation criteria (see Box 8.6). Focusing on impact means that there is likely to be less attention paid to the other DAC criteria, like relevance and sustainability. The unintended consequences of this focus are worth considering.

Jones (2009) identifies two trends within the development sector relating to accountability and impact that we need to watch. The first is that in an effort to determine impact, key funders tend to favour certain types of impact evaluations, commonly referred to as 'the gold standard' (European Evaluation Society, 2007), such as randomized control trials (RCTs). The other trend is that impact evaluations are mostly used for upwards accountability and to justify the implementation of the evaluation (Raitzer and Winkel, 2005; Jones et al., 2009). Practice shows that if you are able to demonstrate impact, funding is more likely to continue, and you are also better able to attract funding. At the same time, we need to be aware that impact evaluations can also be learning-oriented and help inform future (or other) initiatives.

THE ROLE OF M&E IN M4SDI

The strategic guidance process, strategic planning framework (see Chapter 6) and effective operations (Chapter 7) provide the basis for M&E, which in turn informs decision-making processes that help to steer the initiative/organization towards sustainable development impact. M&E can also be used to strengthen collaboration and learning for impact, influence policymaking, or gain the support of stakeholders to help the initiative/organization adapt to change. M&E is also about identifying unintended consequences (positive and/or negative) and gaining insights into how the initiative/organization is performing and where adjustments are needed.

Having the support and commitment of leaders is crucial for the success of any initiative/organization. It also requires team effort to set up and implement an M&E system given that different competencies are needed. For example, technical competencies in M&E design, data collection and analysis, and sense-making are essential, as well as strategic competencies such as systems thinking, facilitating learning and engagement, critical reflection, and communication (see Chapters 4 and 5). Some leaders and practitioners may have to actively develop some of these competencies to support the work of their initiative/organization.

USE AND INFLUENCE OF M&E

The ultimate goal of M&E is to enhance the management of initiatives/organizations and increase impact through M&E use and influence. To find out whether you are in fact doing this, you will need to have a good M&E system in place. It's useful to first articulate the M&E policy as the basis for the M&E framework and plan (see Box 8.2). While conducting your M&E, it is important to keep in mind that the Theory of Change will need to be adapted as the initiative/organization progresses and new information comes to light, particularly when working in a complex context. Crucially, always think through how both the findings and the M&E process itself can contribute to the envisaged impact.

Actively engaging people in using M&E findings, or just going through the process itself, can act as an important vehicle for change. On the concept of use, Henry and Mark (2003: 294) differentiate between four types of use. The first, instrumental use, is considered 'a direct action that has occurred as a result of an evaluation', whilst conceptual use is described as a direct reaction 'to something that is newly learned about an initiative/organization'. They go on to explain that participation in the evaluation procedures results in process use. Finally, symbolic use is when the evaluation itself is used as a basis for action (or inaction) or to justify pre-existing positions. Furthermore, use can also be pre-planned, as in Patton's (1997) mantra of utilization-focused evaluation, or it can emerge as an evaluation unfolds, as findings are generated and opportunities arise.

M&E influence can lead to intangible and tangible results, such as a change in mindset, in the way people act and how they use the results. Table 8.2 draws on the work of Williams (2009), Mark (2009), and Kusters et al. (2011) and provides a selected overview of the influences/consequences of different types of use at the individual, interpersonal and collective levels. It highlights the most important forms of use: direct or instrumental use, process use and relational use. Throughout this chapter a conscious effort is made to develop an M&E system aimed at getting stakeholders to use M&E findings and developing an awareness of the importance of thinking through how the influences or consequences of M&E can affect attitudes and behaviour at the personal, interpersonal and organization levels to bring about impact. Our description of 'influence' is based on Kirkhart's (2000: 7) definition, i.e. influence is 'the capacity or power of persons or things to produce effects on others by intangible or indirect means'. It is therefore broader than use.

Table 8.2 M&E influence and use

TYPE OF USE:	TYPE OF USE:	TYPE OF USE:
Direct (immediate) or instrumental use: Relates to knowledge for decision-making and action (Rich, 1977) e.g. to determine continuation or change in direction for an initiative/ organization.	Process use: The process of carrying out an evaluation is crucial to learning. Patton (2008: 154) says that 'individual changes in thinking, attitude and behaviour… occur among those involved in the evaluation as a result of the learning that occurs during the evaluation process'.	Relational use: Relates to the need to transform relationships, restructure organizations.
Influences affect: Behaviour and action.	Influences affect: Behaviour, actions, thinking, broader aspirations as a result of being engaged in the evaluation process.	Influences affect: Ongoing relationships, (organizational) structures and processes.
Influences at individual/ personal level affect: What individuals will do e.g. take up additional tasks.	Influences at individual/ personal level affect: What individuals will do, think, believe.	Influences at individual/ personal level affect: Role and functioning of an individual in relation to others (e.g. more empowered to fulfil their tasks).
Influences at the interpersonal level affect: What individuals will do together e.g. sharing tasks to achieve a common goal.	Influences at the interpersonal level affect: People's actions, attitudes, understanding in relation to collaboration with others.	Influences at the interpersonal level affect: Role and functioning of groups, networks (e.g. more shared learning).
Influences at collective or organizational level affect: What an institution does e.g. strategic decisions about an initiative, or policy.	Influences at collective or organizational level affect: An organization's actions, values, role.	Influences at collective or organizational level affect: Role and functioning of an institution in society (e.g. learning organization).

Developing an M&E system to support the leadership and management of your development initiative/organization is of utmost importance. Being context-, people-, and learning-oriented will enhance its development. Also, give some thought to the communication processes that support the different steps outlined below, especially in relation to promoting use of M&E findings (see section 'Agree on communication and reporting'). The M&E framework captures the overall set up for the M&E system (Figure 8.1), and the M&E framework can be operationalized into an M&E plan.

The following steps represent an iterative process for developing an M&E system:
1. Assess and establish ability and readiness for M&E.
2. Agree on the purpose and scope of the M&E.
3. Agree on key M&E information needs.
4. Agree on data collection, processing and analysis.
5. Agree on critical reflection and sense-making.
6. Agree on communication and reporting.
7. Plan for implementation.
8. Evaluate and adapt the M&E.

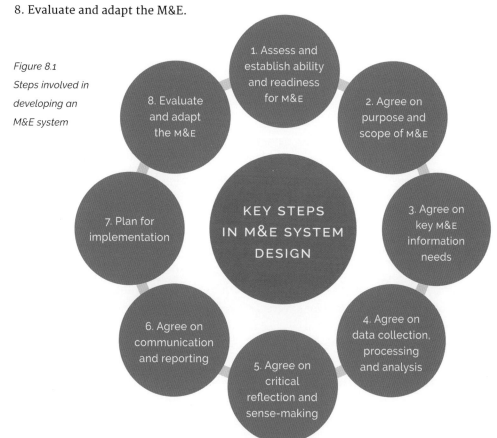

Figure 8.1
Steps involved in developing an M&E system

It is important to note that a description of what the initiative/organization is about, including its Theory of Change, should be done prior to describing the M&E system, framework or plan.

Step 1. Assess and establish ability and readiness for M&E

Establishing ability and readiness is about finding out the extent to which people (staff and stakeholders) are ready and able to engage in M&E. Questions you could ask include:
- Does the initiative/organization have a culture of evaluation? Is there openness to critique and the learning and sharing of experiences?
- Are the necessary competencies in-house to carry out M&E?
- Are there sufficient resources (financial, human, and material) in place?
- Are there external influences that might affect the ability and readiness for M&E?
- Is there support from the leadership within the initiative/organization?
- Is there a willingness to act on findings?
- Are leaders, M&E staff and external evaluators ready to commit to making monitoring and evaluation useful?

Resource constraints (e.g. budget, time, data) and pressures from some influential stakeholders (e.g. political influences and internal pressure from leadership) are important factors that can hamper good-quality monitoring and evaluation (Bamberger et al. 2012).

Working with resource constraints
Budgetary constraints involve not having enough funds for M&E. These constraints can be addressed by: modifying or simplifying the M&E design; clarifying the information needs of stakeholders and focusing on what is essential to know; looking for reliable secondary data; reducing the sample size to what is minimally acceptable for good-quality analysis; reducing the cost of data-collection methods by administering questionnaires yourself, collecting information from groups or online surveys, and direct observation.

Time constraints can often be addressed in different ways, but the option you choose may affect your budget adversely. Most of the points identified above under budgetary constraints can also be used to save time. Other ways to tackle time constraints include: rationalizing data needs (i.e. what information is essential and will be used); seeking reliable secondary data; reducing the sample size; commissioning preparatory studies; hiring more resource persons; revising the format of project records to include critical data for impact analysis; and using modern data-collection and analysis technology.

Data constraints sometimes result from either a failure to collect baseline data prior to implementation of the initiative, or because a comparison group hasn't been identified. There can also be problems associated with the collection of ongoing data, such as missing data points within an existing data set, and data that may be weak in terms of reliability or validity. These data constraints can be addressed by:

- reconstructing baseline data using secondary data, retrospective studies, working with key informants, participatory M&E methods (e.g. time trends, historical profiles, critical incidents, recall), and use of a geographic information system (GIS);
- constructing or reconstructing control groups by using statistical matching techniques and judgemental matching;
- working with non-equivalent group design (most frequently used in quasi-experimental studies).
- collecting data on sensitive topics from groups that are difficult to reach (might prove costly). Ways of working around this include using culturally appropriate methods (e.g. participant observation, focus groups, case studies, key informants, trace studies, snowball samples, socio-metric techniques);
- using multiple methods (triangulation).

Reducing the effect of external influences
Although no evaluation can be completely objective or free of influence, there are steps that you can take to reduce external influences and increase objectivity. For example, political influences can be addressed by ensuring the appropriateness of data-collection methods and the comprehensiveness of the data set, even if there is pressure from funding agencies, for example, to limit the types of data to be collected. Further, ensure that analytical foci and methods appropriately address all data and issues arising during M&E, including those related to funding agencies and other key stakeholder groups. Get leadership support right from the start to foster evaluative thinking, mobilize and facilitate stakeholder engagement and learning, and promote use throughout the M&E process. Without this kind of support, it will be difficult to get a well-functioning M&E system in place. Concretely, this involves attending key meetings and lobbying key partners for vital support.

Establishing an ability and readiness for M&E should therefore be viewed as laying the foundation for developing a sound M&E system for the initiative/organization, and so provide support for the strategic and operational decision-making processes in M4SDI.

Step 2. Agree on purpose and scope of the M&E

Once readiness and ability are established, think about the focus of the M&E. Important questions to ask include: What are we focusing on in the development initiative/organization? Why are we doing M&E? Who should be involved, why and how? What questions do we want to address and how will we use the information? How detailed should the information be? How much funding do we have available? Answering these questions will help you determine the purpose and scope of the M&E.

Purpose relates to why you want to carry out the M&E. The most common reasons include:
- *Accountability:* This has to do with reporting on predefined deliverables. Although complementary in nature, reporting is often seen as being at odds with learning (Guijt, 2010). Accountability can be seen at different levels. Upward accountability involves accounting to funding agencies; internal/sideward accountability is to staff and stakeholders involved in a particular development initiative/organization, and downward accountability means reporting on performance to intended clients.
- *Strategic management:* This relates directly to the improvement of the initiative/organization. Here information is used to make strategic decisions for change, for example, in relation to the improvement of the Theory of Change of a particular initiative, sector, policy or organization.
- *Operational management:* M&E information is also used to adapt operational plans and processes to ensure objectives are being reached within a given time frame.
- *Policymaking or influencing:* M&E data can be used to show what is happening in a particular area or sector and in relation to a particular topic. For example, budget monitoring which has been defined as 'a continuous process by which we ensure an action plan is achieved, in terms of expenditure, and income' (University of St. Andrews, 2010), can be used as a powerful tool to advocate and promote human rights.
- *Knowledge generation:* Information can also be collected on issues that you would wish to understand better and share with others. For example, specific studies can be undertaken to better understand the application of a rights-based approach to development initiatives.

Other reasons for undertaking M&E include:
- *Empowerment of stakeholders:* By being actively engaged in M&E, stakeholders can, for example, increase their capacity to carry out self-assessments, and as a result, they can more effectively influence their own change processes and contribute to a particular development initiative on a timely basis.
- *Development of learning organizations and the generation of knowledge:* When M&E

is carried out in a culture of learning where success and failure are both valued, this can help to improve the performance of an initiative/organization. See also Chapter 3 section 'Learning orientation', where learning organizations are discussed.

· *Enhancement of practical wisdom and good practice judgements:* There are many things you can learn from M&E that do not necessarily result directly in the improvement of the development initiative/organization, but instead help those engaged in these processes to learn lessons that they can apply in different situations.

Often, M&E will cover more than one purpose, but it all depends on the budget and where your priorities lie. For example, for a more learning-oriented organization, strategic management and knowledge generation may be more important than accountability to funders, or operational management. It is also important to think through the use and influence of the M&E by considering exactly how the information will be used by different stakeholders or how M&E could influence their efforts to manage for sustainable development impact (see section 'Use and influence of the M&E').

Scope refers to the boundaries of your M&E system. Different organizations use different sets of criteria to determine scope. Scope is often defined as outlining the issues you and your stakeholders want covered – a certain geographic area, principles and standards, target groups, methods and approaches to be used, time period, and funds. More often than not, your scope will be defined by the resources made available to you i.e. time, money, capacity, and availability and readiness of stakeholders.

Be aware that tensions may exist around any (monitoring and) evaluation undertaken because of the different interests of stakeholders. For example, funders may be primarily interested in accountability issues, whereas you might be more interested in knowledge generation and strategic management issues. And even though it is possible for an M&E system to have different purposes, it is still important to think through use and what it is that you really want to focus on.

Agree on M&E principles and standards

The next step in focusing the M&E is to think about and agree on evaluation principles and standards (Box 8.4) to underpin the M&E processes. See Annex 2 'Making a difference with evaluations' for stories that highlight how principles and standards can act as 'enabling factors' to enhance the impact of evaluations on the lives of people. It is also important to note that much depends on the users of the evaluation, their perspectives and level of engagement.

Below is a list of suggested M&E principles:

BOX 8.4 STANDARDS USED FOR EVALUATION

Utility: The utility standards are intended to increase the extent to which programme stakeholders find evaluation processes and products valuable in meeting their needs.

Feasibility: The feasibility standards are intended to increase evaluation effectiveness and efficiency.

Propriety: The propriety standards support what is proper, fair, legal, right and just in evaluations.

Accuracy: The accuracy standards are intended to increase the dependability and truthfulness of evaluation representations, propositions, and findings, especially those that support interpretations and judgments about quality.

Evaluation accountability: The evaluation accountability standards encourage adequate documentation of evaluations and a meta-evaluative perspective focused on improvement and accountability for evaluation processes and products.

Source: Joint Committee on Standards for Educational Evaluation, 2014

- *Be utilization-focused:* Evaluations should be done for and with specific, intended users (Patton, 2008) so that '… primary intended users select the most appropriate content, model, methods, theory and uses for their particular situation' (*ibid:* 37).
- *Focus on stakes, stakeholder engagement and learning:* Engaging stakeholders, not only in the design and implementation, but also in (learning from) M&E, is crucial for impact. This involves not only understanding stakeholders and their interests or stakes, but also engaging them in the M&E process. This includes learning by sharing and critically reflecting on their own and others' actions, experiences, views and perceptions (see Chapter 3 sections 'People orientation' and 'Learning orientation').
- *Be responsive to the situation (situational responsiveness):* This relates to context orientation, which is about being aware of the environment in which the initiative/organization is operating and the uniqueness of each situation. Adapt M&E to the special characteristics and conditions of a particular situation – a mixture of people, politics, history, context, resources, constraints, values, needs, interests, and chance.
- *Multiple roles in M&E:* Everyone has a role in M&E, and this needs to be made explicit. These roles may include acting as a trainer, facilitator, information broker, communicator, change agent, or problem solver as all these functions cannot be handled by a single person.

Agree with key stakeholders on the extent to which (programme) evaluation standards should guide the evaluation. These standards include utility, feasibility, propriety, accuracy and evaluation accountability (see Box 8.4). Note that the standards will sometimes need to be adapted to the particular situation at hand and that they can sometimes prove conflicting in reality.

Agree on the level of detail

It is important to agree on how much detail is required by different stakeholders to enable them to use the findings. This will also inform the selection of methods and approaches.

Agree on stakeholder engagement and learning in M&E

As mentioned earlier, engaging stakeholders in M&E processes is essential for learning and managing for sustainable development impact as this can build commitment, and support the use of M&E findings. It is important therefore to agree on who to involve in the design and implementation of the M&E. This can be done using a participation matrix, indicating the range of different stakeholders involved, as well as different tasks in M&E design and implementation.

Agree on overall methods and approaches for M&E

A wide range of methods and approaches can be used for M&E and are chosen based on:

- The key M&E questions to be addressed e.g. the methods and approaches needed for a question about efficiency are different from those addressing a question about impact.
- The subject to be monitored and evaluated. Understanding issues where cause-and-effect relationships are well-known (e.g. pneumonia vaccination) can be dealt with using rather simple methods (e.g. counting the number of children vaccinated), whereas more complex issues (e.g. organizational capacity or HIV/AIDS) can be dealt with using a mixed methods approach (see Box 8.5). Particularly where issues are complex, and cause-and-effect relationships are not yet known, it's important to closely monitor what works and what doesn't, as well as what emerges in a changing environment. Often this involves monitoring (safe fail) experiments (see section 'Agree on data collection, processing and analysis', and Chapter 2). If the topic you are dealing with is a sensitive one, different approaches will be needed. For example, sexual reproductive rights-related issues may only be discussed, either individually or in same-sex or same-age groups.
- The context i.e. what is or isn't possible in terms of M&E methods and approaches. Political instability and insecurity pose real threats to monitoring what is going on in the field. Methods may need to be 'quick and dirty', rather than 'scientific' and detailed. They also need to be tailored to the context. For

In evaluation, the choice is never between quantitative or qualitative methods, but rather about using an integrated approach to enhance and validate data, as well as the findings and recommendations, so as to deepen our understanding of the context and processes that lead to the initiative achieving particular outcomes and impacts (CDI, 2013). According to Bamberger (2012: 1), 'mixed methods evaluations (MME) seek to integrate social science disciplines with predominantly quantitative (QUANT) and qualitative (QUAL) approaches to theory, data collection, data analysis and interpretation'.

example, if it is not considered culturally appropriate for male data collectors to talk to women individually, then talking to them in groups may be an option, or better still, work with female data collectors. Also, the context needs to be closely monitored to respond quickly to emerging issues. See also section 'Step 4. Agree on data collection, processing and analysis'.

Agree on core capacities and conditions for M&E
Think through the capacities and conditions needed to support M&E processes. A key question is what can be done to improve these capacities and conditions, with respect to:
- Human capacity: Are the competencies of people needed to carry out M&E in place?
- Incentives: Are staff and stakeholders motivated to engage in M&E? Are roles and responsibilities clearly defined?
- Environment: Is the environment conducive to M&E and the sharing of experiences?
- Finances: Is there enough funding available to carry out M&E?
- Knowledge management and supporting infrastructure: Are knowledge management and sense-making approaches in place to support learning from M&E? Is there a culture of critical reflection and evaluative thinking to help make sense of complex situations and think through the possible consequences of M&E findings and processes? How will the data flow? How will access to data (MIS) be organized?

Based on the responses to the above questions, it may be necessary to lobby for extra funds for M&E, get leadership support, train people in data collection and analysis, set up a database, organize mobile phones for real-time data collection, etc. All these issues will need to be carefully thought out and addressed. See section 'Assess and establish ability and readiness' and Chapter 4.

Step 4. Agree on key M&E information needs

It is important to agree on the key information needs of stakeholders with respect to an initiative/organization. A pitfall of many M&E systems, however, is that they often end up with long lists of indicators that result in large data sets and reports that are often unused. Using M&E questions that have been agreed by stakeholders after reviewing the Theory of Change and logframe, will help you focus on what you need to know and report on impact more easily. Also, M&E questions can address more complex issues, where cause-effect relationships are not known and where it will be difficult to come up with fixed indicators.

The issue of indicators cannot be dealt with before the broad questions are formulated. These broad questions relate to performance, evaluation, strategic or learning questions. Often, these questions are defined around the DAC criteria (see Box 8.6). During the process of agreeing on key M&E questions, follow the suggestions outlined below to develop your questions. Please note that your key stakeholders, especially the primary intended users, will need to agree on these M&E questions.

Review the strategy (e.g. Theory of Change and logframe): Each stakeholder or primary user needs to think about the areas in the Theory of Change and logframe that they are interested in and how they will use this information. This may assist them in future decisions. For example, the management of the initiative may be interested in understanding what works and why, to strategically adapt when reviewing the Theory of Change. This will mean thinking about how the objectives are related, what contextual factors influence changes and the capacities and conditions needed for change to take place. This requires responding to different information needs at different levels of the Theory of Change or objective hierarchy.

Use DAC criteria (OECD, 2016): To evaluate development assistance, use the DAC criteria (impact, relevance, sustainability, effectiveness, efficiency) to guide the formulation of M&E questions (see Box 8.6). Often (external) evaluations are based on DAC criteria, and monitoring provides information to help address these areas. However, not all evaluations need address all five areas. What is important is to agree on which of them to focus on and which questions are more important, so as not to raise expectations too much.

Think through possible influences of the M&E process and findings at the individual, interpersonal and collective levels: For example, would you like individuals to change their attitude, skills and behaviour as a result of the findings? Then include questions that focus on a better understanding of a particular issue e.g. HIV/AIDS.

If you want to use the findings as evidence, e.g. for food security in a particular region of a country to demonstrate a need for policy and government support, then a question on the extent of food insecurity in that particular region would be useful.

Include questions on partnerships: Just as it is useful to formulate M&E questions about the implementation and results of the initiative, it is also useful to ask questions about your partnerships to enhance the effectiveness of your initiative. Through partnerships, it is usually possible to achieve more, particularly in complex situations. A key drawback, however, is that partnerships are often fraught with difficulties. To learn more on how M&E can strengthen partnerships for sustainable development, consult the conference report Partnering for success (CDI, 2016). The MSP guide (Brouwer et al., 2015) also provides further insight into how to make partnerships work.

Decide on useful M&E questions: In collaboration with stakeholders agree on what it is you really need to know. Try not to draw up a long list of key questions. Focus on getting the information that you will use and agree on how this information will be used.

Moving from key M&E questions to indicators and other information needs

M&E questions are the basis for defining indicators and other information needs. This will help to focus these indicators and information needs.

An indicator is defined as 'a quantitative or qualitative factor or variable that provides a simple and reliable basis for assessing achievement, change or performance. A unit of information measured over time that can help show changes in a specific condition' (Guijt and Woodhill, 2002: A-6). 'Making the most of indicators (and seeing their limits) means deciding whether or not to use indicators – or opt for questions – and if so, how to construct and use them to tell the story of change' (Guijt, 2007: 27).

Each M&E question will have a range of indicators or other information needs which together can give a comprehensive answer to the question being evaluated. It is useful to negotiate indicators with stakeholders, especially primary intended users of the evaluation. Stakeholders' views are very important. For example, local poverty indicators may include: types and size of funerals (e.g. in Ghana, Burkina Faso); availability of new clothes for celebrations (many areas); and eating three meals a day (various areas) (Guijt and Woodhill, 2002: 5-22).

There are differences between quantitative and qualitative indicators (see Table 8. 3), and both can help to provide a comprehensive picture of a situation. For example, a qualitative indicator may capture perceptions of people. This is important because people can have different opinions or perspectives about the same situation, people act on their opinions and different opinions are legitimate but not necessarily justifiable to others. Examples of the different types of indicators are described in Table 8.4

Check whether your indicators are SMART (see Box 8.7) even though it may not be easy to meet all of the criteria. In situations where resources are limited, it would be wise not to use indicators that are costly or too difficult to measure.

> **BOX 8.7 SMART CRITERIA FOR INDICATORS**
>
> **Specific:** Is the indicator specific enough to measure progress towards the results?
> **Measurable:** Is the indicator a reliable and clear measure of results?
> **Attainable:** Are the results in which the indicator seeks to chart progress realistic?
> **Relevant:** Is the indicator relevant to the intended outputs and outcomes?
> **Time-bound:** Are data available at reasonable cost and effort?

Table 8.3 Difference between quantitative and qualitative indicators

Quantitative indicators	Qualitative indicators
Measures of quantity (e.g. number of women trained in income-generating skills)	Descriptive; people's judgements and perceptions about a subject (e.g. perceptions about the initiative's impact); explain the 'why' behind numbers

Table 8.4 Types of indicators

	Quantitative	Qualitative
Information	Number of kilometres (km) of road built Number of households with access to clean water	Villagers' perceptions about benefits/ problems of the road Reasons why villagers don't use wells for drinking water
Methods	Direct observation (measuring/counting)	Discussion groups with villagers about how quality of life has changed
Analysis & Reporting	10 km of road built in one year 50% of households using wells for household use	50% of villagers reported that they did not use the wells because the river was closer Stories, text, descriptions, pictures km of road built
	Simple quantitative indicators:	Average yield from crop X in Y areas
	Complex quantitative indicators:	Number of months that households experience food shortages
	Compound indicators:	Number of effectively functioning water user associations
	Proxy indicators:	% of households with bicycles
	Qualitative indicators – open ended:	Perceptions of stakeholders about the overall performance of the project
	Qualitative indicators – focused:	Perceptions of stakeholders about a very specific aspect of the project

When defining indicators and information needs, think about what baseline information is already available, which indicators need additional baseline information and how this information will be collected. Baseline information is information about the initial starting point or situation before any intervention has taken place (see Box 8.8). It can help assess change over time and redefine the development initiative at start up. Some baseline information may already be present, for example, through the situational assessment, or in the form of secondary data, such as reports or statistical data from other organizations. Data may also be public. Some baseline information can be acquired retrospectively, such as through storytelling.

BOX 8.8 NOTE ON THE USE OF BASELINES

Baselines are particularly useful in helping leaders/development practitioners track the progress of their intervention in achieving outputs and outcomes and mapping change. Carrying out a rigorous impact evaluation without having baseline information is very difficult. If you have good baseline data, try as much as possible to collect your data in a consistent manner over the years, to allow for comparisons.

Kusek and Rist (2004: 82) provide eight key questions for establishing baseline information for indicators:
· Where do you get the data?
· What data-collection methods are you using?
· Who will collect the data?
· How frequently will the data be collected?
· How hard is it to collect the information and what are the cost implications?
· Who will analyse the data?
· Who is responsible for reporting the data?
· Who are the users of the data?

Some initiatives use **rolling baselines** during the implementation process. To get a good understanding of the concept, think of an initiative that initially started in Area A and is then rolled out sequentially to two other areas in the next two years. Data collected in Area A will serve as the baseline in the first year in Area A. Data collected in Area B in the following year, year two, will serve as the baseline for Area B, and so on (USAID, 2010).

Methods are all those techniques, tools, processes that are used to monitor and evaluate an initiative/organization. The methods used are aimed at finding answers to questions posed. The way in which methods are selected and used are determined by the methodology. Examples of data-collection methods are widely available. Some recommended sites include the M4SDI and MSP portals and the BetterEvaluation website.

Methodology refers to a set of procedures, methods and processes used to undertake M&E.

Approach is an integrated way of conceptualizing, designing and conducting M&E, which is often underpinned by theories, concepts and values, and includes an integrated set of options to do some or all of the tasks involved in M&E. Examples of evaluation approaches can be found in the list of methods and approaches in the Annexes.

Step 4. Agree on data collection, processing and analysis

Choosing methods and approaches

In this section, we outline the key issues to be aware of when choosing your M&E methods and approaches (see Box 8.9). A mixed methods approach allows you to overcome the limitations of an exclusive reliance on quantitative or qualitative evaluation approaches, as well as other benefits indicated by Bamberger (2012) such as: triangulation of evaluation findings (to check or validate results); development (this involves using the results from one method to improve another); complementarity (using different methods to understand more deeply and gain new insights into the findings); value diversity (including a range of values using different methods). There are emerging alternatives that add to the body of mixed methods approaches, particularly those that are relevant for the evaluation of more complex issues. They include realist/realistic evaluation, contribution analysis, process tracing, people's narratives, participatory assessment of development, and Configurational Comparative Methods. These are included in the list of methods and approaches in Annex 1.

It is important to choose an evaluation approach that best fits the evaluation question that needs to be addressed for a particular initiative/organization in its context. Many of these approaches are described on a number of websites including the M4SDI and BetterEvaluation websites.

To agree upon the design for M&E, you will need to consider the M&E questions; the attributes, or nature of the initiative/organization (e.g. level of complexity, uncertainty and risk), its purpose and context; and available M&E approaches and methods. Given the diversity of evaluation questions that generally come with the attributes of the initiative/organization, the use of one single method or approach will not be sufficient. A key question then is how best to coordinate and exploit the use of different methods and approaches. Consider whether you have leadership support, as well as the time, evaluation competencies, data and resources available, and have thought through political influences, expected use, and level of engagement.

Stern et al. (2012) have developed a framework (Figure 8.2) highlighting this relationship. The kind of questions posed determines how to design (impact) evaluations. For example, a question on attribution may call for experiments and statistical designs, while a question on how the initiative has made a difference calls for theory-based (Box 8.10) and participatory evaluation. The attributes of an initiative are also important e.g. assessing the impact of technical initiatives can be done through experiments using comparison groups, while complex issues like organizational capacity call for theory- or case-based approaches.

BOX 8.10: WHAT IS THEORY-BASED EVALUATION?

According to Birckmayer and Weiss (2000: 407), theory-based evaluation 'explores the how and why of program success or failure'. More specifically, based on a review of their works, theory-based evaluation examines the assumptions underlying the causal chain from inputs and activities to outcomes and impact in great detail. For example, what are the activities, what are their effects, and what does the initiative do next? The evaluation then looks at every step along this pathway to see what happened in reality and to what extent the original theory or causal chain can be validated. To evaluate an initiative, the Theory of Change needs to be made explicit and each part of the causal chain needs to be confirmed using (more often than not) a mix of methods.

Given the limited approaches available, Stern et al. (2012) plea for a broader range of designs and approaches for impact evaluation, not only to include experimental and statistical designs, but other approaches that are able to address the question of how change takes place, and explain the complexities of the initiative and related changes. This argument is also valid for other evaluations addressing e.g. relevance and sustainability.

Stern et al. (2012), present four key
questions that are generally asked in
impact evaluations (see Box 8.11). For
each of these questions, underlying
assumptions and suitable designs are
suggested in Annex 3.

Mixed methods designs
Mixed methods designs are described
in more detail in order to think
through the choice of mixing
qualitative and quantitative methods.
Often, using a mix of methods will
provide more valid data.

Creswell and Clark (2011) describe six major mixed methods designs for research
that can also be used for M&E purposes. The first four are basic mixed methods
designs, while the last two bring multiple design elements together (see Box 8.12).
To understand the differences in the designs, you will need to view them against
the level of interaction, priority, timing and procedures for mixing different
strands of qualitative and quantitative analytical methods. There are two ways
in which qualitative and quantitative strands can interact: 1) both implemented
independently and only brought together when the final findings of the evaluation

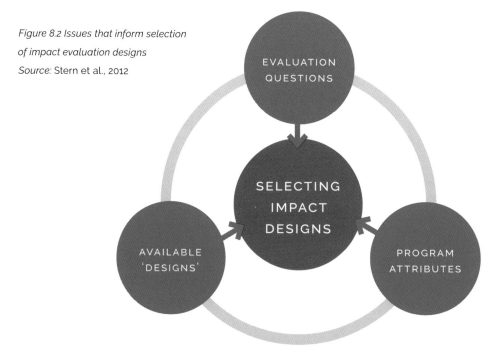

*Figure 8.2 Issues that inform selection
of impact evaluation designs*
Source: Stern et al., 2012

are discussed; and 2) interaction between the two strands, which are mixed before the final findings have been drawn. Priority relates to whether both qualitative and quantitative strands have equal priority or a particular study prioritises one strand above the other.

Timing in mixed methods refers to when data collection and the different strands will take place: concurrent, sequential and multiphase. Creswell and Clark (2011) identify four strategies for mixing strands of qualitative and quantitative analytical methods: merging both data sets, connecting the analysis of one data set to the collection of another; embedding one data form within the larger design; using a framework to join both data sets.

The publication *Introduction to Mixed Methods in Impact Evaluation* by Michael Bamberger (2012) has a number of case studies showing different ways of applying mixed methods designs that you can use for inspiration when developing your own.

Choosing methods for data collection
Based on the agreed key information needs, data collection can either be from primary or secondary data sources. Secondary data are data that have already been collected (e.g. official statistics, previous evaluations, project records) whereas primary data are data yet to be collected in the M&E process. Primary data can either be collected at the individual level (e.g. in cases where sensitive information is being gathered), at the group level (e.g. to encourage learning), or involve observation and physical measurements (e.g. measuring weight, height, or soil fertility). Where possible, it is useful to ensure that data collection methods are participatory, in order to enhance learning and ownership and ultimately contribute to impact. The choice of method will also depend on: the type of information required; how detailed the information needs to be (degree of precision); skills of the people involved (e.g. skills of facilitator in terms of providing suggestions, probing, encouraging, redirecting and taking notes); available resources (time, personnel, finances); sensitiveness of information (more difficult in groups); the extent of validity needed (more problematic in groups); and how the information will be used.

Depending on the type of information required (key information needs), you can use quantitative or qualitative data collection methods, or both, as explained in the previous section. The difference between quantitative and qualitative methods is that quantitative methods directly measure the status or change of a specific variable: they provide direct numerical results and are clear and precise, and are often more scientifically verifiable e.g. surveys, tests or measurements. Qualitative methods, on the other hand, gather information by for example asking people

BOX 8.12 SIX MAJOR MIXED METHODS DESIGNS

The convergent parallel design: Quantitative and qualitative strands are given the same priority. They are implemented and analysed concurrently, after which results are compared, or related to during the overall interpretation.

The explanatory sequential design: This takes place in two interactive phases. In this design, the focus is on the use of quantitative data collection and analysis to address the questions posed. This is then followed by qualitative data collection and analysis to help explain initial quantitative results.

The exploratory sequential design: As its name suggests, it is based on sequential timing. This design starts with qualitative data collection and analysis in the first phase. Quantitative data collection and analysis is then carried out to test or generalize the initial findings.

The embedded design: In this situation, both quantitative and qualitative data are collected and analysed, but a qualitative strand may be added within a quantitative design (e.g. experiment study) or a quantitative strand may be added within a qualitative design (e.g. case study).

The transformative design: Here the design is shaped within a transformative theoretical framework e.g. from a feminist perspective. And this perspective influences all other decisions in terms of interaction, priority, timing and mixing of qualitative and quantitative methods.

The multiphase design: Sequential and concurrent strands are combined over a period of time within the lifetime of an initiative. This design is often used for monitoring and evaluating the initiative during its lifetime. The findings of the different strands feed into each other.

Source: Adapted from Creswell and Clark, 2011

to explain what they have observed, what they do, believe or feel. Qualitative methods include, for example, resource mapping, focus groups, storytelling (such as the most significant change (MSC) technique), and pictures. MSC, for example, identifies changes that people/stakeholders consider personally important, though this is not to be confused with the change desired by the development initiative, and so it works without indicators. At the meta-analysis level, qualitative information can also be quantified.

There are different ways of recording collected data, such as filling forms or tables; using a camera, tape or video recorder; writing answers on cards or flipcharts; and taking detailed notes. Data can also be collected in real-time e.g. by using mobile devices (smart phones) or tablets. Real-time evaluation is especially useful when working in complex contexts, so as to stay tuned in to what emerges and be able to respond quickly e.g. in the humanitarian sector.

Data analysis

Data analysis involves converting collected (raw) data into usable information that is interpreted and validated. It includes looking for trends, patterns, relationships, etc. It is an important part of the M&E process because it shapes the information that is reported and its potential use after critically reflecting on and making sense of these findings so as to inform decision-making (see section 'Agree on critical reflection and sense-making'). Given that data are continually collected throughout the lifespan of an initiative, data analysis is an ongoing process.

Before analysing the data, decide on who to involve in the analysis. Try to involve staff and primary stakeholders as much as possible. Sometimes analysing and summarizing the data collected will be a time-consuming process requiring particular competencies, so you won't be able to involve your stakeholders all the time. Nevertheless, try to keep your stakeholders abreast of the findings and discuss with them any contradictions and gaps identified. Also, decide on the data analysis methods. Any method used will depend on your facilities (e.g. computer) and the type of data being gathered (e.g. qualitative or quantitative data) as well as what question needs to be addressed through these data, (see also section 'Choosing methods for data collection').

Some recommended procedures for quantitative and qualitative data analysis for designing mixed methods studies, inspired by the work of Creswell and Plano Clark (2011), are presented in Annex 4. Key steps include: prepare data for analysis; examine the data; analyse the data; represent and interpret the results; validate the data and findings.

BOX 8.13 REAL TIME EVALUATION

Cosgrave et al. (2009: 10) refer to a real-time evaluation (RTE) as 'an evaluation in which the primary objective is to provide feedback in a participatory way in real time (i.e. during the evaluation fieldwork) to those executing and managing the [initiative]'. RTE allows leaders and development practitioners to look at the situation from a different perspective, enabling them to focus more on the immediate effects than regular monitoring would. Often this type of evaluation is used in the humanitarian sector to respond quickly to chaotic and complex situations or emergencies (see Chapter 2 section 'Understanding complexity').

The main data-collection method in humanitarian aid – where timing and rapid feedback are crucial – is through semi-structured key informant interviews, although group interviews and observations are also used (Brusset et al., 2010: 14-16).

Quantitative data analysis
Quantitative data analysis involves producing numerical data. Quantitative data analysis may involve using data mining, frequency tables, time series (e.g. line chart or bar charts), and statistical methods (BetterEvaluation (no date: a)). The analysis of quantitative data may be based on a single variable (univariate analysis), which is the simplest form of analysis. Bar charts, pie charts and histograms showing the height of children (one variable) of a certain age are examples of this. The analysis may also be bivariate, which explores the relationship between two variables (it is usually easy to do, but time consuming). For example, in this type of analysis you may look at the relationship between height and weight of children of a certain age. To show this type of analysis graphically you could use scatter plots, regression analysis and correlation coefficients. Multivariate analysis involves the analysis of data sets with many variables and an increasing level of complexity. Multivariate analysis gives a broader picture than when looking at just one variable. This is suitable for larger and more complex sets of data and often statistical software packages are used, e.g. Statistical Package for Social Sciences (SPSS) or Statistical Analysis Software (SAS).

The analysis may also use both inductive and deductive methods, given that both methods have their advantages and disadvantages. Deductive methods involve deriving conclusions from general truths by beginning with a theory and then narrowing them down to more specific hypotheses that can be tested by collecting data based on observations made. Inductive methods work the other way around, moving from making specific observations to making broader generalizations (some conclusions) and theories.

Qualitative data analysis
Qualitative data analysis involves working with texts (written or spoken), images (e.g. pictures, video) and observations, to produce textual data. Qualitative data analysis can help to generate explanations, e.g. of how and why things happened, or generate emerging themes and typologies.

A core feature of qualitative data analysis is the coding process. Coding is important because it is a way of organizing and sorting your data so that you can see what is happening to it. There are many ways to go about coding, but generally it involves giving a word, phrase, symbol or number, a coding category. For example, texts (e.g. interviews, notes, observations) are coded to fit into categories.

Different types of analysis can be used. For example, content analysis reduces large amounts of unstructured textual content to manageable data that can respond to

M&E questions (BetterEvaluation (no date: c)). Coded content can be quantitatively analysed for, for example, trends, patterns, similarities, differences (*ibid*: c). Data can also be coded by theme. Framework matrices allow for sorting data across case and by theme, and can be used to summarize and analyse qualitative data in a two-by-two matrix table (*ibid*: i). Analysis can be aided by the visualization of key events, sequences and results, e.g. through the use of timelines and time ordered matrices.

Data analysis equipment and software
Specialized equipment such as calculators or computers and software (e.g. Excel, SPSS, Access, Visio) are needed for these analyses. Simple statistical analysis (such as percentages) can be done using a calculator, while more complex ones, such as survey data, are carried out using Excel or statistical software such as the SPSS, STATA, SAS, R and MIwiN. The StatPages.info(no date) website has links to some freely available statistical software packages like OpenStat, easyreg, epidata, WinIDAMs, MicrOsiris, Epi Info and PSPP. Also, if your team is to be involved in any data entry or analysis that requires specific technical skills, determine whether such experience exists among the staff or if training is necessary. These factors can then be included in the M&E budget and human resource development.

Programs designed to handle qualitative data can speed up the analysis process and make it easier for you to experiment with different codes, test different hypotheses about relationships, and facilitate diagrams of emerging theories and the preparation of research reports (Coffey and Atkinson, 1996). The steps involved in computer-assisted qualitative data analysis parallel those traditionally used to analyse texts such as notes, documents, or interview transcripts: preparation, coding, analysis, and reporting. Examples of qualitative data analysis software are NVivo and ATLAS.ti. For information on options for qualitative and quantitative data analysis visit the BetterEvaluation website.

Step 5. Agree on critical reflection and sense-making

How can we make sense of the information gathered and analysed and use it to make improvements and enhance the impact of our initiatives? Critical reflection is a process of reviewing what happened in the past and the actions taken, and also involves thinking deeply in order to draw lessons, learning from what worked and what did not work. Sense-making is the ability to make sense of situations by trying to understand connections in complex situations. Critical reflection and sense-making therefore offer a way for us to question and analyse experiences, observations, theories, beliefs and/or assumptions with our stakeholders. Although critical reflection is closely linked to quantitative or qualitative analyses,

BOX 8.14 KEY QUESTIONS IN CRITICAL REFLECTION

You can learn a lot from initiatives/ organizations, once the 'right' questions are asked:

What is happening?

Why is this happening?

So, what are the implications for the development initiative/ organization?

Now what will we do next?

Bob Williams (2009) has created a list of questions that can be used to get a deeper understanding of initiatives:

• What happened, to whom and in what circumstances?
• What generalizations do you draw from this; what exceptions are there; how can those exceptions be explained (and not explained away)?
• What contradictions do you observe (i.e. complete the sentence: On the one hand…, on the other hand…)? Assuming these contradictions are true, what sense do you make of them?
• Which of these events did you not expect to happen? What does that say about the assumptions you made regarding the development initiative?
• What did not happen that you expected to see in your data? What does that say about the assumptions you made regarding the initiative?
• What remains a puzzle? What would you have to do to clarify or address the situation?

it moves beyond that by documenting and sharing decisions and ensuring that these decisions are implemented. This is because in critical reflection and sense-making we question what is normally taken for granted, particularly assumptions regarding the development initiative about what worked and what did not, but also why not and what next. Taking time to think critically and make sense of M&E information will therefore help us to understand experiences and data in a more in-depth way, create new insights and agree on further action.

What can we do to improve critical thinking and sense-making in M&E processes? As a first step, we can challenge ourselves and learn to ask probing questions (see Box 8.14).

To promote learning, however, we need to create an environment where stakeholders can freely share their thoughts and ideas. Examples of ways to create a learning environment include analysing the organization's learning culture; noting and addressing obstacles to learning; making full use of the learning cycle (see Chapter 3); engaging in learning at all levels. To engage people in learning requires taking into account learning preferences at various levels – individual, team, project, programme, organization, societal/stakeholders – and building in regular critical reflection moments. Also, dialogue and generative listening are useful in sense-making processes (see Chapter 5).

Making M&E activities more reflective

Critical reflection can be done at the individual level in our everyday M&E activities, by capturing lessons learned with the initiative's stakeholders, and planning for an integrated sequence of reflective events. Individual reflection promotes critical reflection during group events, such as annual project reviews or monthly meetings with implementing partners. Ensuring critical reflection in groups can serve to: uncover new information; limit biases; build a clear picture of a situation, event or process, and reach consensus; ensure well-reasoned, meaningful actions; and facilitate action that has broad ownership. A checklist to make meetings reflective is provided in Box 8.15. Leaders/development practitioners have a key role to play in stimulating critical reflection processes at the individual, group and organizational levels.

There are many ways to critically reflect and make sense of data and analysis generated. This can be done, for example, during formal meetings such as review meetings (quarterly, annually, mid-term) or supervision missions. Informal meetings can take place during field visits and informal discussions with clients and other stakeholders. They can be internal events, carried out by staff and key stakeholders involved in the development initiative, or external events carried out by evaluators, funders, or other interested parties (see Box 8.16). In planning

---

BOX 8.15 CHECKLIST FOR REFLECTIVE GROUP MEETINGS

Before the meeting:
Decide who is to be at the meeting.
Agree on scheduling and allow enough time to reflect on new information, with meetings frequent enough for timely decision-making.
Agree on what M&E findings are to be discussed.

Source: Adapted from Guijt and Woodhill, 2002

During the meeting:
Ensure everyone has the same agenda and that expectations are clear.
Share responsibilities, build skills and create a team spirit.
Ask staff/stakeholders to raise problems or dilemmas they are facing and invite everyone to find solutions.
Encourage analysis of a critical incident or issue of importance.
At regular intervals, include constructive feedback exercises.
Make sure outputs of the meeting are action-oriented.

In an IFAD-supported agricultural programme in Zanzibar, lessons learned at different levels fed into each other. At the field level, farmers had weekly meetings where they could discuss progress, lessons learned and challenges. Some of these challenges were addressed at these meetings, but some challenges required external assistance. At the district level, again programmes and related problems were discussed, and project staff, district officials and farmer representatives discussed how to overcome the problems.

Whatever problems could be solved at the district level would be discussed at project management level and where necessary other stakeholders were brought on board to help solve some of the problems farmers faced in improving agricultural productivity. During the annual review and planning meeting with stakeholders, the most important successes and failures were presented and discussed, as well as ways forward for the next year. This was then fed into the next annual work plan and budget.

regular reflective events, feedback loops are important and information can be shared through the use of innovative methods such as mobile phones. Pilot projects such as the 'Low-cost mobile-enabled feedback mechanism for solicited and unsolicited feedback' implemented by World Vision UK, International NGO Training and Research Centre (INTRAC) and the Social Impact Lab (2016) demonstrated that vulnerable target groups are willing to engage in two-way feedback despite constraints such as illiteracy and limited access to mobile phones.

Arkesteijn et al. (2015: 1) call for reflexive evaluation approaches that 'challenge systemic stability and support processes of learning and institutional change' and indicate that reflexive evaluation approaches 'may well complement current system approaches in development evaluation practice'.

Figure 8.3 Key steps in communicating and reporting for use
Source: Based on Stetson, 2008

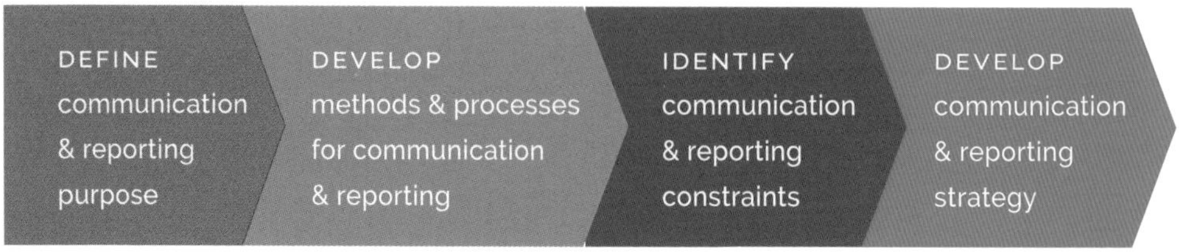

| DEFINE communication & reporting purpose | DEVELOP methods & processes for communication & reporting | IDENTIFY communication & reporting constraints | DEVELOP communication & reporting strategy |

Step 6. Agree on communication and reporting

Communication and reporting are an intrinsic part of the M&E process, and of managing for sustainable development impact as a whole. Getting the whole communication process right can be quite challenging. For example, the word 'evaluation' can evoke a gamut of emotions, most notably anxiety, and result in resistance to change and limited use of M&E findings e.g. for improved management and action. Chapter 5 provides useful insights in enhancing communication. In this section, however, the focus is on communication to effectively interact with stakeholders and communicate and report M&E findings for their improved use (e.g. in programme design). Much of the information in this section has been inspired by the work of Stetson (2008) and Torres et al. (2005).

Key steps in communicating and reporting for use

The steps presented below will help you develop an appropriate communication strategy to promote learning and use within the initiative/organization. This includes: defining the communication and reporting purpose; selecting the communication and reporting methods; identifying the communication challenges and developing a communication and reporting strategy to support use and influence (see Figure 8.3).

BOX 8.17 QUESTIONS TO ASK DURING THE M&E PROCESS

- Who are the key stakeholders?
- On what issues do they need to be informed? At what stage of the (monitoring and) evaluation process? Why?
- Which stakeholders need to be included in the critical reflection and sense-making processes? When?
- Which stakeholders are to be involved in the decision-making processes (i.e. for garnering support, developing recommendations, or determining the future direction of the initiative?

Define the communication and reporting purpose

During the initial stages of the M&E system design, agreements will have been made with key stakeholders/primary users of the M&E regarding what they want to know and how they intend to use the M&E process and findings e.g. is it for awareness creation, gaining support, or for improvement of the initiative? Some questions to ask during the M&E process are suggested in Box 8.17. The answers to these questions will help you determine the purpose of your communication and reporting for M&E.

Develop methods and processes for communication and reporting

Communication is the thread that binds everything together in M4SDI. This is particularly true for M&E where we are concerned with promoting and enhancing the use of M&E findings. This section builds on Chapter 5, the Communication chapter.

Just as stakeholders have specific information needs, they may also have particular needs with respect to how information is communicated. For example, a programme manager may want full reports, while a funder or policymaker may be mainly interested in the executive summary. Partner agencies may be more interested in details about the services that they have provided in a particular development initiative. In cases where you might want to use the findings to influence e.g. policymaking, producing elaborate reports may not be appropriate. Instead, consider preparing policy briefs or organizing policy events, see Chapter 5 section 'Communication methods and processes'.

Learning models, discussed in Chapter 3, are also useful in showing how people learn in different ways. For example, some people learn through experimentation, others through concrete experiences, while some prefer to take a step back and reflect on experiences. This means that stakeholders or intended users who learn through experimentation will, for example, benefit from case studies and handouts that they can use and refer to later on. And those who prefer concrete experiences will benefit from hands-on activities, observations, and role play. For evaluation to be meaningful, you will need to involve your intended users/stakeholders during the evaluation process. And to promote use, you will need to bear in mind who your intended users are and the way they learn. One way to address this is to agree upfront with your stakeholders, especially the primary intended users of the evaluation, what findings they are interested in. Often this relates to specific information needs formulated by stakeholders during M&E design. Communicating with stakeholders requires knowing how, when and where you can reach them.

Useful ways of communicating findings include collaborative communication processes involving stakeholders in the design, implementation and sense-making of findings, as well as the formulation of recommendations and conclusions. These processes present opportunities to actively engage your stakeholders and facilitate group learning to support M&E use. Dialogue and stimulating generative listening are useful for sense-making and informed decision-making. Other important ways of communicating findings for use include: maintaining close contact with key decision-makers and leaders; keeping them up-to-date on interim evaluation findings on how the initiative can be improved, and deciding whether there needs to be a change in strategy or whether the initiative needs to stop altogether. Keeping regular contact with stakeholders to thank them for their participation, as well as letting them know how the process is going, will strengthen commitment and use of the evaluation. Other steps include: developing management responses and monitoring their implementation; providing space for dialogue on the findings (e.g. annual stakeholder reviews); developing policy briefs with clear recommendations for strategic and operational changes and how these changes will be managed.

Box 8.18 provides some ideas about communication and reporting methods that may lead to different degrees of interaction with your users and even facilitate learning (see also Table 5.4). There are a variety of methods, such as cartoons, short reports, and summaries which can be tailored to the needs of the intended users. Reports and summaries that are written in clear, jargon-free language are usually desirable (unless otherwise indicated). Try to use graphs and charts to illustrate points; list positive and negative findings; and include qualitative, contextual data as well as quantitative data and specific recommendations to make your report informative, visually appealing and easy to read. Also, think about new ways of communication, such as the seven new ways of communicating findings presented by Glenn O'Neill (2012): summary sheets, findings tables, scorecards, interactive webpages, photo stories, blogs and multimedia video reports. The BetterEvaluation website also offers some novel ways. Whatever the communication methods/techniques or strategies used, bear in mind that their main objective is to help users assimilate and use information generated from M&E.

Ensure accessibility
When thinking through the design of the communication and reporting methods, also think about the accessibility of these methods. For example, people may have auditory disabilities, they may be colour blind or have other visual impairments. The 1-3-25 principle is also useful – present the findings in a logical and consistent manner using a 1-page outline, a 3-page executive summary and 25 pages to present the findings and methodology. Make sure to simplify the layout of your report by eliminating unnecessary charts, emphasizing headings, writing summary statements and using descriptive, catchy titles.

Ensure transparency
In order to ensure accountability and learning, it is important to be transparent about the M&E findings, what these mean for the organization and/or stakeholders involved, and what will be done in response to the findings. This will also enhance their use.

Identify communication and reporting constraints
Some of the most common obstacles to communication include the general anxiety around M&E, the failure to plan from the start, and organizational culture.

Stronger efforts on the part of leadership/management will therefore be needed to get the support of staff. Other communication challenges can arise as a result of not communicating with stakeholders regularly and in a timely fashion. Factors such as a lack of commitment and disinterest can lead to findings not being used at all. Try to get some funds to cover report production, verbal presentations, or dissemination to strengthen the communication process.

Be sensitive to negative perceptions on M&E. It's important to find out why people are negative, in order to formulate an appropriate strategy. Sometimes underlying problems need to be addressed, such as loss of institutional memory due to rapid staff turnover. When leaders do not want to openly share performance findings, you may want to involve other influential staff or stakeholders, but it's important to engage leadership early in the M&E process so that findings do not come as a surprise. Ways of overcoming these obstacles include understanding the context and culture of the initiative/organization, and actively communicating with staff from the start. Other ways of tackling obstacles and enhancing communication are proposed in Chapter 5.

Develop a communication and reporting strategy
Many of the key elements that you need to develop your communication and reporting strategy have been discussed earlier as well as in Chapter 5 section 'Developing a communication strategy'. They include having an idea about: what the M&E is about and why it is needed; who the primary intended users of the M&E findings are and their characteristics; the information needs of the these stakeholders; the most appropriate communication methods for each user

group; an implementation plan. In addition to this, identify who is responsible for preparing the communication strategy and developing a budget and other resources to support its implementation.

Step 7. Plan for implementation

All the elements discussed above can now come together to form a strategic (M&E) framework which provides the overall guidelines for M&E. However, it will need further development to become a fully operational M&E plan. In this plan, explain how the M&E for the initiative works, set out the purpose of the plan, the Theory of Change for the initiative (strategic planning framework), the information needs, indicators, data collection and analysis methods and sources of information, roles and responsibilities, capacities and conditions, knowledge management/ data flows, critical reflection events and processes, communication processes and feedback mechanisms. The M&E plan will also need to be integrated into operational plans for the initiative/organization to achieve efficiency and make M&E less of a burden to staff.

Additionally, it is useful to work out all the methods and tools you need to support your M&E, such as interview guides, record sheets to collate data, guidelines for facilitators of participatory methods for data collection and analysis, etc. Another useful implementation tool is the M&E matrix, which can be used to systematically link evaluation questions to indicators, and related methods and processes for data collection, data analysis, sense-making and communication of findings. There is a good example of a M&E matrix in the IFAD Managing for impact in rural development guide (Guijt and Woodhill, 2002: Annex C) that you can consult to guide you in developing the M&E matrix for your initiative. A proposed format for the matrix is also given in Table 8.5.

Table 8.5 Format for an M&E matrix

Evaluation question	Indicators & other information needs	Data collection methods and pro-cesses	Data analysis methods and pro-cesses	Sense-making methods and pro-cesses	Communi-cation and reporting methods and pro-cesses

Step 8. Evaluate and adapt the M&E

It is important to periodically review and adapt your M&E. In the beginning, you will need to fine-tune the system in order to meet the particular needs of those involved. We live in a dynamic environment, so you will also find that you will have to adjust your information needs in response to changing contexts and strategies. Review your M&E system regularly, preferably on a yearly basis, in collaboration with key stakeholders involved in the process.

If time and resources allow, take the opportunity, along with the stakeholders involved in the process, to critically reflect on the M&E process, its outcome and the extent to which expectations have been met. Some of the questions you could ask are: What did we do well? How can we do better? What lessons can we draw from this?

The following points will help you assess how well your M&E is faring and check the extent to which:
- the articulated Theory of Change underpins the rationale for getting engaged in this initiative;
- the Theory of Change/strategic framework (objectives, purpose, intended processes, etc.) is translated into operational practice;
- the operations monitoring processes – activities and outputs – are functioning (Are we doing things right?);
- the objectives monitoring processes – outcomes and impact – are functioning (Are we doing the right things?);
- the context monitoring processes – relevant trends and developments that influence the initiative/organization – are functioning (Are we connected/relevant/ proactive?);
- the processing and storage of data/information and the related arrangements for accessibility are functioning;
- the analysis and sense-making processes are functioning;
- the communication processes are functioning;
- the translation into management decision-making or adaptive management is happening;
- the feedback mechanisms from key stakeholders are in place.

These questions can also be used as the basis for a more thorough M&E design process. The questions are meant to cover the key areas that make M&E an effective and efficient instrument in project performance management.

Table 8.6 provides ideas on what may happen if M&E is not well designed or functioning. You can use these ideas to test your own M&E system.

Table 8.6 What happens if M&E is not well designed and functioning?

Purpose & scope	Information needs	M&E methods	Critical reflection	Communication & reporting	Capacities & conditions	Result
Not clear	ok	ok	ok	ok	ok	Incoherent untargeted M&E
ok	Unclear / unspecified (per stakeholder)	ok	ok	ok	ok	Not knowing what you need to know
ok	ok	Inappropriate	ok	ok	ok	Not gathering what you need to gather
ok	ok	ok	Insufficient	ok	ok	Inadequate understanding of change process
ok	ok	ok	ok	Ineffective	ok	Loss of stakeholder commitment
ok	ok	ok	ok	ok	Inadequate	Great ideas, but it just doesn't happen

Other aspects to look at in your M&E include its 'connectedness' with the other core processes – strategic guidance and effective operations (i.e. how sufficiently well the M&E system covers the areas that need to be considered), as well as organizational learning processes. Review different parts of the system and check how well the different elements are connected to the strategy of your initiative/ organization, and adapt where necessary. Further, it is important to systematically track the extent to which M&E recommendations and related decisions have been followed up, and if not, why.

SUMMARY

Monitoring and evaluation are crucial in M4SDI. For M&E to inform strategic and operational decision-making, it is essential to create an environment where people can learn and be actively engaged, and monitor and adapt to what works (or not) and what emerges in an often complex context. Theories of Change are an important starting point for the development of a well-functioning M&E system, which in turn informs the adaptation of these Theories of Change. A supportive leadership that engages in M&E is also important.

To develop your M&E system, you will need to: assess and establish ability and readiness for M&E; agree on purpose and scope of the M&E; agree on key information needs; agree on data collection, processing and analysis; agree on critical reflection and sense-making; agree on communication and reporting; plan for implementation; and evaluate and adapt the M&E process. Having an M&E system is invaluable in helping to find out whether things are going well and whether the initiative/organization is doing things right. For example, is the system able to adequately support decision-making processes? Are operations going well and are the internal systems such as the MIS and financial systems functioning well? Is the initiative relevant and proactive in the way it operates? Is it able to make sense of what is happening on the ground and keep abreast of developments? Is there good communication flow internally and externally? Are feedback processes working?

In carrying out impact evaluations and other types of evaluation (e.g. for relevance and sustainability), we need to be careful that we are not overly dependent on any one approach or method. Mixed methods are preferred because of their integrated approach to evaluation, resulting in a deeper and broader understanding of issues regarding the initiative. Although M&E is important for accountability and impact purposes, it is also essential for learning in order to enhance strategic decision-making processes, influence policy, and gain the support of stakeholders to respond and adapt in a complex context and manage towards sustainable development impact.

CHAPTER 8

CHAPTER 9

THE POWER OF M&E TO BRING ABOUT TRANSFORMATIONAL
CHANGE: THE SRSP STORY, PAKISTAN

MY PERSONAL JOURNEY IN INSTITUTIONALIZING M4SDI IN
NARO, UGANDA

DEALING WITH COMPLEX SYSTEMS AND POWER THROUGH
ENGAGEMENT AND LEARNING: BENEFIT PARTNERSHIP,
ETHIOPIA

M4SDI STORIES OF CHANGE

The M4SDI approach has been used by leaders and development practitioners in diverse settings and across sectors. This chapter highlights stories from people who have used the M4SDI approach in challenging and complex situations.

The story from SRSP, Pakistan, shows the importance of strong leadership in a large programme, and how, with good understanding of M&E, they developed and used context-specific M&E to transform the organization and the communities they serve. The story from a large research organization in Uganda shows us how, with vision and perseverance, it is possible to enhance staff capacity and bring about a change in culture. The story from Ethiopia not only shows us the importance of working with people, but also the challenges in engaging staff and stakeholders, with their diverse backgrounds from the start of a large development initiative.

M4SDI is not just about guiding planning, implementation, and monitoring and evaluation processes. It is also about working with people with different backgrounds and interests in often rapidly changing contexts. To manage for sustainable development impact requires visionary leadership, passion and dedication, and recognition of the role people can play in positively contributing towards sustainable change.

Masood Ul Mulk,
Chief Executive Officer,
SRSP

Syed Aftab Ahmad,
Programme Manager
Operations and Humanita-
rian programme, SRSP

Atif Zeeshan Rauf,
Programme Manager,
Planning Monitoring
Evaluation and Research,
SRSP

THE POWER OF M&E TO BRING ABOUT TRANSFORMATIONAL CHANGE: THE SRSP STORY, PAKISTAN

SRSP's integration of M&E to support change efforts have raised the credibility of the organization, attracted funding from multiple sources, and transformed the institution as well as the lives of the people it serves.

The Sarhad Rural Support Programme (SRSP) is one of the largest NGOs working in North-West Pakistan. Established in 1989, the development organization initially focused on poverty alleviation in Khyber Pakhtunkhwa. Later, it broadened its operations into humanitarian work, and extended its coverage to the Federally Administered Tribal Areas region. Today, SRSP is a vibrant organization with 50 offices, 1300 staff, serving roughly 36,000 communities and an annual budget of US$40 million.

The Chief Executive Officer, Masood Ul Mulk, describes how difficult the first 10 years were for SRSP. The "seed money" the donor promised never came because of the changed geo-political situation after the end of the Afghan war of the eighties. In this period the government helped by entrusting SRSP with the implementation of part of its large area development programmes. This gave the organization the geographical spread and outreach in communities. But within five years the relationship with the government had broken down and the organization lost its credibility with both donors and the government, mostly because multi-stakeholder interests could not be handled. By 2000 SRSP had lost its major donors and public credibility, and was on the verge of collapse.

So how did SRSP become a dynamic, successful organization?

Since Masood Ul Mulk has been at the helm of SRSP for the last 15 years, it has grown tremendously. Masood Ul Mulk is an M&E professional, and clearly a visionary. From the very onset of his tenure, he has been strategically steering the organization. In his previous position as an M&E professional at a well-resourced development programme, he was able to experience first-hand how crucial a good M&E system was to the credibility of an organization. He also saw how important information generated from M&E activities could help guide change processes, and facilitate understanding the needs of stakeholders. Undaunted by what he saw at SRSP, he started debates within the organization about the need to set up systems to support the work of the organization. Masood Ul Mulk also set about getting funding to build up basic capacities within the organization, focussing particularly on strengthening competencies in finance, auditing, and M&E in an effort to attract funders. As part of strategic planning processes, he and his staff looked for opportunities that would result in improving the livelihoods of people in the region, and adapted the organization accordingly.

If opportunity doesn't knock, build a door yourself (Milton Berle)
In 2005 there was an earthquake disaster in the region, and SRSP was ready to play its part. Management and staff developed a programme to help the people affected. A key part of the programme was to build 60,000 houses for the communities. An important conclusion from a World Bank evaluation was that SRSP had a 92–93 per cent compliance rate for building standards, which is commendable. This finding was crucial for SRSP because it signalled that the organization was a credible partner. In later years, the organization also successfully dealt with the problem of internally displaced people, showing that it had the capacity to effectively combine humanitarian work with its development activities. This did not go unnoticed. The government and the European Union, KfW Development Bank, AusAID and UN agencies indicated that they were willing to work with SRSP in the region. As systems improved within SRSP, it was able to share more information with donors and partners, and this attracted even more funding. At one point, in one year SRSP worked with up to 42 donors providing a range of services.

Additional funding for SRSP also meant opportunities to continue building capacities and further enhance their M&E system. 'This helped in two ways,' says Masood Ul Mulk. 'It addressed the issue of upward accountability. Donors, policy-makers and decision-makers are far away and we are working in a conflict zone. We needed to develop a strong M&E system to show them what we are doing, how we are doing it and be able to meet the reporting demands of donors (which can get pretty complicated if you have to work with multiple donors!). Two, downward accountability – we need to work closely with communities and respond to their needs based on feedback.' In fact, because SRSP believes so strongly in enhancing capacities and in creating conditions for development, they maintain close relations with communities beyond the project life cycle. They have also formed strategic partnerships with government agencies at different levels that enable them to extend support in areas where there is no funding. SRSP has also commissioned external evaluations of their projects and circulated the findings among donors and partners in an effort to mobilize resources to expand their services, enhance effectiveness of their organization and address long-term sustainability concerns.

It is clear that there are many reasons for the success of SRSP, but when asked to identify the key factors responsible for its success, Atif Zeeshan Rauf, Programme Manager, Planning Monitoring Evaluation and Research, indicated that, 'Mr Ul Mulk has been one of the major driving forces behind the improved M&E system at SRSP'. However, in conversation with Atif Zeeshan Rauf and Syed Aftab Ahmad, it doesn't take long to realise that they too, along with a few selected colleagues working in M&E, have also been very instrumental in helping the organization to become what it is today.

Integrating M&E into every aspect of the organization and building systems to support this process has taken considerable time and effort, but there is now a strong link between M&E and decision-making processes, the engagement of primary stakeholders and partners and donors, and achievements on the ground. To develop this integrated system, management and staff had to take a multifaceted approach. This was only possible because top management and change agents were deeply committed to the process. The strategy involved investing considerably in staff and building their competencies in critical areas such as PME and other specialist areas. For example, at least three members of staff, including Atif Zeeshan Rauf have attended the Managing for Impact course by Wageningen Centre for Development Innovation. Other staff members have been sent for training to other institutes. This has had a major impact on SRSP because they have been given the room to experiment and implement what they have learned. This has enabled the organization to become stronger and more adaptable to change.

The organization has been able to further transform itself by recruiting new, younger staff willing to carry out the change processes. And by strengthening the organizational capacity of primary stakeholders via outreach programmes to improve literacy, entrepreneurship, and awareness of primary stakeholders on issues that impact them directly through, for example, stakeholder consultations. Efforts have also been made to create an environment where people are motivated, can enjoy their work, free from politics and are valued for their long-term institutional memory. 'Nothing is more motivating than seeing the difference you are making to the lives of people', says Atif Zeeshan Rauf. Perhaps this is true for many staff given the low staff turnover.

SRSP serves a region that is diverse both in its geography and people. Getting local staff from these areas has had the added benefit of the organization being better able to understand the people and their needs. With the rapid expansion of SRSP it is widely recognized that staff cannot monitor everything, and that having a network of community volunteers and community resources who can liaise with the organization has been crucial.

Gender issues are also of paramount concern to SRSP. Despite the conservative nature of the region, the organization has found innovative ways to meet the needs of women in the communities. For example, if the women need water or assistance in enterprise development, then a project is built around their practical needs. A good example of this is the creation of a community investment fund aimed at building the capacity of women's groups in a decentralized way and providing seed funding.

Access to relevant, timely information is also a key reason why the organization has been so successful in meeting the needs of its clients and funders. For example, after the earthquake in 2005, Syed Aftab Ahmad, who has responsibility for humanitarian operations, developed an innovative M&E system, which helped the organization to effectively monitor, almost in real time, what was happening on the ground. This helped the organization to keep track of developments, identify gaps on a continuous basis and helped agencies to assess what they could contribute to. In addition to this, SRSP now shares information about its activities, using social media (e.g. Facebook, Twitter, YouTube and Instagram) to promote their achievements and success stories.

Transparency, tailoring M&E to meet the needs of the users, building capacities of staff, empowering primary stakeholders, and partnership, have become hallmarks of the programme. SRSP's integration of M&E to support change efforts have raised the credibility of the organization, attracted funding from multiple sources, and transformed the institution as well as the lives of the people it serves. As a testimony to the outstanding work the organization has been doing in providing green energy in remote communities and impacting lives, SRSP received the Green Oscar Ashden Award in 2015.

Engaging stakeholders in dialogue
Source: SRSP

Sylvester Baguma,
Principal Knowledge
Management Officer and
M&E Specialist, Directorate
of Agricultural Technology
Promotion, National
Agricultural Research
Organisation - Secretariat

MY PERSONAL JOURNEY IN
INSTITUTIONALIZING M4SDI IN NARO,
UGANDA

What struck me about the approach in particular was the way in which it integrates existing methods and approaches for planning, monitoring and evaluation from a people-, learning- and context-oriented perspective.

In 2006, I had the opportunity to participate in an IFAD-funded initiative, the Strengthening Managing for Impact Programme (SMIP), aimed at testing the extent to which the managing for sustainable development impact approach could be used to enhance the impact of pro-poor interventions. The initiative was implemented in East and Southern Africa from 2006 to 2010. The exposure I got was invaluable and has left an indelible mark on my professional life. I came to appreciate that managing development initiatives and organizations was not simply a matter of applying a particular management approach and successfully carrying out project activities. Managing an initiative/organization for sustainable development impact calls for the institutionalization of management approaches tailored to meet the specific needs of the initiative/organization. What struck me about the approach in particular was the way in which it integrates existing methods and approaches for planning, monitoring and evaluation from a people-, learning- and context-oriented perspective. I became even more convinced of the workability of the approach when I saw the impact of the initiative on the ground.

Currently, I work as the Principal Knowledge Management Officer at the National Agricultural Research Organisation (NARO) in Uganda. At the time of my involvement with SMIP, I had another job function within the organization and I remember then that I was deeply concerned about mounting pressures on NARO to demonstrate results and impact of agricultural research agendas. This spurred me to critically reflect on ways my organization could respond effectively to these demands bearing in mind my experiences under SMIP. It was then that I decided to develop an action plan to introduce the M4SDI approach to my organization with the hope that my colleagues would eventually come to see its merit. Unfortunately, I only got as far as presenting a briefing paper and conducting a sensitization seminar. However, once I'd taken the time to critically reflect on why my plan was not enthusiastically received, I realized that it was because NARO did not have the requisite capacities and conditions to implement the approach.

This did not deter me and I decided to take a slightly different approach. So whenever I was given the opportunity to give a talk, I would also highlight the importance of managing agricultural research organizations and agendas for results and how the M4SDI approach could help in this regard. And although many colleagues appreciated my "sermons", I was unable to muster much support from the research managers.

Nevertheless, I persisted in my efforts. I tried many times to convince management to send some members of staff to CDI in an effort to promote awareness of the M4SDI approach and how it can enhance the work of NARO as well as develop much needed planning, monitoring and evaluation competencies. Eventually one member of staff was trained, but she left the organization shortly thereafter. In 2013, I spotted a rare opportunity to apply to Nuffic for funding to support tailor-made courses and subsequently submitted a proposal to train NARO top management in the M4SDI approach. My proposal was successful, and in June 2015 a member of CDI staff and I trained 25 staff members (mainly M&E officers and a few top managers) over a course of two weeks. In my opinion, NARO's "eureka" moment came around that time when at the end of the training workshop NARO managers resolved to develop and fund a proposal to train staff. And in October 2015 we conducted a one-week training course for all of NARO's top managers (24 in total).

The trainings have led to a number of changes at NARO. For the first time in the history of the organization, roughly 10% of its budget has been allocated to support M&E activities. A task team has been put in place to ensure that M4SDI is institutionalized, and the Capacity Development and Mentoring Programme is playing a key role in this process. For example, three training courses for 92 staff have taken place between December 2015 and January 2017. New staff have been recruited to enhance M&E practice and strengthen strategic guidance and effective operations processes. Much time and energy have also gone into putting in place systems, processes and procedures to support effective operations. Creating an organization that is people-, learning- and context-oriented has not been easy, but we have made enormous strides. Attention is also being given to developing effective communication skills within the organization.

NARO and its research institutes are currently in the process of developing strategic plans for their respective organizations using a range of tools and methods. It has been wonderful to observe how management and staff have been putting their training into action, conducting situation analyses and developing their Theories of Change (or revising them) in order to understand complex issues and develop an appropriate plan. All this is being done with the vibrant participation of key stakeholders.

Institutionalizing the M4SDI approach in NARO has clearly not been easy. Initially, I encountered a lot of resistance, but patience, persistence and a strong desire to see my organization become stronger, more resilient and have more impact have paid off. However, no man is an island. Our success is also due to supportive leadership, the commitment of like-minded colleagues and a willingness of management and staff to embrace change.

NARO staff screening of cassava varieties for resistance to cassava brown streak disease.
Source: NARO

Simone van Vugt,
CDI, Wageningen University
& Research, Coordinator of
the BENEFIT Partnership
Dawit Alemu, Manager,
BENEFIT Partnership
Seblewengel Tesfaye,
M&E Specialist, BENEFIT
Partnership

DEALING WITH COMPLEX SYSTEMS
AND POWER THROUGH ENGAGEMENT
AND LEARNING: BENEFIT
PARTNERSHIP, ETHIOPIA

The M4SDI approach has been invaluable in helping to manage the BENEFIT Partnership and meet challenges as they arise, especially in relation to engaging staff and stakeholders from diverse backgrounds.

Agriculture is crucial to the Ethiopian economy. According to the Foodsecurityethiopia.nl platform, the combined support of the Netherlands Embassy in Ethiopia and its partners for small-scale farmers and the commercial sector is bridging traditional areas of aid and trade in Ethiopia. In December 2015, the Bilateral Ethiopian-Netherlands Effort for Food, Income and Trade (BENEFIT) Partnership, was launched to improve sustainable food production, incomes, markets and trade among rural households. The Partnership is ambitious, aiming to reach around 3 million smallholder farmers with improved agricultural practices and technologies, 230 cooperatives and associations and 2,500 small- and medium-sized enterprises and entrepreneurs by 2019. It also expects to train 1,800 research and extension staff at various levels and hopes to facilitate the direct investment of 22 Dutch/international companies. The Partnership has been working in policy dialogue and advocacy, developing strategic partnerships with knowledge-based institutions, private-sector institutions and commodity platforms and has conducted studies to support evidence-based policy-making in the seed sector and address major bottlenecks hampering the uptake of technologies within the sector.

The BENEFIT Partnership encompasses a coordinating unit and four projects: the Integrated Seed Sector Development (ISSD) project; the Capacity Building for Scaling up of Evidence-Based Best Practices in Agricultural Production in Ethiopia (CASCAPE) project; the Ethiopia-Netherlands Trade Facility for Agricultural Growth (ENTAG) project; and the Sesame Business Network (SBN) project. Prior to being incorporated into the BENEFIT Partnership, ISSD, CASCAPE and SBN had been operating in Ethiopia for a number of years and have had some measure of success in enhancing knowledge-sharing, learning, the uptake of innovations and widespread collaboration among a variety of stakeholders. A key idea behind the BENEFIT Partnership is that by placing all these projects under one umbrella, synergies will arise in expertise and collaboration at the policy and implementation levels and result in greater impact on the ground.

CHAPTER 9

However, for this type of partnership to work successfully, understanding the complex context in which the projects operate is very important. It is also imperative to be alert to the many changes taking place, ranging from political tensions and conflicts to changes in the prices of commodities and selected crops (e.g. sesame, wheat). This includes understanding who the many stakeholders are, their interests and power relations. With respect to the internal environment, it involves trying to understand the dynamics within the respective projects, what the issues of concern are and how to harmonize, for example, the different M&E and MIS systems which were designed to meet the needs of the specific projects.

According to Simone van Vugt, Dawit Alemu and Seblewengel Tesfaye, the M4SDI approach has been invaluable in helping them manage the Partnership and meet challenges as they arise, especially in relation to engaging staff and stakeholders from diverse backgrounds. From the very onset of the Partnership, they have been keen to create a learning environment where BENEFIT partners and key stakeholders can freely discuss successes and failures, and re-think and co-develop a Theory of Change based on the four projects and coordination unit. This also includes developing related indicators and strategies.

To aid the process, an M&E think tank comprising managers and coordinators with strong links to the communication staff has been set up and an overarching M&E system is being developed in collaboration with key stakeholders such as the donor, managers and coordinators. This system also incorporates the project-based M&E systems for ISSD, CASCAPE, ENTAG and SBN. Strong considerations in shaping the system to meet current needs include the ToC for the Partnership, donor accountability requirements, and indicators agreed by the donor and key stakeholders based on available funding.

The Partnership faces other challenges. It has been a juggling act trying to deal with multiple stakeholders and engaging them in core processes. Power relations within and outside the Partnership are complex and it is difficult to work out how to empower stakeholders given their own interests, context and funder requirements. Other issues that the team have been dealing with include determining whether the information is reliable, which information to share and how much to share and with whom, in order to avoid information being used by powerful actors to the detriment of others.

Members of the coordinating unit have found that, to meet these challenges and manage effectively, tremendous time has to be spent communicating with stakeholders regularly, convincing them of the need for change and involving them in various processes (e.g. ToC and M&E) in order to get them to buy into the change process. In addition to unstructured monitoring of the external environment, biannual meetings are held internally to monitor context. Meetings are also held among team members to discuss issues that affect project operations. Furthermore, the unit stimulates teamwork through learning events that enable the sharing of cross-cutting or specific themes per project and the development of baselines to monitor the effects of the Partnership.

Also, the team is continuously learning from what works and what emerges, and improving internal systems based on their interaction with stakeholders. They realise the importance of asking powerful questions: Why are the changes happening or not happening? What are the triggers and leverage points that we, together with others, can "push" and "pull" to bring about change? What are the triggers (people, environment, economic, social and political elements) beyond our influence, and yet unknown, which may have an effect on the envisaged changes? Whose changes are we trying to influence? How can we monitor, learn and react in relation to the projects we are implementing? What are the bigger questions we want to pursue and with what kind of methods and tools? What are our own paradigms and perceptions? What are the power dynamics in the areas we are working?

Asking these questions, and engaging people in learning processes helps them to better understand and make sense of the complex system in which they work, including the power dynamics. It also helps them to be systemic in their approach and to remain focussed and be able to respond, in part, to challenges such as power relation concerns, and multiple stakeholder interests, donor requirements, and what information to share with whom. However, with time the team hopes that the internal support systems also develop and become integrated into the Partnership, and that learning and the flexibility to respond to change in a complex context will become part and parcel of the culture of the BENEFIT Partnership. The investment in people in the BENEFIT Partnership is already bearing fruit, through strengthened relationships and team spirit, and this will help support managing for sustainable development impact in the face of complexity.

Wheat from breeder seed
Source: Mirjam Schaap, CDI

CHAPTER 9

ANNEXES

---

1. LIST OF SELECTED METHODS AND APPROACHES FOR M4SDI

2. MAKING A DIFFERENCE WITH EVALUATIONS

3. EVALUATION QUESTIONS AND EVALUATION DESIGNS

4. RECOMMENDED QUANTITATIVE AND QUALITATIVE DATA ANALYSIS PROCEDURES FOR DESIGNING MIXED METHODS STUDIES

From the previous chapters, we have seen that to make full use of the M4SDI
approach, we will need to draw on a range of M&E methods and approaches. For an
explanation of what we mean by methods and approaches see Chapter 8 Box 8.9
'Methods, methodology, approach (M&E): What's the difference?'

M4SDI is not about creating a new set of methods and approaches; rather, M4SDI
makes use of existing tried and tested methods and approaches. The choice of
methods and approaches used will need to address a particular purpose and
connect to context specifics, including stakeholder backgrounds, interests and
preferences. In the table below, we suggest a number of methods, approaches
and options, which we have found to be useful in a range of situations. It is by no
means a comprehensive list. For an expanded list of methods and approaches and
how to use them, visit our M4SDI portal. Other useful websites include the MSP
portal and the BetterEvaluation website. The MSP tool guide (Brouwer et al. 2015) is
also a good resource to use.

Chapter	Topic	Methods, approaches, options
2. Dealing with change in complex systems	Systems thinking, complexity	Critical systems heuristics Cynefin framework Developmental evaluation Narratives/storytelling Rich picture | Ritual dissent Soft systems methodology
3. Key orientations	People orientation: teamwork, dealing with diversity and power	Belbin team roles Conflict styles (Thomas Kilmann conflict mode instrument) Option one-and-a-half | Power ranking Team development (Tuckman)
	Learning orientation	Kolb's learning styles Reflection methods (manual)
	Context orientation	Dialogue | Institutional analysis Narratives, storytelling Rich picture | Risk management
4. Capacities and conditions	Change management	Five colours of change Four quadrants of change
	Facilitation	Reflection methods (manual) Facilitating multi-stakeholder partnerships (MSP guide)
	Leadership competency	Situational leadership
	Organizational capacity assessment/ development	5Cs framework 7-S model Appreciative inquiry
	Strategic foresight competency	Scenario analysis/planning
	Strategic thinking	Brainstorming | Creativity tools | Guided fantasy Scenario analysis/planning Soft systems methodology Six thinking hats (De Bono) Wheel of multiple perspectives
5. Communication	Communication	Asking powerful questions Generative listening Giving feedback Non-violent communication (NVC) Silence | Socratic dialogue

Chapter	Topic	Methods, approaches, options
6. Strategic guidance	Situation analysis (see the data collection section for methods you can use to support your analysis)	Appreciative inquiry Drivers and constrainers of change Force field analysis Scenario analysis Soft systems methodology Supply chain analysis Sustainable livelihoods security framework Value chain mapping
	Stakeholder analysis	Actor analysis matrix (RAAKS) Actor matrix Alignment, influence and interest matrix Fast arrangement mapping Needs-fears mapping Network mapping or net-mapping
	Strategic planning	Appreciative inquiry Assumption-Based Planning Logical Framework Approach/logical framework matrix (logframe) Outcome mapping Scenario planning Theory of Change Visioning
7. Effective operations	Financial planning and management	Budget Critical Path Method Expense Tracking Sheet
	Human resource management	Contracts, agreements Employee evaluation forms Screening
	Operational planning	Gantt chart Timeline charts
	Procurement and contract management	Contracts, agreements, procurement policies
8. Monitoring and evaluation	M&E approaches and options	Appreciative inquiry Beneficiary assessment Case study Collaborative outcomes reporting Configurational Comparative Methods Democratic evaluation Developmental evaluation Empowerment evaluation Experimental approaches: RCTs Horizontal evaluation Innovation history Institutional histories

6

7

	Livelihood Asset Status Tracking
	Most significant change technique
	Outcome harvesting
	Outcome mapping
	Participants assessment of development (PADev)
	Participatory evaluation
	Participatory Impact Assessment and Learning Approach (PIALA)
	Quasi-experimental approaches
	Realist evaluation | Real-time evaluation (RTE)
	Reflexive monitoring in action | SenseMaker
	Social Return on Investment (SROI)
	Theory-based approaches for causal inference: process tracing, contribution analysis
	Utilization-Focused Evaluation
Data collection	Balanced scorecard
	Community institutional and resources mapping
	Diaries, journals, self-reported checklists
	Focus groups | Hierarchical card sorting
	Interviews: key informant, structured, semi-structured interviews
	Institutional analysis
	Livelihood Asset Status Tracking
	Mobile data collection
	Observation | Photography
	Prioritizing and ranking
	Problem definition worksheet
	Problem tree | Questionnaires
	Rich picture | Social mapping | Stories/narratives
	Surveys | SWOT analysis
	Timeline | Trend line
	Tools for institutional, political and social analysis of policy
Data analysis	Numeric analysis
	Qualitative data analysis software packages
	Quantitative data analysis software packages
	Textual analysis
Critical reflection and sense-making	Delphi method | Dialectical methods of inquiry
	Ladder of inference
	Left hand column exercise
	Reflection methods (manual)
	Ritual dissent | Stories without an ending
Communicating and reporting M&E findings	Creative forms of presenting your findings (e.g. stories, pictures and drawings)
	Final report
	Presenting findings at staff forums and conferences
	Storyboards | Theatre | Video for development

8

ANNEXES

A group of evaluators from different parts of the world obtained a grant from EvalPartners to collect stories of positive impact on people's lives. From the stories compiled, eight 'enabling factors' were identified, most of which are closely related to evaluation principles and standards (Evaluations the Make a Difference, 2015: 6-11):

1. **Focus on evaluation impact** (all of the stories): The stories highlighted the importance of evaluations being utilization-focused. The evaluation standard on utility states that evaluations should be carried out in a way that promotes use and impact.

2. **Give voice to the voiceless** (the Nepal story Listening to the Listeners and the Mexican story If You Don't Ask, You Won't See It): These stories reinforce the importance of the principle of stakeholder (beneficiaries) engagement from the start and the propriety standard (i.e. effectively serving the needs of your stakeholders).

3. **Provide credible evidence** (the Papua New Guinea story Evaluation in Action: the Milne Bay Emergency Phone Service): The standard on accuracy underscores how important it is for the evaluation to capture clearly and accurately the perspectives of key stakeholders and gather hard evidence on the initiatives.

4. **Use an approach that supports positive thinking and action** (the Papua New Guinea story): This relates to the principle of being situational-responsive. It involves recognizing what works, what should be continued, scaled up, adapted or stopped.

5. **Ensure users and intended beneficiaries are engaged through a participatory approach to evaluation** (the Netherlands story Positive Sisters: a Transformative Journey, and from Canada The Power of Community-owned Data): Here the utility standard is important and related to the principle of engagement, where community participation was important in increasing evaluation impact.

6. **Embed evaluation within the initiative/organization** (the Kenya story Learning and Earning: Training That Works): This ensures that evaluations are built into the initiative/organization at an early stage when data are collected and there is feedback on results regularly, so that stakeholders can make adjustments way before the final report is even written. This shows the importance of engaging stakeholders in a process of learning and adapting and responding to changes throughout the life of an initiative/ organization.

7. **Really care about the evaluation** (stories from Papua New Guinea, Mexico and the Netherlands): This demonstrates that once people are fully engaged they can become really committed and learn from the evaluations so that they can make better decisions.

8. **Champion the evaluation with decision-makers** (Sri Lanka story Salvaging Sri Lanka's Small and Medium Businesses): How an evaluation led to rapid change. This points to the principle of engaging and (targeting) key stakeholders, including decision-makers (some of whom are possible champions) and ensuring there is leadership support for evaluation and related change processes.

Source: Evaluations that Make a Difference, 2015

Key impact evaluation questions	Related evaluation questions	Underlying assumptions	Requirements	Suitable designs
To what extent can a specific (net) impact be attributed to the intervention in this setting?	· What is the net effect of the intervention? · How much of the impact can be attributed to the intervention? · What would have happened without the intervention?	· Expected outcomes and the intervention itself clearly understood and specifiable. · Likelihood of primary cause and primary effect. · Interest in a particular intervention rather than generalization.	· Can manipulate interventions. · Sufficient numbers (beneficiaries, households, etc.) for statistical analysis.	· Experiments (e.g. randomized control trials, quasi-experimental designs). · Statistical studies (e.g. statistical modelling, longitudinal studies). · Hybrids with 'Case'-based and participatory designs.
Has the intervention made a difference on its own?	· What causes are necessary or sufficient for the effect? · Was the intervention needed to produce the effect? · Would these impacts have happened anyhow?	· There are several relevant causes that need to be disentangled. · Interventions are just one part of a causal package.	· Comparable cases where a common set of causes are present and evidence exists as to their potency.	· Experiments. · Theory-based evaluation, see Box 8.10 (e.g. Contribution Analysis, Theory of Change). · Case-based designs e.g. Qualitative Comparative Analysis (QCA).
How has the intervention made a difference?	· How and why have the impacts come about? · What causal factors have resulted in the observed impacts? · Has the intervention resulted in any unintended impacts? · For whom has the intervention made a difference?	· Interventions interact with other causal factors. · It is possible to clearly represent the causal process through which the intervention made a difference – may require 'theory development'.	· Understanding how supporting & contextual factors connect intervention with effects. · Theory that allows for the identification of supporting factors – proximate, contextual and historical.	· Theory-based evaluation especially 'realist' variants. · Participatory approaches (e.g. empowerment evaluation, policy dialogue, Collaborative Action Research).
Will the intervention work elsewhere?	· Can this 'pilot' be transferred elsewhere and scaled up? · Is the intervention sustainable? · What generalizable lessons have we learned about impact?	· What has worked in one place can work somewhere else. · Stakeholders will cooperate in joint donor/beneficiary evaluations.	· Generic understanding of contexts e.g. typologies of context. · Clusters of causal packages. · Innovation diffusion mechanisms.	· Participatory approaches. · Natural experiments. · Synthesis studies (e.g. realist-based synthesis, narrative synthesis).

Source: Stern et al., 2012: 48.

ANNEX 4. RECOMMENDED QUANTITATIVE AND QUALITATIVE DATA ANALYSIS PROCEDURES FOR DESIGNING MIXED METHODS STUDIES

Quantitative data analysis procedures	Qualitative data analysis procedures

PREPARE DATA FOR ANALYSIS

• Develop a coding system using numeric values suitable for input into a quantitative statistics program. • Create and refine coding categories: this is important because it helps you determine the number and kinds of distinctions made within a variable and how you differentiate them. For example, if you are looking at the variable 'wealth' you might decide on having 3 categories – high or middle income, poor. • Code the data. • Enter the data into your statistics program. • Scrutinize the database to see if the coded values are correctly coded and whether there are outliers. • Recode your data. • Prepare the codebook.	• Take time to organize your documents and data collected. • Transcribe all your data (text) obtained in the field, e.g. from taped interviews, diaries, notes, etc. • Prepare the data so that it can be analysed. • If you intend to use a qualitative software program, e.g. NVivo, you can pre-code variables/questions so that you can do auto-coding in the program.

EXAMINE THE DATA

• Manually go through the data. • Write down your main observations, your analyses. • Determine if there are any trends or patterns.	• Read everything to get a sense of the data gathered. • Make notes on the main ideas, concepts, themes. • Prepare your qualitative codebook; in your guidelines try to use the terms and semantics of the respondents as well as linguistic cues, as this increases accuracy in the way coders apply codes to text (MacQueen, 1998).

ANALYSE THE DATA

• Select the most appropriate statistical test. • Analyse your data so that you can test your hypotheses or address your evaluation questions. • Document your inferential tests, effect sizes and confidence intervals. • Use a quantitative statistics program.	• Code the data: auto-coding for information generated through pre-coded questionnaires. Also, code data into new 'nodes' e.g. around particular topics or themes. This can also be categorized into sub-themes ('child nodes'). • Make sure you use data from different sources, including interviews, observations, documents, etc. • You can work with pre-coded variables ('nodes') and develop new variables or nodes. • A qualitative software program can be used to analyse your data (e.g. NVivo). This type of program will mainly help you to organize your data in line with particular topics or themes. You will still need to analyse the results yourself, preferably in collaboration with those who were involved in the data collection process so that they can help explain some of the findings.

Quantitative data analysis procedures	Qualitative data analysis procedures

REPRESENT AND INTERPRET THE RESULTS

· Results can be represented in statements, tables, figures. This will help in explaining and interpreting the results and respond to the evaluation questions. · Where possible, compare findings with previous evaluation studies.	· Results can be represented by way of descriptions/narratives, visual models, figures, preferably by category or by the evaluation question. · Where possible, compare findings with previous evaluations or studies.

VALIDATE THE DATA AND FINDINGS

Reliability is concerned with whether the method or tool used to measure your research object is consistent and dependable. Validity refers to how well the concept being measured fits with what is actually measured (e.g. if you want to measure agricultural productivity but you are actually measuring production then your measurement would not be valid) and whether the means of measure are accurate. · It is important to use external standards to validate data and findings. · Ensure that you validate and check the reliability of results from a similar method, applied in a different context. · Check the validity and reliability of the data used in the evaluation. · Determine the internal validity (reasons for the outcomes) and external validity (ability to utilize, with confidence, the findings in other situations) of the findings.	Reliability of qualitative data is concerned with whether data are collected in a consistent manner that makes them dependable/trustworthy. Validity is concerned with the quality and rigour of the evaluation – how well you have captured what is 'real' to the people being studied · Try to use standards that are relevant to the evaluators, participants and reviewers. · Employ validation strategies (triangulation): This ideally would have been done already by integrating data from different sources in the data to be coded (see above). Stakeholder validation workshops, management meetings, getting opinions from experts and key informants can be used as a means of validating data. · Involve key stakeholders in the validation and sense-making of findings. This will help support the use of the findings.

Source: Adapted from Creswell and Plano Clark, 2011

Accountability: Obligation, e.g. of an organization, funding agency, or development initiative, to demonstrate to stakeholders that work has been conducted in compliance with agreed rules and standards or to report fairly and accurately on performance results vis-à-vis mandated roles and/or plans. Accountability is not only upward, e.g., to funders, but it is also downward to primary stakeholders and sideward to key stakeholders.

Activities: These are the means through which outputs are produced (logframe).

Adaptive management: A process that integrates the design, management, and monitoring and evaluation of a development initiative to provide a framework for testing assumptions, adaptation and learning. This implies guiding an initiative/organization towards change, whilst learning from and adapting to a changing context.

Annual work plan and budget (AWPB): This is used in effective operations and lays the groundwork for developing more detailed work plans (e.g. on a quarterly or monthly basis).

Assumptions (logframe): These are external factors which may positively or negatively influence the initiative events described by the narrative summary in the logframe, including any external phenomena beyond the control of the initiative/organization.

Assumptions (ToC): These are statements about how and why we expect a set of changes to come about as depicted in the pathways of change. They form the basis of a Theory of Change (ToC), explaining our thought processes, reasoning and how we arrive at certain conclusions. They are hard to articulate because they are deeply held perceptions that have become 'rules of thumb' that are taken for granted. There are four types of assumptions: causal links; operations and the external context; paradigm or world view; dominant belief systems.

Baseline information: This is information about the initial starting point or situation before any intervention has taken place.

Capabilities: Are the collective abilities of an initiative/organization to do something either within its system or externally. Capabilities are the result of conditions and collective competencies of an initiative/organization. (Adapted from Keijzer et al., 2011)

Capacities and conditions: Are about shaping the readiness of leaders and practitioners to engage in and manage a development initiative/organization towards sustainable development impact.

Capacity: This is the emergent outcome of a system. It is the combination of the individual competencies of leaders, staff of an initiative/organization, development practitioners and other key stakeholders involved in an initiative/organization, the collective capabilities, assets and relationships that enable an initiative or organizational system to create social value. (Adapted from Baser and Morgan, 2008)

Capacity development: The process through which the capacity of an initiative/organization and key stakeholders is enhanced. It is also the change that focuses on improvement in the wider society or environment. (Adapted from Baser and Morgan, 2008)

Communication: Is the way in which we convey our ideas, thoughts and actions. It is integral to all the M4SDI processes and is the basis for good relationships and collaboration, which is especially important when working in complex contexts. Complexity calls for dialogue.

Communication strategy: Helps guide the initiative's/organization's communication process, outlining how to communicate with stakeholders both internally and externally to enhance learning, build consensus, knowledge and decision-making capacities to facilitate strategic guidance, effective operations and M&E processes for impact. It is not cast in stone, as circumstances relating to an initiative/organization can change, and you may have to modify it or even change it entirely.

Competencies: This refers to the energies, mindsets, skills and motivations of leaders, development practitioners and other key stakeholders. (Adapted from Keijzer et al., 2011)

Complex system: Has large numbers of interacting elements; the interactions are nonlinear, and minor changes can have disproportionately major consequences; it is dynamic (Brouwer et al 2015: 96).

Complexity: Is related to the nature of the relationship between cause and effect, and this requires different forms of analysis, planning, monitoring and management. Complex contexts are dynamic, often unpredictable and cause-effect relationships can only be known in hindsight.

Conditions: Are the circumstances internally and externally that come about as a result of, for example, a combination of assets, connections, formal and informal policies, resources, culture, power relations, principles or values.

Conflict: Involves a disagreement between two parties. It can emerge gradually, or develop rapidly in response to significant events.

Context orientation: This is about understanding and responding to the internal and external environments in which an initiative/organization operates. This includes understanding: the wider setting (e.g. political dynamics, policies, future trends, key actors, etc.); the specific context (e.g. community setting); organizational structures and processes underpinning the initiative/organization; and the dynamics of staff and stakeholders.

Critical reflection: Involves thinking deeply in order to draw lessons, learning from what worked and what did not work, why this happened and what this means. Critical reflection and sense-making are a way to question and analyse experiences, observations, theories, beliefs and/or assumptions.

Development initiative: An initiative focused on empowerment and eliminating poverty. This can be a project, programme, partnership, network, or any other initiative.

Developmental evaluation: 'Supports innovation development to guide adaptation to emergent and dynamic realities in complex environments. Innovations can take the form of new projects, programs, products, organizational changes, policy reforms and systems interventions' (Patton 2011: 1).

Dialogue: A 'conversation in which people think together in a relationship, suspend their judgment, and together create something new (new social realities). People who are in dialogue set out to understand the other person's perspective, even if they don't agree with it (Brouwer et al 2015: 96).

Effective operations: Are about turning strategic plans and ideas into practical implementation procedures and measures that relate to every aspect of the initiative/ organization (i.e. project management, finance management, human resource management, operational planning, procurement and contract management, maintenance management, information management, and coordination and communication).

Effectiveness: A measure of the extent to which a project attains its objectives at the goal or purpose level, i.e. the extent to which it has attained, or is expected to attain, its relevant objectives efficiently and in a sustainable way.

Efficiency: A measure of how economically inputs (funds, expertise, time, etc.) are converted into outputs.

Evaluability: This is the extent to which an initiative can be evaluated in a credible and reliable way.

Evaluation: There are many definitions for evaluation. One definition by Scriven (1991: 1) describes evaluation as 'the process of determining the merit, worth and value of things, and evaluations are the product of that process'. At the other end of the spectrum is Patton (2008: 39) who

describes programme evaluation as 'the systematic collection of information about the activities, characteristics, and results of programs to make judgments about the program, improve or further develop program effectiveness, inform decisions about future programming, and/or increase understanding'.

Evaluation or performance question: A question that helps guide the information seeking and analysis process, to help understand the performance of an initiative/ organization. (Adapted from Guijt and Woodhill, 2002: 4-3)

Evaluative culture: This refers to an initiative/organization that: engages in regular and systematic critical self-reflection, and which challenges and improves the work it is doing; engages in evidence-based learning done in a structured manner; learns lessons not only from successes, but also from mistakes; stimulates knowledge-sharing among staff and partners/ key stakeholders; and encourages innovation. (Adapted from Mayne, 2008)

Evaluative thinking: This is critical thinking applied within the context of evaluation that involves identifying assumptions, posing powerful questions, pursuing deeper understanding through reflection and perspective taking, and informing decisions in preparation for action. (Adapted from Buckley et al., 2015)

Generative listening: This is the highest level of listening (of four levels) identified by Scharmer (2008). It goes far beyond the downloading, factual and empathic listening levels. At this fourth level of listening, we generate new understanding and insights, not only about the current situation but also about future pathways.

Goal: This refers to broad (sustainable development) issues to which the initiative/organization seeks to contribute (logframe).

Impact: This is defined as the positive and negative changes produced by a development initiative/organization, directly or indirectly, intended or unintended. This involves the main impacts and effects resulting from the

initiative/organization on sustainable development (OECD, 2016).

Indicator: A quantitative or qualitative factor or variable that provides a simple and reliable basis for assessing/indicating achievement, change or performance.

Inputs: These concern what is actually needed to run the activities, including the budget (logframe).

Iterative process: Involves going back and revising steps in a process.

Knowledge Management: A range of practices used in organizations to identify, create, represent, distribute and enable adoption of insights and experiences which comprise knowledge, either embodied in individuals or embedded in organizational processes or practice (Kusters et al., 2011).

Learning orientation: This is about creating an environment where learning takes place at the individual, group, organizational and societal levels. This includes not only understanding, but also sense-making to inform strategic and operational decision-making.

Logical framework approach: An analytical, presentational and management approach that involves problem analysis, stakeholder analysis, developing a hierarchy of objectives and selecting a preferred implementation strategy. It helps to identify strategic elements (inputs, outputs, purpose, goal) and their causal relationships, as well as the external assumptions (risks) that may influence success and failure of a development initiative (Kusters et al., 2011).

Logical framework matrix (or logframe): A matrix that is often used as a summary (consisting of four rows and four columns) and to communicate how change is expected to happen. The logframe is a planning tool that assumes a linear cause-and-effect relationship.

Managing for Development Results (MfDR): An approach that centres on gearing all human, financial, technological and natural resources - domestic and external - to achieve desired development results. It shifts the focus from inputs (e.g., money) to measurable results (e.g. what can be achieved with the money) at all phases of the development process (Kusters et al. 2011).

Managing for Sustainable Development Impact (M4SDI):
An integrated approach, results-oriented management approach, which can be used across a range of sectors and domains in a variety of contexts, and aims to contribute towards the Sustainable Development Goals (SDGs). It seeks to integrate ideas and practices from a range of approaches and methodologies for planning, monitoring and evaluation, using appropriate methods or tools that engage people in a process of learning and adaptation. It is specifically aimed at strengthening the readiness of leaders, decision-makers and development practitioners to effectively manage their initiatives/organizations in complex settings.

Meaningful participation: This involves engaging stakeholders to such an extent that it is relevant to them and that they are prepared to take action, leading to change.

Means of verification (MOV): This refers to how (methods) you collect data.

Monitoring: A continuous process of data collection and analysis for performance indicators in order to compare a development initiative's progress with its intended results.

Monitoring and evaluation (M&E):
Although monitoring and evaluation are different processes, they are intricately linked and go hand in hand. M&E supports strategic guidance and effective operations processes and includes providing insights into managing responsibly in terms of focusing on the envisaged sustainable development impact, tracking progress, keeping an eye on dynamics in the internal and external context, and facilitating strategic decision-making. An important feature of M&E is the process itself, as it can help enhance learning about what works and what emerges, so as to inform strategic and operational decision-making.

M&E approach: This is an integrated way of conceptualizing, designing and conducting M&E, which is often underpinned by theories, concepts and values, and includes an integrated set of options to do some or all of the tasks involved in M&E.

M&E framework: Relates to the strategic plan for M&E. The framework is important for guiding monitoring and evaluation within a programme, or across programmes in an initiative/organization. It is based on the M&E policy. (Adapted from BetterEvaluation n.d.)

M&E matrix: This is part of the M&E plan and provides detailed information about how the initiative's/organization's strategy (e.g. Theory of Change) and operational plan and its context will be monitored and evaluated. (Adapted from BetterEvaluation n.d.)

M&E method: Are all those techniques, tools and processes that are used to monitor and evaluate an initiative/organization.

M&E methodology: Refers to a set of procedures, methods and processes used to undertake M&E.

M&E plan: Relates to the operational plan for M&E, and is based on the M&E framework. (Adapted from BetterEvaluation n.d.)

M&E policy: Outlines the definition, concept, role and use of monitoring and evaluation within an organization/initiative. (Adapted from BetterEvaluation n.d.)

M&E system: An integrated system of reflection and communication that supports implementation of an initiative. A well-functioning M&E system manages to integrate the more formal, data-oriented side commonly associated with the task of M&E, with informal monitoring and communication. (Adapted from Guijt and Woodhill, 2002: 4-3)

Multi-stakeholder partnership (MSP): 'A process of interactive learning, empowerment and participatory governance that enables stakeholders with interconnected problems and ambitions, but often differing interests, to be collectively

innovative and resilient when faced with the emerging risks, crises, and opportunities of a complex and changing environment' (Brouwer et al., 2015: 18).

Nonviolent communication (NVC): It is a powerful tool used to resolve conflict based on the principles of non-violence.

Output: This is the intended benefit – what an initiative/organization hopes to achieve (logframe).

People orientation: This is about acknowledging the central role that human interactions play in complex development processes. This involves engaging people meaningfully to understand and work with others in complex contexts involving different interests, perspectives, relationships, and power dynamics.

Primary intended users: People who are responsible for applying the evaluation findings and implementing the evaluation recommendations.

Public procurement: Is described as 'the process by which public authorities, such as government departments or local authorities, purchase work, goods or services from companies' (European Commission, 2017).

Public-private partnerships: These are mechanisms or long-term arrangements that governments enter into with the private sector to provide works and services to the public.

Purpose (of M&E): The reasons for carrying out M&E e.g. accountability, strategic or operational management, policymaking, knowledge development.

Relevance: The extent to which the objectives of an initiative are consistent with the target group's priorities or needs and, where applicable, the donor's policies.

Results-based management (RBM): An approach to management whereby it is ensured that processes, products and services contribute to the achievement of clearly stated results, through integrated processes of planning, implementation and monitoring and evaluation.
Scaling: This refers to 'strategies

and approaches… [aimed at realizing] the potential of relatively isolated inventions, innovations, and developments benefitting people and situations more widely' (Wigboldus and Brouwers, 2016: 16).

Scope: This refers to the boundaries of an M&E system.

Self-evaluation: Evaluation aimed at promoting learning through the sharing of experiences and reflection so as to bring about change within the individual or organization.

Sense-making: The ability or attempt to make sense of situations by trying to understand connections in complex situations, and involves questioning and analysing experiences, observations, theories, beliefs and/ or assumptions with our stakeholders. More specifically, sense-making is the process of creating awareness and understanding in situations of high complexity or uncertainty for the purpose of decision-making.

Situation analysis: This is a process of analysing the problems or opportunities an initiative/organization aims to address and its causes and consequences.

Situational leadership: Has to do with level of flexibility needed in the leadership style in relation to the maturity of the people being led and the details of the task at hand.

Situational responsiveness: This is the ability of an initiative/organization to respond to internal and external factors and adapt to changes or developments in its environment.

Source of verification: This refers to where you can find data (e.g. reports).

Stakeholder: An agency, organization, group or individual with a direct or indirect interest (stake) in a development initiative, or one who affects or is affected, positively or negatively, by the implementation and outcome of a development initiative.

Strategic guidance: This is about how to manage strategic processes towards sustainable development impact. It includes understanding the situation and its context, making explicit assumptions about how

change happens (ToC) and developing strategies towards agreed (visions of) changes. It also includes navigating within a complex and changing context, using information generated through M&E, as well as providing leadership with strategic thinking, strategic foresight and systems thinking.

Sustainability: The likelihood that the positive effects of a project (such as assets, skills, facilities or improved services) will persist for an extended period after the external assistance ends.

System: consists of interrelated elements with a boundary that determines what is inside of a system and what is outside.

Systems thinking: The ability to view problems and events in relation to whole systems (Brouwer et al 2015). It is about making sense of complexity.

Terms of reference (ToR): Define the tasks and parameters that the evaluation should adhere to, indicating the objectives, planned activities, expected outputs, budget, timetable and responsibilities.

Theory of Action (ToA): It is an operational Theory of Change or strategy for a particular initiative. It shows how an initiative is designed to bring about the desired change.

Theory of Change (ToC): It is concerned with the dynamics of change within a particular context and the causes of change, regardless of any planned intervention. At the heart of a good ToC is the explicit inclusion of values underlying views or perspectives on how change happens, and the assumptions around change and the drivers of change.

Theory-based evaluation: Examines the assumptions underlying the causal chain from inputs and activities to outcomes and impact in great detail.

Transdisciplinarity: Refers to the integration of academic knowledge from various disciplines and non-academic knowledge. Throughout the research process academic and non-academic stakeholders are in dialogue. Societal renewal takes place more and more at the interface

of disciplines with synergy between multiple actors.

Triangulation: This involves using a mix of approaches (e.g., mixed methods, team members or information sources) to cross-check data for validity and reliability.

Utilization-Focused Evaluation: Evaluation done for and with specific intended primary users for specific, intended uses (Patton, 2008: 37).

Work plan: Document containing detailed information on which activities are to be carried out within a given timeframe, how the activities will be done and how they relate to the strategy. For each activity and output there are verifiable indicators, means of verification and assumptions. (Adapted from Guijt and Woodhill, 2000).

ACRONYMS AND ABBREVIATIONS

AWPB Annual Work Plan And Budget

CDI Wageningen Centre for Development Innovation, Wageningen University & Research

DAC Development Assistance Committee (OECD)

EC European Commission

Logframe Logical Framework Matrix

M4SDI Managing For Sustainable Development Impact

M&E Monitoring and Evaluation

MDGs Millennium Development Goals

OECD Organisation for Economic Cooperation and Development

PME Planning, Monitoring And Evaluation

PPP Public-Private Partnership

SDGs Sustainable Development Goals

ToA Theory of Action

ToC Theory of Change

REFERENCES

Chapter 1

Brouwer, J.H., Woodhill, A.J., Hemmati, M., Verhoosel, K.S., and van Vugt, S.M. (2015) *The MSP Guide: How to Design and Facilitate Multi-Stakeholder Partnerships*, Wageningen University and Research – Centre for Development Innovation, Wageningen and Practical Action Publishing, Rugby. Available from: http://www.mspguide.org/msp-guide (accessed 18 January 2017).

Buanes, A. and Jentoft, S. (2009) 'Building Bridges: Institutional Perspectives on Interdisciplinarity', *Futures* 41.7: 446-454.

Guijt, I. and Woodhill, J. (2002) *Managing for Impact in Rural Development: A Guide for Project M&E*, International Fund for Agricultural Development, Rome. Available from http://tinyurl.com/h72dbj2 (accessed 31 December 2016).

OECD (2016) DAC *Criteria for Evaluating Development Assistance* [online]. Available from: http://tinyurl.com/z6rfmvx (accessed 3 March 2017).

Shahin, J., Meyer, T., Kloza, D., Biedenkopf, K. (2014) *Building Bridges, Breaking Barriers: The Smart Approach to Distance between Disciplines in Research Projects* [online], European Commission. Available from: http://tinyurl.com/j2e9s69 (accessed 2 March 2017).

Wigboldus, S. with Brouwers, J. (2016) *Using a Theory of Scaling to Guide Decision Making. Towards a Structured Approach to Support Responsible Scaling of Innovations in the Context of Agrifood Systems*. Wageningen University and Research, Wageningen. Available from: http://tinyurl.com/jlu4bp9 (accessed 2 March 2017).

Chapter 2

Brouwer, J.H., Woodhill, A.J., Hemmati, M., Verhoosel, K.S., and van Vugt, S.M. (2016) *The MSP Guide: How to Design and Facilitate Multi-Stakeholder Partnerships*, Wageningen University and Research – Centre for Development Innovation, Wageningen and Practical Action Publishing, Rugby. Available from: http://www.mspguide.org/msp-guide (accessed 18 January 2017).

Eyben, R., Kidder, T., Rowlands, J. and Bronstein, A. (2008) 'Thinking About Change for Development Practice: A Case Study from Oxfam GB', *Development in Practice* 18(2).

Green, D. (2016) *How Change Happens*, Oxford University Press, Oxford.

Hummelbrunner, R. (2011) 'Systems Thinking and Evaluation', *Evaluation* 17(4): 395-403.

Kurtz, C.F. and Snowden, D.J. (2003) 'The New Dynamics of Strategy: Sense-making in a Complex and Complicated World', *IBM Systems Journal*, 42(3). Available from: http://tinyurl.com/yj2jhzu (accessed 6 March 2017).

Patton, M.Q. (2011) *Developmental Evaluation: Applying Complexity Concepts to Enhance Innovation and Use*, Guilford Press, New York, London.

Rogers, E.M. (2003) *Diffusion of Innovations*, 5th edn, Free Press, New York, NY.

Rotmans, J., Kemp, R. and van Asselt, M. (2001) 'More Evolution than Revolution: Transition Management in Public Policies', Foresight 3(1).

Rowlands, J. (1997) *Questioning Empowerment: Working with Women in Honduras*, Oxfam UK, Oxford and Ireland.

Senge, P. (2006) *The Fifth Discipline: The Art and Practice of the Learning Organization*, rev. edn, Random House, London.

Snowden, D.J. and Boone, M. (2007) 'A Leader's Framework for Decision Making', *Harvard Business Review*, November 2007: 69–76.

Stroh, D.P. (2015) *Systems Thinking for Social Change: A Practical Guide to Solving Complex Problems, Avoiding Unintended Consequences and Achieving Lasting Results*, Chelsea Green Publishing, Vermont.

Waddell, S. (2001) 'NGO's Role in Business Strategies', *Corporate Ethics Monitor*, 13(3).

Waddell, S. (2014) *Addressing the World's Critical Issues as Complex Change Challenges: The state-of-the-field*, Networking Action and Ecosystems Labs.

Williams, B. and Hummelbrunner, R. (2010) *Systems Concepts in Action: A Practitioner's Toolkit*, Stanford University Press, Stanford, California.

Chapter 3

Ambrose, S.A., Bridges, M.W., DiPietro, M., Lovett, M.C. and Norman, M.K. (2010) *How Learning Works: 7 Research-Based Principles for Smart Teaching*, Jossey-Bass, San Francisco.

Argyris, C. and Schön, D.A. (1974) *Theory in Practice: Increasing Professional Effectiveness*. Jossey-Bass, San Francisco.

Arnstein, S.R. (2004) *A Ladder of Citizen Participation* [online]. Available from: http://tinyurl.com/o8byqv4 (accessed 25 February 2017).

Belbin (2015) 'Team Roles in a nutshell', Belbin® [website] <http://tinyurl.com/jftxflk> (accessed 28 February 2017).

Britton, B. (2002) *Learning for change: Principles and Practices of Learning Organisations*, Swedish Mission Council. Available from: http://tinyurl.com/hxyygso (accessed 25 February 2017).

Brouwer, H. and Woodhill, J. with Hemmati, M., Verhoosel, K. and van Vugt S. (2015) *The MSP Guide: How to Design and Facilitate Multi-Stakeholder Partnerships*, Centre for Development Innovation, Wageningen UR, Wageningen.

Burns, D., Howard, J., Lopez-Franco, E., Shahrokh, T. and Wheeler, J. (2013) *Work with Us: How People and Organisations can Catalyse Sustainable Change*, IDS, Brighton. Available from: http://tinyurl.com/zkywcfl (accessed 7 February 2017).

CTA (2012) *Information and Communication Management Strategy Development: A Toolkit for Agricultural* and Rural Development Organisations: Facilitator's Guide, CTA, Wageningen.

Cornwall, A. (2008) 'Unpacking "Participation": Models, Meanings and Practices', Community Development Journal 43:269–283.

CULCokpalad (2015) Leadership and Change [blog] <http://tinyurl.com/jqla353> [accessed 23 February 2017].

FAO (2005) Negotiation and Mediation Techniques for Natural Resource Management, Engel, A. and Korf, B. (eds) Livelihood Support Programme (LSP): An interdepartmental programme for improving support for enhancing livelihoods. FAO, Rome. Available from: http://tinyurl.com/h8nohka [accessed 25 February 2017].

Fisher, R., Ury, W. and Patton, B. (1991) Getting to Yes: Negotiating Agreement Without Giving In, 2nd edn, Houghton Mifflin. Available from: http://tinyurl.com/gprja66 [accessed 8 February 2017].

Hart, R. (1992) Children's Participation: From Tokenism to Citizenship, UNICEF International Child Development Centre, Florence. Available from: http://tinyurl.com/hoo5fbt [accessed 25 February 2017].

Hersey, P. and Blanchard, K. (1993) Management of Organizational Behavior: Utilizing Human Resources. Prentice-Hall Inc, Englewood Cliffs, New Jersey.

Honey, P. and Mumford, A. (1986) The Manual of Learning Styles, Peter Honey Publications Ltd, Maidenhead, Berks.

IDS (2013) Participatory Methods [website] <http://tinyurl.com/h7dk8g6> [accessed 27 February 2017].

IDS (2016) 'Participation', Institute of Development Studies [website] <http://www.ids.ac.uk/team/participation> [accessed 8 February 2015].

James, R. and Wrigley, R. (2007) Investigating the Mystery of Capacity Building: Learning from the Praxis Programme, Praxis Paper 18, International NGO Training and Research Centre, Oxford. Available from: https://tinyurl.com/jpa2xr4 [accessed 12 December 2016].

Kilmann Diagnostics (2016) An overview of the Thomas-Kilmann Conflict Mode Instrument (TKI) [website] <http://tinyurl.com/qxq3ny5> [accessed 12 December 2016].

Kolb, D. (1984) Experiential Learning: Experience as the Source of Learning and Development, Prentice Hall, Englewood Cliffs, New Jersey.

Kotter, J. (2013) 'Leading Change: Why Transformation Efforts Fail', Harvard Business Review. Available from: http://tinyurl.com/h5bmxs4 [accessed 25 February 2017].

Kusters, C.S.L., van Vugt, S.M., Wigboldus, S.A., Williams, B., and Woodhill, J. (2011) Making Evaluations Matter: A Practical Guide for Evaluators, Centre for Development Innovation, Wageningen University & Research Centre, Wageningen.

Manning, C. (2015) Defining conflict resolution [online], Carolyn Manning Consulting Services. Available from: https://tinyurl.com/hd9gdf4 [accessed 8 February 2017].

Mindell, A. (1995) Sitting in the Fire: Large Group Transformation Using Conflict and Diversity, Deep Democracy Exchange. Florence, Oregon and San Francisco, California.

Moore, C.W. (2014) The Mediation Process: Practical Strategies for Resolving Conflict, 4th edn, Jossey-Bass, San Francisco.

Narayan, D. with Patel, R., Schafft, K., Rademacher, A. and Koch-Schulte, S. (2000) Voices of the Poor: Can Anyone Hear Us? The World Bank and Oxford University Press, Inc. Available from: http://tinyurl.com/jpzywwo [accessed 7 February 2017].

NERIS Analytics Limited (2017) 'Personality Types' [website] <www.16personalities.com> [accessed 27 February 2017].

Oxford Dictionary (2016) 'Learning' [website] <https://en.oxforddictionaries.com/definition/learning> [accessed 8 February 2017].

Oxford Policy Management (2013) A Framework for Analysing Participation in Development, Norwegian Agency for Development Cooperation, Oslo. Available from: https://tinyurl.com/j849qun [accessed 12 December 2016].

Pretty, J. (1995) 'Participatory Learning for Sustainable Agriculture', World Development 23/8: 1247–1263.

Sarabdeen, J. (2013) 'Learning Styles and Training Methods', IBIMA Communications 2013: 1–9. Available from: https://tinyurl.com/z24jh3o [accessed 10 February 2017].

Senge, P. (2006) The Fifth Discipline: The Art and Practice of the Learning Organization, rev. edn, Random House, London.

Tilbury, D. (2011) Education for Sustainable Development: An Expert Review of Processes and Learning, UNESCO. Available from: http://tinyurl.com/7uxagkp [accessed 25 February 2017].

Tillett, G. (2000) Resolving Conflict: A Practical Approach, Oxford University Press.

Tritter, J.Q. and McCallum, A. (2006) 'The Snakes and Ladders of User Involvement: Moving Beyond Arnstein', Health Policy, 76/2, Elsevier Limited, Ireland.

Tuckman, B. (1965) 'Developmental Sequence in Small Groups', Psychological Bulletin, 63:384–399

Tuckman, B. and Jensen, M. (1977)' Stages of small group development revisited', Group and Organizational Studies, 2:419–427.

University of Leicester (2016) Honey and Mumford [online]. Available from http://tinyurl.com/ox4bxrz [accessed 25 November 2016].

Wageningen University & Research (2012a) 'Managing for Sustainable Development Impact: Tools and Methods' [website] <http://www.managingforimpact.org/tools> [accessed 27 February 2017].

Wageningen University & Research (2012b) 'Multi-stakeholder Partnerships: Tools and Methods' [website] <http://www.mspguide.org/tools-and-methods> [accessed 27 February 2017].

Chapter 4

Baser, H. and Morgan, P. with Bolger, J., Brinkerhoff, D., Land, A., Taschereau, S., Watson, D. and Zinke, J. (2008) *Capacity, Change and Performance, Study* report, Discussion Paper No. 59B, ECDPM, Maastricht. Available from: http://tinyurl.com/hv4aypf [accessed 7 October 2016].

Brouwer, J.H., Woodhill, A.J., Hemmati, M., Verhoosel, K.S., and van Vugt, S.M. (2015) *The MSP Guide: How to Design and Facilitate Multi-Stakeholder Partnerships*, Wageningen University and Research - Centre for Development Innovation, Wageningen and Practical Action Publishing, Rugby. Available from: http://www.mspguide. org/msp-guide [accessed 18 January 2017].

Conway, M. (2009) 'Strategic thinking: What it is and how to do it' [Slideshare presentation]. Available from: http://tinyurl.com/zz8c6oy [accessed 24 January 2017].

Conway, M. (2016) *Foresight Infused Strategy: A How-to Guide for Using Foresight in Practice*, Thinking Futures, Melbourne.

DFID (1999) *Sustainable Livelihoods Guidance Sheets* Nos 1–8, Department for International Development, London.

Engleberg, I. and Wynn, D. (1997) *Working in Groups: Communication Principles and Strategies*, Houghton Mifflin, Boston.

European Centre for Development Policy Management (2009) 'Capacity change and performance: Insights and implications for development cooperation', in M.W. Blokland, G.J. Alaerts, J.M. Kaspersma, M. Hare (eds) *Capacity Development for Improved Water Management*, UNESCO-IHE for Water Education and UN-Water Decade Programme on Capacity Development [online]. Available from: http://tinyurl.com/h87s4g7 [accessed 19 January 2017].

Fisher, B.A. (1980) *Small Group Decision Making*, 2nd edn, McGraw-Hill, New York.

Fowler, A. and Ubels, J. (2010) 'The multi-faceted nature of capacity: Two leading frameworks', in J. Ubels, N. Acquaye-Baddoo and A. Fowler (eds) *Capacity Development in Practice*, Earthscan Ltd, London. Available from: http://www.bibalex.org/Search4Dev/files/388410/225853.pdf [accessed 28 December 2016].

Gorzynski, B. (2009) *The Strategic Mind: The Journey to Leadership through Strategic Thinking*, 1st edn, Management Book 2000 Limited, Oxford.

Helmer, O. (1967) *Analysis of the Future: the Delphi Method* [online]. Available from: http://tinyurl.com/jqs2fn6 [accessed 28 January 2017].

Hersey, P. and Blanchard, K. (1998) *Management of Organizational Behavior: Leading Human Resources*, Prentice-Hall, Englewood Cliffs, NJ.

Keijzer, N., Spierings, E., Phlix, G. and Fowler, A. (2011) *Bringing the Invisible into Perspective, Reference Document for Using the 5Cs Framework to Plan, Monitor and Evaluate Capacity and Results of Capacity Development Processes*, ECDPM, Maastricht. Available from: http://tinyurl.com/nj9vrkt [accessed 28 December 2016].

Kelly, H.H. and Thibaut, J.W. (1954) 'Experimental studies of group problem solving and process', in G. Lindzey (ed.) *Handbook of social psychology*, 11: 735-785, Addison Wesley, Reading, MA.

Kolb, J.A., Jin, S. and Song, J. (2008) 'A model of small group facilitator competencies', *Performance Improvement Quarterly* 21(2): 119-133 [online], Wiley. Available from: http://onlinelibrary.wiley.com/doi/10.1002/piq.20026/pdf [accessed 18 January 2017].

Kotter, J.P. (2007) 'Leading change: Why transformation efforts fail', *Harvard Business Review*. Available from: http://tinyurl.com/jb37pu8 [accessed 17 January 2017].

McKinsey & Co. (2008) 'Enduring Ideas: The 7-S framework', *McKinsey Quarterly March* 2008. Available from: http://tinyurl.com/zo2jwex [accessed 19 January 2017].

Muir, J. (1911) *My First Summer in the Sierra* [online]. Available from: http://vault.sierraclub.org/john_muir_exhibit/writings/favorite_quotations.aspx [accessed 29 January 2017].

Mulder, M. (2012) 'Competence-based education and training – About frequently asked questions', *The Journal of Agricultural Education and Extension* 18.4: 319–327.

OECD (2005 & 2008) *The Paris Declaration on Aid Effectiveness and the Accra Agenda for Action* [online]. Available from: http://tinyurl.com/pg2478c [accessed 19 January 2017].

OECD (2010) *Capacity Development: A DAC Priority*. Available from: http://tinyurl.com/hg4czs8 [accessed 19 January 2017].

OECD (2012) OECD *Environmental Outlook to 2050: The Consequences of Inaction*, OECD Publishing, Paris. Available from: http://dx.doi.org/10.1787/9789264122246-en [accessed 28 January 2017].

Palmer, D. and Kaplan, S. (2007) *A Framework for Strategic Innovation: Blending Strategy and Creative Exploration to Discover Future Business Opportunities*, [White paper] Innovation Point. Available from: http://tinyurl.com/zupn9c2 [accessed 24 January 2017].

Pauling, L. as quoted by Crick, F. (1995) in 'The impact of Linus Pauling on molecular biology', [presentation] Pauling Symposium, Oregon State University.

Rockefeller Foundation and Global Business Network (2010) *Scenarios for the Future of Technology and International Development* [online]. Available from: http://tinyurl.com/hzvmsu5 [accessed 19 January 2017].

Staiger-Rivas, S., Le Borgne, E., Victor, M., Hagmann, J., Sette, C. and Kosina, P. (2015) 'Group facilitation in CGIAR: Experiences and lessons from international agricultural research organizations', *Knowledge Management for Development* Journal 11(1): 77–90. Available from: http://tinyurl.com/zqgt5ts [accessed 17 January 2017].

Wageningen University & Research (2016) *Research and Results* [online]. Available from: http://tinyurl.com/he4ewdt [accessed 28 December 2016].

Chapter 5

BetterEvaluation (2013) *Report and Support Use of Findings*. Available from: http://tinyurl.com/gv56e4b [accessed 21 February 2017].

Brouwer, J.H., Woodhill, A.J., Hemmati, M., Verhoosel, K.S. and van Vugt, S.M. (2015) *The MSP Guide: How to Design and Facilitate Multi-Stakeholder Partnerships*, Wageningen University and Research – Centre for Development Innovation, Wageningen and Practical Action Publishing, Rugby. Available from: http://www.mspguide.org/msp-guide [accessed 18 January 2017].

Communication Theory (2010) 'Shannon and Weaver Model of Communication' [online]. Available from: http://tinyurl.com/3jgqlgg [accessed 3 March 2017].

Dervin, B. (1981) 'Mass Communication: Changing Conceptions of the Audience' in Rice, R.E. and Paisley, W.J. (eds) *Public Communication Campaigns*, pp. 71–88, Sage Publications, Beverly Hills.

Hanlon, D. and Rigney, J. (2011) *Generated Listening: Subtleties to Prepare Your Inner-Self for the Art of Receiving*, Australian Institute of Training and Development. Available from: http://tinyurl.com/zdksfqv [accessed 21 February 2017].

Leeuwis, C. and Aarts, N. (2011) 'Rethinking Communication in Innovation Processes: Creating Space for Change in Complex Systems', *Journal of Agricultural Education and Extension*, 17/1, Routledge, Taylor & Francis, London.

PuddleDancer and Center for Nonviolent Communication (2009) *Key Facts About Nonviolent Communication* (NVC) [online]. PuddleDancer Press. Available from: http://tinyurl.com/zqb7atz [accessed 21 February 2017].

Rosenberg, M.B. (2003) *Nonviolent Communication: A Language of Life*, PuddleDancer Press, Encinitas, California.

Scharmer, C.O. (2008) *Uncovering the Blindspot of Leadership, Leader to Leader*. Available from: http://tinyurl.com/hm48ah9 [accessed 21 February 2017].

Shannon, C.E. and Weaver, W. (1964) *The Mathematic Theory of Communication*, 10th edn, University of Illinois Press, Urbana. Available from: http://tinyurl.com/jjnp24r [accessed 21 February 2017].

The Communications Network (2010) *Are We There Yet? A Communications Guide* [online]. Asibey Consulting. Available from: http://tinyurl.com/39kmza7 [accessed 21 February 2017].

Torres, R.T., Preskill, H., and Piontek, M. (2005) *Evaluation Strategies for Communicating and Reporting: Enhancing Learning in Organizations*, 2nd edn, Sage Publishing, Thousand Oaks, California.

Vogt, E.E., Brown, J., and Isaacs, D. (2003) *The Art of Powerful Questions: Catalyzing Insight, Innovation and Action*, Whole Systems Associates, California. Available from: http://tinyurl.com/h2gmvgf [accessed 21 February 2017].

Chapter 6

Brouwer, J.H., Woodhill, A.J., Hemmati, M., Verhoosel, K.S., and van Vugt, S.M. (2016) *The MSP Guide: How to Design and Facilitate Multi-Stakeholder Partnerships*, Wageningen University and Research – Centre for Development Innovation, Wageningen and Practical Action Publishing, Rugby. Available from: http://www.mspguide.org/msp-guide [accessed 18 January 2017].

Cognitive Edge (2017) 'Ritual dissent' [website] <http://cognitive-edge.com/methods/ritual-dissent/> [accessed 14 January 2017].

Van Es, M., Guijt, I., and Vogel, I. (2015) *Hivos ToC Guidelines: Theory of Change Thinking in Practice - A Stepwise Approach*, Hivos, The Hague. Available from: http://tinyurl.com/hr53xh2 [accessed 29 December 2016].

Funnell, S.C. and Rogers, P.J. (2011) *Purposeful Program Theory: Effective Use of Theories of Change and Logic Models*, John Wiley & Sons, San Francisco, California.

Guijt, I. (2013) ToC Reflection Notes 3: *Working with Assumptions in a Theory of Change Process*. Available from: http://tinyurl.com/hbdl5h3 [accessed 17 February 2017].

Kotter, J.P. (2007) 'Leading change: Why transformation efforts fail', *Harvard Business Review*. Available from: http://tinyurl.com/jb37pu8 [accessed 17 January 2017].

Mintzberg, H. (2000) *The Rise and Fall of Strategic Planning*, Pearson Education, Harlow, Essex.

Mintzberg, H., Ahlstrand, B., Lampel, J. (1998) *Strategy Safari: A Guided Tour Through the Wilds of Strategic Management*, The Free Press, Simon and Schuster, New York.

Nickols, F. (2016) Strategy IS Execution: *What You Do Is What You Get*. Available from: http://www.nickols.us/strategy_is_execution.pdf [accessed 28 December 2016].

Rogers, P. (2014) *Theory of Change, Methodological Briefs: Impact Evaluation 2*, UNICEF Office of Research, Florence. Available from: http://tinyurl.com/gl2oc2a [accessed 17 February 2017].

Tregoe, B.B. and Zimmerman, J.W. (1980) *Top Management Strategy: What It Is and How To Make It Work*, Simon and Schuster, New York.

Vermeulen, S., Woodhill, J., Proctor, F.J. and Delnoye, R. (2008) *Chain-Wide Learning for Inclusive Agrifood Market Development: A Guide to Multi-stakeholder Processes for Linking Small-Scale Producers with Modern Markets*, International Institute for Environment and Development, London and Wageningen University and Research Centre, Wageningen. Available from: http://tinyurl.com/hbz7t6f [accessed 29 December 2016].

Vogel, I. (2012) *Review of the Use of the 'Theory of Change' in International Development: Review Report*, UK Department of International Development (DFID). Available from:

http://tinyurl.com/hs2arsn [accessed 29 December 2016].

Wageningen University & Research (2012a) 'Managing for Sustainable Development Impact: Tools and Methods' [website] <http://www.managingforimpact.org/tools> [accessed 27 February 2017].

Wageningen University & Research (2012b) 'Multi-stakeholder Partnerships: Tools and Methods' [website] <http://www.mspguide.org/tools-and-methods> [accessed 27 February 2017].

Wageningen University & Research (2015) *Theory of Change* [online]. Available from: http://tinyurl.com/hwltqvr [accessed 17 February 2017].

Wigboldus, S. with Brouwers, J. (2016) *Using a Theory of Scaling to Guide Decision Making: Towards a Structured Approach to Support Responsible Scaling of Innovations in the Context of Agrifood Systems*, Wageningen University and Research, Wageningen. Available from: http://tinyurl.com/jlu4bp9 [accessed 17 February 2017].

Chapter 7

Cambridge Dictionary (2017) 'Tendering' [online]. Available from: http://dictionary.cambridge.org/dictionary/english/tendering [accessed 23 January 2017].

European Commission (2015) *Public Procurement: Guidance for Practitioners*, EC Directorate-General for Regional and Urban Policy Competence Centre Administrative. Available from: http://tinyurl.com/q2kotr9 [accessed 31 December 2016].

European Commission (2016) *Practical Guide* [online]. Available from: http://tinyurl.com/pdr4368 [accessed 23 January 2017].

European Commission (2017) *Public procurement* [online]. Available from: http://tinyurl.com/z4ge6sy [accessed 23 January 2017].

Guijt, I. and Woodhill J. (2002) *Managing for Impact in Rural Development: A Guide for Project M&E*, International Fund for Agricultural Development (IFAD), Rome. Available from: http://tinyurl.com/h72dbj2

[accessed 31 December 2016].

Gupta, H. (2011) *Management Information Systems: An Insight*, International Book House PVT Ltd, New Delhi.

Kobbacy, K.A.H. and Murthy, D.N.P. (2008) 'An overview', in K.A.H. Kobbacy and D.N.P. Murthy (eds), *Complex System Maintenance Handbook*, pp. 3–20, Springer-Verlag, London.

United Nations Commission on International Trade Law (2014) *UNCITRAL Model Law on Public Procurement*, United Nations, New York. Available from: http://tinyurl.com/z5m6bre [accessed 31 December 2016].

Chapter 8

Alkin, M.C. and King, J. A. (2016) 'The Historical Development of Evaluation Use', *American Journal of Evaluation* 14: 568–79.

Arkesteijn, M., Mierlo, B. van and Leeuwis, C. (2015) 'The Need for Reflexive Evaluation Approaches in Development Cooperation', *Evaluation* 21.1: 99–115.

Bamberger, M. (2012) 'Introduction to Mixed Methods in Impact Evaluation', *Impact Evaluation Notes 3*, InterAction, Washington, DC. Available from: https://tinyurl.com/hv5durg [accessed 6 January 2017].

Bamberger, M., Rugh, J., Mabry, L. (2012) *RealWorld Evaluation: Working Under Budget, Time, Data and Political Constraints*, 2nd edn, Sage Publications, Thousand Oaks, California.

BetterEvaluation (no date: a) *Analyse data* [website] <http://tinyurl.com/mwzy8vv> [accessed 18 March 2017]. BetterEvaluation (b) *Communicating evaluation findings* [website] <http://tinyurl.com/ky9eyjf> [accessed 13 March 2017].

BetterEvaluation (c) *Content analysis* [website] <http://tinyurl.com/mz5uwzz> [accessed 19 March 2017].

BetterEvaluation (d) *Evaluation approaches* [website] <https://tinyurl.com/zrvkwye> [accessed 3 March 2017].

BetterEvaluation (e) *Evaluation framework* [website] <http://tinyurl.com/jfuh8h5> [accessed 15 March 2017].

BetterEvaluation (f) *Evaluation plan* [website] <https://tinyurl.com/jqe3o8h> [accessed 3 March 2017].

BetterEvaluation (g) *Evaluation policy* [website] <http://tinyurl.com/h7v9alg> [accessed 15 March 2017].

BetterEvaluation (h) *Evaluation matrix* [website] <http://tinyurl.com/k7yj5tu> [accessed 15 March 2017].

BetterEvaluation (i) *Framework matrices* [website] < http://tinyurl.com/lz6pphv> [accessed 19 March].

BetterEvaluation (j) *Methods for monitoring and evaluation* [website] <http://tinyurl.com/msyc7pg> [accessed 18 March 2017].

Birckmayer, J.D. and Weiss, C.H. (2000) 'Theory-Based Evaluation in Practice: What do we learn?', *Evaluation Review* 24 (4): 407-31.

Breckon, J. (2016) 'An Evidence Base for Evidence-Informed Policy', *Significance*, The Royal Statistical Society.

Brouwer, J.H., Woodhill, A.J., Hemmati, M., Verhoosel, K.S., and van Vugt, S.M. (2016) *The MSP Guide: How to Design and Facilitate Multi-Stakeholder Partnerships*, Wageningen UR – Centre for Development Innovation (CDI), Wageningen and Practical Action Publishing, Rugby. Available from: https://tinyurl.com/hfnnhoo [accessed 18 January 2017].

Brusset, E., Cosgrave, J., and MacDonald, W. (2010) 'Real-time Evaluation in Humanitarian Emergencies', in L.A. Ritchie and W. MacDonald (eds), 'Enhancing Disaster and Emergency Preparedness, Response, and Recovery Through Evaluation', *New Directions for Evaluation* 126: 9–20.

Buckley, J., Archibald, T., Hargraves, M. and Trochim, W.M. (2015) 'Defining and Teaching Evaluative Thinking: Insights from Research on Critical Thinking', *American Journal of Evaluation*, 36(3): 375–388, Sage Publishing. Available from: http://tinyurl.com/hxh8la6

[accessed 11 March 2017].

CDI (2012) *Developmental Evaluation: Applying Complexity Concepts to Enhance Innovation and Use*, Conference report, CDI, Wageningen University & Research, Wageningen. Available from: http://edepot.wur.nl/216077 [accessed 16 March 2017].

CDI (2013) *Impact Evaluation: Taking Stock and Looking Ahead*, Conference report, CDI, Wageningen University & Research, Wageningen. Available from: http://tinyurl.com/zcxwl2m [accessed 29 September 2016].

CDI (2016) *Partnering for Success*, Report of Conference on 'How Monitoring and Evaluation Can Strengthen Partnerships for Sustainable Development', 17–18 March 2016, Wageningen University & Research, Wageningen. Available from: http://tinyurl.com/zepnb75 [accessed 3 March 2017].

Coffey, A. and Atkinson, P. (1996) *Making Sense of Qualitative Data: Complementary Research Strategies*, Sage Publications, Thousand Oaks, California.

Coryn, C.L.S. and Westine, C. (2015) *Contemporary Trends in Evaluation Research*, Sage Publications Ltd, London, UK.

Cosgrave, J., Ramalingam, B., and Beck, T. (2009) *Real-Time Evaluations of Humanitarian Actions: An ALNAP Guide*, Pilot version, ALNAP. Available from: http://www.alnap.org/resource/5595 [accessed 18 March 2017].

Creswell, J.W. and Plano Clark, V.L. (2011) *Designing and Conducting Mixed Methods Research*, 2nd edn, Sage Publications, Thousand Oaks, California.

European Evaluation Society (2007) EES Statement: *The Importance of a Methodologically Diverse Approach to Impact Evaluation – Specifically with Respect to Development Aid and Development Interventions*, EES Secretariat, Nijkerk. Available from: http://tinyurl.com/j28ohmr [accessed 3 March 2017].

EvalPartners (2017) *International Mapping of Associations* [website]

<http://tinyurl.com/zq298sk> [accessed 11 March 2017].

Eyben, R. (2013) *Uncovering the Politics of 'Evidence' and 'Results': A Framing Paper for Development Practitioners*, bigpushforward.net. Available from: http://tinyurl.com/jua79zz [accessed 16 March 2017].

Guijt, I. (2007) *Assessing and Learning for Social Change: A Discussion Paper*, Learning by Design and Institute of Development Studies. Available from: https://tinyurl.com/gq3hegj [accessed 29 September 2016].

Guijt, I. (2010) 'Accountability and Learning', in J. Ubels, N.A. Acquaye-Baddoo and A. Fowler (eds), *Capacity Development in Practice*, pp. 277–91, EarthScan, London. Available from: http://tinyurl.com/j9h3sk7 [accessed 6 January 2017].

Guijt, I. and Woodhill, J. (2002) *Managing for Impact in Rural Development. A Guide for Project M&E*, International Fund for Agricultural Development, Rome. Available from: http://tinyurl.com/h72dbj2 [accessed 6 January 2017].

Henry, G.T. and Mark, M.M. (2003) 'Beyond Use: Understanding Evaluation's Influence on Attitudes and Actions', *American Journal of Evaluation*, 24 (3): 293–314.

Joint Committee on Standards for Educational Evaluation (JCSEE) (2014) *Program Evaluation Standards Statements* [website] <http://tinyurl.com/joxd6xp> [accessed 3 March 2017].

Jones, H. (2009) 'The "Gold Standard" is Not a Silver Bullet for Evaluation', *Opinion*, Overseas Development Institute (ODI), London. Available from: <http://tinyurl.com/zsxzr04> [accessed 3 March 2017].

Jones, N., Steer, L., Jones, H. and Datta, A. (2009) *Improving Impact Evaluation Production and Use*, ODI, London. Available from: http://tinyurl.com/mjxo85y [accessed 18 March 2017].

Kahan, B. and Goodstadt, M. (2005) *The IDM Manual: A Guide to the IDM (Interactive Domain Model) Best Practices Approach to Better Health*

[website], Section on IDM terminology, IDM Best Practices, <http://tinyurl.com/k4ffamp> [accessed 31 January 2017].

Kusek, J.Z. and Rist, R.C. (2004) *Ten Steps to a Results-Based Monitoring and Evaluation System: A Handbook for Development Practitioners*, The World Bank, Washington, DC. Available from: http://tinyurl.com/gsvwhha [accessed 3 March 2017].

Kusters, C., van Vugt, S., Wigboldus, S., Williams, B. and Woodhill, J. (2011) *Making Evaluations Matter: A Practical Guide for Evaluators*, CDI, Wageningen UR, Wageningen.

Mark, M.M. (2009) 'Evaluation, Method Choices, and Pathways to Consequences', in K. Ryan and J. Cousins (eds), *The Sage International Handbook of Educational Evaluation*, pp. 55–73, Sage Publications, Thousand Oaks, California.

Mayne, J. (2008) 'Building an Evaluative Culture for Effective Evaluation and Results Management', *ILAC Working Paper 8*, Institutional Learning and Change Initiative, Rome. Available from: http://tinyurl.com/h74x469 [accessed 11 March 2017].

Mierlo, B.C. van, Regeer, B., Amstel, M. van, Arkesteijn, M.C.M., Beekman, V., Bunders, J.F.G., Cock Buning, T. de, Elzen, B., Hoes, A.C., and Leeuwis, C. (2010) *Reflexive Monitoring in Action: A Guide for Monitoring System Innovation Projects*, Wageningen University & Research Communication and Innovation Studies, Wageningen and Athena Institute, VU University Amsterdam. Available from: http://edepot.wur.nl/149471 [accessed 16 March 2017].

OECD (2016) DAC *Criteria for Evaluating Development Assistance* [website] <https://tinyurl.com/z6rfmvx> [accessed 3 March 2017].

O'Niel, G. (2012) *7 New Ways to Present Evaluation Findings* [blog] <http://tinyurl.com/gpxeykb> [posted 3 October 2012] [accessed 5 March 2017].

Patton, M.Q. (1997) *Utilization-Focused Evaluation*, 3rd edn, Sage Publications, Thousand Oaks, California.

Patton, M.Q. (2008) *Utilization-Focused Evaluation*, 4th edn, Sage Publications, Thousand Oaks, California.

Patton, M.Q. (2011) *Developmental Evaluation: Applying Complexity Concept to Enhance Innovation and Use*, The Guildford Press, New York, NY.

Patton, M.Q. (2014) *Evaluation Flash Cards: Embedding Evaluative Thinking in Organizational Culture*, Otto Bremer Foundation, St Paul, MN. Available from: https://tinyurl.com/jk2pt2e [accessed 18 March 2017].

Raitzer, D., and Winkel, K. (2005) *Donor Demands and Uses for Evidence of Research Impact: The Case of the Consultative Group on International Agricultural Research (CGIAR)*, CGIAR Standing Panel on Impact Assessment, Science Council Secretariat, Rome.

Rich R.F. (1977) 'Uses of Social Science Information by Federal Bureaucrats: Knowledge for Action Versus Knowledge for Understanding', in C. H. Weiss (ed.), *Using Social Research in Public Policy Making*, Lexington Books, Lexington, MA.

Rist, R.C. and Stame, N. (eds) (2011) *From Studies to Streams: Managing Evaluative Systems*. Transaction Publishers, New Brunswick, NJ, and London, UK. Available from: http://tinyurl.com/z6mpkuz [accessed 2 October 2016].

Scriven, M. (1991) *Evaluation Thesaurus*, 4th edn, Sage Publications, Thousand Oaks, California. StatPages.info (no date) *Free Statistical Software* [website] <https://tinyurl.com/j4wlkno> [accessed 3 March 2017].

Stern, E., Stame, N., Mayne, J., Forss, K., Davies, R., and Befani, B. (2012) *Broadening the Range of Designs and Methods for Impact Evaluations*, Department for International Development (DFID) Working Paper 38, DFID, London. Available from: http://tinyurl.com/gmw2ojo [accessed 6 January 2017].

Stetson, V. (2008) *Communicating and Reporting on an Evaluation: Guidelines and Tools* [website], Catholic Relief Society, Baltimore, MD and the American Red Cross Washington, DC.

Available from: http://tinyurl.com/zto5sfk [accessed 18 March 2017].

Torres, R.T., Preskill, H., Piontek, M. (2005) *Evaluation Strategies for Communicating and Reporting: Enhancing Learning in Organizations*, 2nd edn, Sage Publications, Thousand Oaks, California.

UN (2017) *Sustainable Development Goals* [website], United Nations Statistics Division, New York, NY, <https://unstats.un.org/sdgs/> [accessed 11 March 2017].

USAID (2010) *'Baselines and Targets', Performance Monitoring and Evaluation Tips 8*, 2nd edn, USAID. Available from: http://tinyurl.com/z4048wt [accessed 3 March 2017].

University of St Andrews (2010) *Financial Operating Procedure: Budget Monitoring*. Available from: http://tinyurl.com/zzr3vqg [accessed 3 March 2017].

Wageningen University & Research (2012a) *Managing for Sustainable Development Impact: Tools and Methods* [website] <http://www.managingforimpact.org/tools> [accessed 27 February 2017].

Wageningen University & Research (2012b) *Multi-Stakeholder Partnerships: Tools and Methods* [website] <http://www.mspguide.org/tools-and-methods> [accessed 27 February 2017].

Weiss, C.H. (1977) 'Introduction', in C.H. Weiss (ed.), *Using Social Science in Public Policy Making*, D.C. Heath, Lexington, MA.

Williams, B. (2009) Input cited in C. Kusters, S. van Vugt, S. Wigboldus, B. Williams and J. Woodhill (2011) *Making Evaluations Matter: A Practical Guide for Evaluators*, CDI, Wageningen.

Woodhill, J. (2007) 'M&E as Learning: Rethinking the Dominant Paradigm', in J. De Graaff, J. Cameron, S. Sombatpanit, C. Pieri and J. Woodhill (eds), *Monitoring and Evaluation of Soil Conservation and Watershed Development Projects*, CRC Press, Taylor & Francis Group, Enfield, NH.

World Vision UK, International NGO Training and Research Centre

(INTRAC) and the Social Impact Lab (2016) *Low-Cost Mobile-Enabled Feedback Mechanism for Solicited and Unsolicited Feedback*. Available from: http://tinyurl.com/hv9chu7 [accessed 5 March 2017].

Chapter 9

BrainyQuote.com (nd) Milton Berle quotes. Available from: https://tinyurl.com/gwkhca4 [accessed 9 March].

Foodsecurityethiopia.nl *Why this platform?* [website] http://tinyurl.com/zstx7qb [accessed 3 March 2017].

The National Agricultural Research Organisation (2014) About NARO [online]. Available from: http://www.naro.go.ug/ [accessed 9 March 2017].

Annexes

Baser, H. and Morgan, P. with Bolger, J., Brinkerhoff, D., Land, A., Taschereau, S., Watson, D. and Zinke, J. (2008) *Capacity, Change and Performance*, Study report, Discussion Paper No. 59B, ECDPM, Maastricht. Available from: http://tinyurl.com/hv4aypf [accessed 21March 2017].

BetterEvaluation (no date) *BetterEvaluation* [website] <http://tinyurl.com/n8trj9s> [accessed 21 March 2017].

Brouwer, J.H., Woodhill, A.J., Hemmati, M., Verhoosel, K.S., and van Vugt, S.M. (2016) *The MSP Guide: How to Design and Facilitate Multi-Stakeholder Partnerships*, Wageningen UR – Centre for Development Innovation (CDI), Wageningen and Practical Action Publishing, Rugby. Available from: https://tinyurl.com/hfnnhoo [accessed 18 January 2017].

Buckley, J., Archibald, T., Hargraves, M. and Trochim, W.M. (2015) 'Defining and Teaching Evaluative Thinking: Insights from Research on Critical Thinking', *American Journal of Evaluation*, 36(3): 375–388, Sage Publishing. Available from: http://tinyurl.com/hxh8la6 [accessed 11 March 2017].

Creswell, J.W., and Plano Clark, V. L. (2011) *Designing and Conducting Mixed Methods Research*, 2nd edn, Sage Publications, Thousand Oaks, California.

European Commission (2017) *Public procurement* [online]. Available from: http://tinyurl.com/z4ge6sy [accessed 21 March 2017].

Evaluations that Make a Difference (2015) *Evaluations that make a difference*. Available from: http://tinyurl.com/zr4b654 [accessed 4 March 2017).

Guijt, I. and Woodhill J. (2002) *Managing for Impact in Rural Development: A Guide for Project M&E*, International Fund for Agricultural Development (IFAD), Rome. Available from: http://tinyurl.com/kbq3x8b [accessed 21 March 2017].

Keijzer, N., Spierings, E., Phlix, G. and Fowler, A. (2011) *Bringing the Invisible into Perspective, Reference Document for Using the 5Cs Framework to Plan, Monitor and Evaluate Capacity and Results of Capacity Development Processes*, ECDPM, Maastricht. Available from: http://tinyurl.com/nj9vrkt [accessed 21 March 2017].

Kusters, C., van Vugt, S., Wigboldus, S., Williams, B. and Woodhill, J. (2011) *Making Evaluations Matter: A Practical Guide for Evaluators*, CDI, Wageningen UR, Wageningen.

MacQueen, K. M., McLelland, E., Kelly Kay, K., and Milstein, B. (1998) Codebook Development for Team-Based Qualitative Research, *Cultural Anthropology Methods*, 10 (2): 31-6. Available from: http://tinyurl.com/gqqx838 [accessed 3 March 2017].

Mayne, J. (2008) 'Building an Evaluative Culture for Effective Evaluation and Results Management', *ILAC Working Paper 8*, Institutional Learning and Change Initiative, Rome. Available from: http://tinyurl.com/h74x469 [accessed 11 March 2017].

OECD (2016) *DAC Criteria for Evaluating Development Assistance* [online]. Available from: http://tinyurl.com/z6rfmvx [accessed 3 March 2017].

Patton, M.Q. (2008) *Utilization-Focused Evaluation*, 4th edn, Sage Publications, Thousand Oaks, California.

Patton, M.Q. (2011) *Developmental Evaluation: Applying Complexity Concept to Enhance Innovation and Use*, The Guildford Press, New York, NY.

Scharmer, C.O. (2008) *Uncovering the Blindspot of Leadership, Leader to Leader*. Available from: http://tinyurl.com/hm48ah9 [accessed 21 February 2017].

Scriven, M. (1991) *Evaluation Thesaurus*, 4th edn, Sage Publications, Thousand Oaks, California.

Stern, E., Stame, N., Mayne, J., Forss, K., Davies, R., and Befani, B. (2012) *Broadening the range of designs and methods for impact evaluations*, Department for International Development (DFID) Working Paper 38, DFID, London, UK. Available from: http://tinyurl.com/gmw2ojo [accessed 6 January 2017].

Wageningen University & Research (2012a) *Managing for Sustainable Development Impact: Tools and Methods* [website] <http://www.managingforimpact.org/tools> [accessed 27 February 2017].

Wageningen University & Research (2012b) *Multi-Stakeholder Partnerships: Tools and Methods* [website] <http://www.mspguide.org/tools-and-methods> [accessed 27 February 2017].

Wigboldus, S. with Brouwers, J. (2016) *Using a Theory of Scaling to Guide Decision Making: Towards a Structured Approach to Support Responsible Scaling of Innovations in the Context of Agrifood Systems*, Wageningen University and Research, Wageningen. Available from: http://tinyurl.com/jlu4bp9 [accessed 17 February 2017].

THANK YOU

CDI co-workers: Herman Brouwer, Hedwig Bruggeman, Nikki Buizer, Caroline Desalos, Marianne van Dorp, Valerie Eijrond, Femke Gordijn, Joost Guijt, Marion Herens, John Hollands, Judith Jacobs, Dieuwke Klaver, Chris van Kreij, Astrid Mastenbroek, James Mulkerrins, Bram Peters, Marco Meurs, Matilda Rizopulos, Marlene Roefs, Mirjam Schaap, Karen Verhoosel, Simone van Vugt, Anja Wolsky, all support staff for the M4SDI courses 2002–16 and the M&E on the Cutting Edge conferences 2009–16 at CDI, Wageningen University & Research.

Others: Syed Aftab Ahmad, SRSP; Ismael Akhalwaya, Presidency of South Africa; Dawit Alemu, Benefit; Kwadwo Asenso-Okyere, IFPRI; Yona Baguma, NARO; Willem Bettink, IFAD; Ferko Bodnar, IOB; Karel Chambille, Hivos; Rick Davies, M&E consultant; Shashi Dijkerman; Marjan van Es, Hivos; Helen Gilma, IFAD; Ian Goldman, Presidency of South Africa; Dieneke de Groot, ICCO; Irene Guijt, OXFAM GB; Mwatima Juma, IFAD; Ibrahim Khadar, CTA; Zaki Khamis Juma, IFAD; Jean-François Kobiané, University of Ouagadougou; Marlène Läubli Loud, LAUCO; Cees Leeuwis, Wageningen University & Research; Philip Macnaghten, Wageningen University & Research; Ramzy Magambom, ISSD Uganda; Andreas Mbinga, IFAD; Arnoud Meijberg, Farm Africa; Christopher Moore, CDR Associates; Masood Ul Mulk, SRSP; Jessie Mvula, Grow Africa; Thevan Naidoo; Fumiko Nakai, IFAD; Maureen Nyachwaya, Farm Africa; Zenda Ofir; Mine Pabari, IUCN; Michael Quinn Patton; Jim Riordan, Grow Africa; Patricia Rogers, University of Melbourne; Ruerd Ruben, Wageningen University & Research; Dave Snowden, Cognitive Edge; Orlando Sosa, IPPC, FAO; Elliot Stern, University of Bristol; Leanne Stewart, IPPC; Ros Tennyson, PBA; Seblewengel Tesfaye, Benefit; Issaka Traoré; Yuca Waarts, Wageningen University & Research; Christine Webster, CTA; Gill Westhorp, Community Matters; Bob Williams; Jim Woodhill; Atif Zeeshan Rauf, SRSP; Elias Zerfu; all presenters and participants of the M4SDI courses 2002–16 and the M&E on the Cutting Edge conferences 2009–16 at CDI, Wageningen University & Research; all the people we engaged with during the course of our work; our families and friends.

We would also like to thank the many people we met during our project/programme activities. Any errors in the text are the sole responsibility of the authors.